Rowland Hamilton

Money and Value

An Inquiry into the Means and Ends of Economic Production

Rowland Hamilton

Money and Value
An Inquiry into the Means and Ends of Economic Production

ISBN/EAN: 9783744720199

Printed in Europe, USA, Canada, Australia, Japan

Cover: Foto ©Suzi / pixelio.de

More available books at **www.hansebooks.com**

MONEY AND VALUE

AN INQUIRY INTO

THE MEANS AND ENDS OF ECONOMIC PRODUCTION

WITH AN APPENDIX

ON THE DEPRECIATION OF SILVER AND INDIAN CURRENCY

BY

ROWLAND HAMILTON

London:

MACMILLAN AND CO

1878.

CONTENTS.

CHAPTER II.

(*Money.*)

EXTENDED USES OF METALLIC MONEY AND OF SUBSTITUTES FOR IT.

CHAPTER III.

(*Value.*)

ON THE NATURE OF EXCHANGE VALUES—PROPERTY AND
CAPITAL.

CHAPTER IV.

(*Value.*)

CONDITIONAL OWNERSHIP—CREDIT AND BANKING.

APPENDIX I.

SOME FURTHER REMARKS ON LOCAL AND GENERAL CURRENCY.

APPENDIX II.

THE DEPRECIATION OF SILVER AND THE INDIAN CURRENCY.

INTRODUCTION

THE activity of our varied industries and the vast extent of our commerce have always been a source of reasonable pride in this country : and now more than ever justly so : for without these aids to the support of our population these little islands could hardly expect to maintain their position as one of the great powers which influence the destinies of the world.

It is strange that notwithstanding this sentiment so little is generally understood of the conditions and principles which govern the true organisation of industry. Many works have been written of late years, some very superficial, but some with very great ability, showing " how things are done in the City ; " indeed during the recent period of spurious financial excitement an amazingly intimate acquaintance with the mere forms of business was to be met with in society which could not be supposed to have a very discriminating interest in productive undertakings. By an error very characteristic of the time, purely *technical* knowledge was taken to be pre-eminently practical. Instruments which can only be safely used by those who know how to use them, and why and when they should be employed, were perverted in a way which led to much loss, misery, and demoralisation, and with an equal want of wisdom and discrimination, the blame was thrown upon the forms or instruments, rather than upon those who had misused them through ignorance, recklessness, or flagrant dishonesty of purpose.

One of the main objects of the present work is to explain something of the true nature of that which has to be done, and the responsibilities which must be incurred, by those who would earn a share in the gains of beneficial industry. It does not so much concern me to show how interest can be obtained by putting money in a bank, as to afford some insight into the nature of the varied kinds of work which must be successfully carried out before any return can be secured at all, or apportioned to those who have severally contributed to its production. I do not by any means disparage the services of those who have lucidly explained the mechanism of finance, but it is well sometimes to direct popular attention from forms to the realities which lie behind them. This is, in its degree, nothing more than the old alternation between the realistic and the nominal conceptions of things which have in turn done so much to extend and duly to define the range of our knowledge.

It would be vain to attempt to make this subject popular in the common acceptation of the term, but I have spared no pains in the endeavour to make my exposition as clear, as concise, and as free from technical language as is consistent with the due consideration of all its manifold bearings. The subject is necessarily somewhat dry and complex ; as far as possible I have avoided overlaying it with details except where it seemed well to introduce them for the purpose of illustration, or where questions of permanent interest turned upon the points thus specifically referred to. It may seem needless to the reader, as indeed it did at one time to myself, to combine the notice of metallic money so fully with the inquiry into the actual work of production ; but so many fallacies, so many truths half expressed and wholly misunderstood, are associated with the precious metals, that I found my task could be more thoroughly accomplished by keeping this branch of the subject in mind throughout. For it may thus most clearly be shown both what such money can and what it can *not* do ; and this is at present of the more consequence because the large increase in the supply of it, which is now attracting so much attention, will cause perturbations that will more or less affect many branches of industry, and questions regarding it are sure to be intruded with an exaggerated sense of their importance into regions far beyond and other than those which are actually affected by changes of this description. I have therefore given a somewhat unusual prominence to the discussion of specific money, even in matters which otherwise might as well have been considered without any direct reference to it, although my object has rather been to demonstrate how special and limited are its functions in that work of production which is of real importance to the welfare of mankind.

The abuses to which our industrial system is subject have only been very casually touched upon. To elucidate the true uses of money and of credit will afford the most effectual remedy for those perversions and hallucinations which have so repeatedly led to the most lamentable waste of our national resources. If those who are capable of taking an intelligent interest in the subject, and who are in their degree the leaders of public opinion, can more adequately realise what are the essentials necessary for the success of any undertaking, the conspicuous absence of these essentials will afford the best warning both to themselves and those who are guided by their judgment. Forms, however well devised, will be constantly simulated, and indeed rather afford a cover to the aggressor than any protection to those whose interests may be attacked. It is only by some discriminating knowledge of the principles which lie behind them that security can be attained. Those indeed who are fairly carrying on the work which the country requires may be much embarrassed and straightened by precautionary restrictions entailing losses and expenses which the ordinary profits of industry can ill afford to bear, but such formalities are no obstacle to an unscrupulous adventurer, with whom such minor considerations of cost or convenience can have but little weight. Frauds there always will be ; but if those who are now so often the subjects of them would look a little more closely, and inquire a little more closely, into the work which has actually to be done, the law would soon be able to come to very definite issues with the Spoilers, whether the *suggestio falsi* or the *suppressio veri* has been the means of the deception attempted. Either they have obtained money under false pretences or they have not. If they have, a properly chosen jury of their country-men, or a court taking evidence as a jury, should best be able to deal appropriately with their criminality. If not, what more is to be said than that those who attempt to get the gains of produc-tion without incurring the risks or the labour rightly associated with them are justly doomed to disappointment ? I have nothing to say to those whose real object is to get some one else's money by any means which shall not place them within the clutches of the law. Their own hands, are not clean. Let them take what the law gives them. But they are altogether outside of the circle of productive and self-sustaining industry with which I am now concerned. When its conditions are better understood and more honestly acted upon the field of their operations will be very greatly curtailed.

The most complete and outspoken fidelity, "*uberrima fides*," should beyond all doubt be rigidly required of those who assume the responsibility of

employing other people's money. It is not enough
that Promoters or Directors refrain from deception.
They are bound to use due care and diligence that
the nature of the schemes which they undertake
should be rightly understood. But nothing is to
be gained by rashly bringing forward charges of
fraud or falsehood. For when it comes to the
point, a natural sense of justice recoils from holding
any man guilty of such flagrant offences unless
clear proof of ill intention can be adduced. What
is specially required in dealing with such matters
is, that "recklessness" and "negligence" should
be recognised as very grave faults, involving a
liability to an appropriate penalty, both in law and
in public estimation. But there are two sides to
this question. Upright and capable men will
neither claim prescience nor put themselves in a
position to be held answerable for the want of it
by the operation of any one-sided law which
ignores the fact that risks and reverses are inseparable from all industrial enterprizes.

But while thus avoiding the consideration of
palpable and acknowledged perversions of the
industrial system, I have not set forth any transcendental theory of morals. On the contrary, men
in their dealings with each other must be taken
for what they are, not for what they ought to
be. The sole aid which the theory of value may
render to a higher morality is by unmasking the
vain pretence of virtue, and showing how with the

means of making good their choice in their own hands, men wilfully give effect to far other preferences' than those which they affect to desire. If we all as "consumers" are not well served, we may depend upon it that some portion of the blame rests with ourselves.

More generally my intention has been to set forth the basis of facts which underlies the appearances presented both by the currency and the various forms by which value is expressed in the terms of it. There is little of novelty to be expected in going over ground which has already been so frequently traversed, but the views which I have presented are from a somewhat different standpoint from that which has been usually taken.

I have sought to go back to the reasons which in the course of ages have led to that universally acknowledged consensus of opinion which has made the precious metals the common measure of value throughout the world : for these reasons still exist in the order of Nature, and so effectually govern the limits of their use and of their value that any attempt to control or regulate the one or the other by artificial means can end only in failure and confusion.

Further, I have constantly endeavoured to convey the idea of the great work of material production as it moves in unceasing and ever-changing activity around us :—to exhibit capital as maintained only by continuous reproduction, and the conditions under which its consumption is implied by the various obligations expressing the use of credit; keeping before the mind continually the cardinal truth that though labour is the basis of all value in exchange, that value must ever depend upon the intelligent adaptation and adjustment of natural resources to the felt and acknowledged wants of mankind. The conclusions deduced are little in accordance with that common desire to acquire sudden wealth by some dazzling speculation which has given birth to a system of "financing" that has earned for the word a sinister signification peculiarly its own.

On the other hand, a wider field is thus opened up to the view of those who do not shrink from the labour and self-denial which wins success by a rational obedience to natural law. The task may not be an easy one—

> *Pater ipse colendi*
> *Haud facilem esse viam voluit:*

—but the toil is lightened by the hope of ample recompense. For the sake of precision it may be needful to assume the fixity of conditions which have to be made the subject of careful analysis, but it is not the less true that, even during the time taken to complete every work of production, these conditions have been modified for better or worse according to the measure of success with which that work has been carried out. We are not living under any dead law of rigid necessity. It would indeed be a dismal Science which taught that the faithful use of man's best faculties of mind and body could avail nothing for the relief of man's estate.

On some points, especially regarding value and production, I have disregarded the limits usually assigned to the scope of Political Economy, though I trust I have made my argument sufficiently clear to avoid any confusion as to the commonly received meaning of the terms used. But why is it, I may ask, that a science which has done so much for humanity has made so little progress even among men whose capacity and disposition well qualify them to deal with the subjects of which it treats? Its utility seems, as it were, arrested within certain narrow and partial bounds. Is it not that it has clung too long to restrictions which are useful only as an expedient by which a new and untried field of inquiry may be more thoroughly investigated? The reasonableness, indeed the necessity of this method in the early stages of every new science may be freely admitted. Adam Smith in his great work on the *Wealth of Nations* fittingly confined himself to the investigation of material considerations, the just recognition of which must form the basis of every stable civilisation and especially that of a race of free men. Nor can objection be taken to any one who may deduce logically to the utmost the effects of the desire of wealth as the great motive power of any supposed society, nor does the exclusive assumption made imply any incapacity to give due weight to all the other considerations which together form the bases of State polity. But surely work such as this, however useful it may be within its own range, is essentially technical. The designation of Political Economy assumed broader grounds, and the results of investigations in a field thus limited are surely rather adapted to aid in the construction of an enlarged Science which should be presented for the use of those who are not specialists, developed with a due regard to the relative importance of other correlated truths, and thus claim and take its fitting place in the hierarchy of Sciences designed to subserve all the varied needs of concrete humanity.

How these manifold needs can best be satisfied, how they should be regulated, and what ought to be the ends and objects to which men should devote that balance of energy which is not required to maintain their struggle for life, are questions coming rather within the range of Physics, Physiology, and the Moral Sciences. But admitting that the special function of Political Economy is not to decide upon the higher problems of utility, but rather to set forth the law of justice and of necessity as regards the voluntary interchange of services as between man and man, it surely should not be considered beyond its province to show how far the quantity of labour devoted to material production is governed by laws of physical necessity ; how far a change of " will " can modify the existing conditions of industrial organisation ; and finally, how far material considerations may be dispensed with or made altogether subordinate in determining the objects to which men may devote their energies and their aspirations. A theorem obstructed by the notion of the accumulation of wealth as the limit of its inquiries does not readily rise to these higher purposes. There is no due place for life to be found within its borders.

Nevertheless it must be remembered also, that it has to declare with rigid fidelity the facts which come within its province. It cannot recognise inchoate intentions which have not strength enough to influence acts. The fruits of the earth are not yielded to our good intentions or to our fervent desires, but to our serviceable toil, and this rigid law and its analogies are the bases of all true economic science. Hence it is that its teaching will ever be obnoxious to all those whose ambition is greater than their power—to those who undervalue labour, the fruits of which they willingly appropriate —to all, in short, who dream of attaining great ends by feeble sacrifices and with inadequate means.

It is in accordance with these views that I have ventured to submit a few remarks, after the conclusion of my more special subject, on the economic side of some of the fundamental social questions of the day. An influential school of economists hold that over-population is already the necessary cause of the poverty which weighs down so large a portion of the community. I contend rather that our manifold resources, rightly applied, are as yet fully adequate, and for many years to come may be adequate, to make increasing numbers a source of just pride and of strength to our country.

.*. Various accidents have somewhat delayed the issue of this volume. It was planned and commenced before I knew of the publication of Professor Stanley Jevons's book on *Money and the Mechanism of Exchange,* in the International Science Series. I abstained from reading his work until my own treatise was completed for the press. Such minor coincidences as there are in matters of detail, whether of agreement or dissent, are -therefore altogether fortuitous. The Professor, in dealing with the mechanism of exchange, approaches the general subject of Money from a different direction, and is, for the most part, on different ground from that which I have traversed. His intimate acquaintance with the whole literature of the subject makes his work most valuable for reference, and will suggest many subjects of reflection to the student.

On a few of the points, however, of which he has treated I will venture to submit some very brief comments.

The questions of decimal coinage and international money may well be left with those who have devoted so much time and ability to these subjects. All that I would deprecate in the movement is that an over eager desire for uniformity should accept coins as international when the bases on which their values rested were not thoroughly identical. This would merely remove a difficulty from statistical tables at the expense of the accuracy of the facts recorded. Moreover, it will surely be a very small and doubtful gain to adjust the small differences in monetary units while systems of weights and measures are not assimilated. For the value of statistical tables depends much on their continuity, and repeated corrections for changes brought about in detail would only make confusion worse confounded.

The construction of a "tabular standard of value" is a subject of peculiar interest at the present time. I have referred to it casually in the Appendix on the Depreciation of Silver. The Professor proposes that such a standard should be deduced from an average of prices of a large and well selected number of commodities, on the assumption that the true price of gold must at all times vary inversely with that of "all commodities," and apparently that such variation is in fact the cause of any general change in prices. There are no doubt temporary conditions which affect the purchasing power of gold used as money at different times and in different places. It does not attain to its world-wide average of relative value without many casual fluctuations above and below the mean to which it inevitably tends. But in a still larger degree does the elastic machinery of credit admit of a very general expansion or contraction of prices within any limited period or area. The varying temper of commercial enterprize in its most generalized form, deals largely with mere transfers in estimated terms of value, and the validity of the prices thus assumed are not proved till the final aggregate results of many comparatively long operations are tested by experience. When, as has always been the case, a commercial crisis discloses a large amount of long pre-existing insolvency, the inference surely is rather that general prices have been unduly inflated by a misuse of credit than that they have been enhanced by any change in the value of gold itself. The utility of gold as a common measure and standard rests, as I maintain, on the fact that its value is governed by a far wider range of causes, and is comparatively exempt from (though of course in degree influenced by) such casual elements of perturbation.

I must demur, moreover, to the conclusion that the value of gold was more than doubled during the first half of the century, at least in so far as it is based only upon the corresponding fall in the average of general prices. For this allows nothing for the immense development of industry which led to so large an increase in individual productive power. This power is indeed the most important element in the question. If we suppose class A to provide food and class B all other necessaries, it follows that each produces twice as much as it requires for its own uses, and the consumption of A and B may alike be represented as $\frac{1}{2}a + \frac{1}{2}b$. But if they can so far increase their production as to be able to admit C into the association, each will require $\frac{1}{3}$ only of its own production for its own use, and, as the common measure of labour shows the same value in exchange for the increased production, that of the several items of it must be expressed by $\frac{1}{3}$ instead of $\frac{1}{2}$. But this local development does not affect the value of gold, the supply of which is derived from so many different regions, and its stability, rather than its depreciation, is to be inferred from a marked fall in local prices under such conditions. This principle will hold good, though the fractions which would represent the actual results may be infinitely complex and variable. During the subsequent period there is much reason to suppose that causes very much the converse of these have come into operation. I by no means say that gold has not risen and fallen, but I do submit that the fact cannot be positively inferred, and, *à fortiori* that the extent of any change in value cannot be measured merely by a comparison with general prices, however ably deduced. It would be very deceptive so to manipulate the standard as needlessly to hide or obscure such important factors as an increase or decrease in the actual cost of production.

Professor Jevons further contemplates the expediency of using this tabular standard of value for money debts "say of more than three months' standing." The essential point involved here was noticed by anticipation in Ch. II. § 23. If such current debts were payable in weights of gold varying according to the proposed standard as its indications were published from time to time, prices would be fixed according to the anticipated requirement to find a greater or less amount of the metal or coin in which the debts were actually to be discharged. The effect of this would be to counteract the natural ebb and flow of bullion by means of which its value is made to depend on a world-wide average of demand and supply. Our currency would be practically so far isolated while the prices on which the proposed average is to be deduced would be settled with reference to a constantly varying weight of metal.

We should, I fear, ere long, be landed in utter confusion: the more so as there would be an uncertain gap between the money in which all importers and wholesale dealers had to pay their longer obligations and that in which their transactions had to be carried out to the end by retailers and consumers.

But while I consider this proposal altogether untenable, I should be glad if any word of mine could add weight to Professor Jevons's recommendations in favour of organising our national statistics by the most efficient methods possible. Public money might well be expended on a matter of so much general importance. The objections to the use of such a standard for current transactions do not apply to its application to many obligations extending over lengthened periods of time, which indeed in not a few cases might quite as conveniently be made to depend upon the actual purchasing power of current money, as upon any direct reference to the value of gold.

R. H.

FEBRUARY, 1878.

MONEY AND VALUE.

CHAPTER I.

(*Money.*)

THE PRIMARY USES OF METALLIC MONEY

ERRATA.

Page 80, line 8, *for* "unexceptional" *read* "exceptional."

,, 278, line 3, note, *for* "*alieno nc*" *read* "*alienum non.*"

,, 320, line 33, *for* "elapse" *read* "lapse."

,, 351, note, *for* "A.D. 1847, 5/2$\frac{11}{16}$" *read* "5/9$\frac{11}{16}$."

,, 371, line 3 from bottom, note, *for* "108·4" *read* "106·4."

,, 385, line 25, *for* "evidently," *read* "eventually."

phrases. Like as in the old cabalistic lore the word
or symbol was tortured to yield an occult knowledge
of the thing signified till its true meaning was not
only missed, but overlaid and even totally lost, so
men still look to the mere forms which money
assumes for an explanation of the many irregular
results caused by the working, not only of untrammelled human passions and ignorant desires, but
of such motives only so partially controlled as

B

or coin in which the debts were actually to be discharged. The effect of this would be to counteract the natural ebb and flow of bullion by means of which its value is made to depend on a worldwide average of demand and supply. Our currency would be practically so far isolated while the prices on which the proposed average is to be deduced would be settled with reference to a constantly varying weight of metal.

We should, I fear, ere long, be landed in utter confusion: the more so as there would be an uncertain gap between the money in which all

of so much general importance. The objections to the use of such a standard for current transactions do not apply to its application to many obligations extending over lengthened periods of time, which indeed in not a few cases might quite as conveniently be made to depend upon the actual purchasing power of current money, as upon any direct reference to the value of gold.

R. H.

February, 1878.

MONEY AND VALUE.

CHAPTER I.

(*Money.*)

THE PRIMARY USES OF METALLIC MONEY.

THERE are few subjects which are at once of so much general interest, and yet so little popularly understood, as "money." The use of it in some form or other has come down to us from the most remote ages of antiquity, and would almost seem to have brought with it, even to the present day, some of the fantastic superstitions of alchemy or necromancy, which are none the less pernicious from being reclothed in modern and quasi-scientific phrases. Like as in the old cabalistic lore the word or symbol was tortured to yield an occult knowledge of the thing signified till its true meaning was not only missed, but overlaid and even totally lost, so men still look to the mere forms which money assumes for an explanation of the many irregular results caused by the working, not only of untrammelled human passions and ignorant desires, but of such motives only so partially controlled as to distort and obscure their manifestation by every variety of artifice and disguise. Whenever conventional morality is unreal, pedantic and one-sided, and positive morality consequently lax, confused and hypocritical, the test of money may expose the hollowness of its pretensions. Whenever arbitrary power attempts to override the inclinations and will of the governed, money often affords the most effectual means of baffling and evading the oppression. Whenever impatience or credulity attempts to realize desired ends without the use of adequate means, it is money again which may demonstrate most forcibly the inevitable failure. All the subtlety and ingenuity alike of well- or ill-intentioned folly rebels against a test so unintelligent, yet so impartial. But very much as almost every fallacy under the sun may receive the apparent support of numerical statistics although the rules of simple arithmetic are absolute and incontrovertible, so schemes for the manipulation of money may be so devised as to give colour to those very delusions and deceptions which the test of money, when rationally applied, is best calculated to dispel. Again, there is a constant tendency to confound the nature of the agent with that of the purposes to which it is applied and the results attained by it. The money which is so intimately associated with every relation of life, thus, by innumerable false analogies, comes to be confounded with the true causes which give rise to success or failure. It represents the concrete outcome of delicately adjusted labour in various stages ; but is taken to be the efficient cause of such results. In a certain limited sense this is reasonable enough, and reflects that state of mutual interdependence and mutual trust which is essential to all higher states of social development. But it is because so many of the mutual relations of society are and must be expressed in the terms of money, that a clear comprehension of the scope, the limits, and the intent of such terms becomes of so much importance.

2. I shall not ask my readers to follow me into the polemics of the " currency question," or into any inquiry into the innumerable fallacies by which the subject has been complicated. If we can only succeed in keeping to the simple facts as to what money does and can do in the world's work, such mystifications and delusions will be altogether avoided. My endeavour will be to state as clearly and concisely as I can what money is, and what are the functions of the precious metals in relation to it, though as we can sometimes best indicate the boundaries of a country by naming the regions which lie just beyond its limits, so the functions of money may sometimes be most readily explained by showing what it can *not* do, and what obligations cannot be expressed by means of it. I must crave patience if I begin by stating what may seem to be mere truisms, for it is often the case that where fundamental truths are not stated because they are trite, they are ere long tacitly ignored because they

CHAP. I.

The scope of the inquiry.

have not been brought forward. Moreover, it will be found that the chief effort of mind required for the consideration of the question is to keep in view simple primary truths in their full integrity, and in their due relative importance. The danger of going astray arises not so much from the difficulties of the road as from the glamour which surrounds it.

The nature and basis of Value.

3. Before entering fully upon my argument, let me call to mind very briefly some of the fundamental conditions under which life, and especially life in a highly civilized state, has to be maintained.

(a.) There is no proposition of political economy which has a more general bearing on all social questions than that the "capital" which supports all life and labour is constantly in course of consumption, and can be replaced only by the persistent and well-directed application of that labour which it supports. For the most part the fruits of the soil are yielded, and their consumption must be reckoned, in annual cycles, though mankind would fare badly if the surplus of abundant harvests was not stored to meet the deficiencies of years of scarcity. The several products of pastoral and agricultural industry are yielded at very different intervals. The rate of consumption of food, of clothing, of dwellings, of machinery (or, so-called fixed capital), varies in numberless ways and degrees, though the correlation of production and consumption, of work and waste, of the conservation and dissipation of energy, runs through all Nature.

(*b.*) Further, the utility of all things which we require does not depend merely on their inherent qualities, but upon their adjustment and adaptation to our several wants. Even those things most necessary to support life are required only in certain limited quantities. Life itself may depend upon the continuity of the supply, and obvious precautions will be taken to prevent any intermission of it ; still stores held for this purpose are so much dead weight, and excessive hoards are utterly useless. Nothing can be said to have an absolute value, or to be more useful than another, without regard to its relation to the existing aggregate of our needs.

(*c.*) Lastly it may be stated, as a general condition of the world in which we live, that a man's labour, without overtaxing his health or strength, will obtain for him from Nature a far more ample return than will suffice for the primary wants of himself and of those naturally dependent on him ; especially if he concentrate his energies on any one kind of production, he obtains far more than he can consume of that particular product. This holds good even in a rude agricultural state, and, *a fortiori*, where the efficiency of labour has been economised and increased by the arts of higher civilization. There may be a scarcity, of food for instance, as compared with the aggregate numbers of a community: that is a different question, arising rather from the exceptional poverty or inadequacy of the "natural agents" which it may possess; but there is not the less a surplus of productive energy because it may appear in the form of an excess of the power of labour which is in want of fitting occupation. The accretion of economic *rent* exemplifies this position, though there may be a large surplus of produce without any such accretion. Inducements and facilities for the division of labour are very deeply seated in the order of Nature, and the palpable advantages of it are largely increased by the cultivation of special faculties and aptitudes; but with this specialisation the work of adaptation and adjustment must go on with greater powers and also with more manifold complexity.

It is not enough that such well-known principles should be acknowledged. They must be realized as conditions under which our thoughts must work in order to carry out the analyses required for the elucidation of the subject. What, for instance, can be more common than trite reflections on the instability of all mundane affairs; while the idea of continuous adjustment according to the order of Nature is set aside for one of immobility, so conceived as to give place to blind faith in mere formal precedents, which has often misdirected the efforts and impeded the progress of mankind.

Money is that which confers a special power of choice.

4. The primary idea of money is that of something by the possession of which a certain power of choice or selection is conferred. Barter means the exchange of one thing for some other; but sale (by which it is implied that one of the terms of the exchange made is expressed in money) means

more than this. The thing parted with is exchanged, not for any other specific thing, but for that which will in effect give the owner the command over many other things.   Anything that can be used for this general purpose, in so far as it is so used, is *money*.   If any one substance more than another becomes vested with this property of general exchangeability it acquires an intrinsic and quite independent value arising from this newly developed property alone.   It may still in part supply certain special wants as before, for its inherent qualities remain the same, though those which fit it for the one purpose are not necessarily conterminate with those which fit it for the others.

An obvious corollary of this proposition is that money can only represent values according to the preferences which those who successively hold it may chose to exercise according to their estimate of the relative advantages to be derived from owning possessions of one kind rather than another. Its own special use is to give effect to a wider range of interchanges than those which can be simultaneously made ; but its indications cannot transcend the current opinions of relative value which are for the time dominant.

Even if we suppose a primitive state of society, where cattle could be exchanged for many other desired objects with more readiness than corn or any other less portable form of wealth, we have clearly an inducement to keep cattle over and above the numbers required for food or clothing or any such purposes. The excess need not be specifically set apart, and is as well adapted as ever to supply these original wants; but there are no wants of the kind left to supply. This new element of value would assuredly be felt and recognised, though it might not very clearly be defined, and would be based solely on the practical estimate, however roughly formed, of the trouble of rearing and keeping the increased number of cattle on the one side, and the intensity of the desire on the other, to command the choice of whatever could be obtained for them, and, among other considerations, a sense of power would be associated with the possession of cattle tending greatly to their accumulation, not only with no direct reference to their original uses, but even in excess of the number which could be sold as a means of gratifying wants of any other description.

5. I have dwelt upon this point because it seems to me that the intrinsic utility of the precious metals, as based upon their pre-eminent adaptability for use as money has hardly been recognised with sufficient clearness, and an occasion is thus given to attribute to them an occult, or an absolute value not rationally based upon, and limited by, the uses which they actually subserve. Mr. Tooke seems very fairly to represent the current opinion of his day when he " admits " that "the value of the precious metals as money must depend ultimately on their value as materials for jewelry or plate, since if they were not used as commodities they

could not circulate as money;" and further that "the primary cause of the utility of gold is its use as the material for plate. The secondary cause is its use as money." Mr. J. S. Mill, also, in his chapter on money in his *Principles of Political Economy*, lays some stress upon the statement that "the strongest inclination in a rude state of society is for personal ornaments," and that in such a state "every one was eager to accumulate as great a store as possible of things at once costly and ornamental."

The striking qualities of the precious metals no doubt attracted attention to them in remote ages far beyond historic times, and they thus became very widely and generally recognised, but the very earliest records refer to their use as money, and there seems no reason to doubt that their peculiar fitness for this special purpose constituted their chief value from almost the very first dawn of civilization, though then, as now, the nature of the work they did may have been very imperfectly understood. The rude tribes of the present day have no special liking for gold as an ornament, even when they are familiar with it, until they have found out practically that it has a "purchasing power" and a peculiar value which is not visible on the face of it. There are then new and very powerful motives to exhibit it for purposes of ostentation, but the gratification derived is largely owing to the sense of a power held in reserve—the power, that is, which gold has potentially as money.

The fallacy expressed in the first quotation is that the use of the precious metals as money does not suffice to make them "commodities," as if as a matter of fact the use of such money were not in itself one of the greatest of conveniences. A man keeps coin in his pocket, or a banker treasure in his vaults, or a patriarch shekels in his tent for common and clearly recognisable uses, which have nothing whatever to do with any notion of converting them into plate or ornaments. Uses of either kind are quite adequate independently to create effective demand, but in fact, as we shall more clearly see hereafter, the special value of plate or ornaments is something superadded to the general value of gold or silver as bullion, and the aggregate value depends for the most part not so much on the fact that these metals are thus diverted from their uses as money, as that they may readily be reverted to them. The uses of the precious metals are so peculiar and exceptional, that it is often convenient to speak of them on the one side, and of all other commodities on the other; but the opposition is casual only, and, as far as gold and silver are used as money at all, they are commodities used because they are best fitted for certain purposes, to which therefore they have come to be universally applied.

Metals
more
suited for
general
purposes
less fitted
for money.

6. The very fact that the inferior metals can be used, not merely as ornaments, but also more generally for common purposes of life, renders them less suitable as money; for the wider range of

competition to which they are thus exposed makes them more liable to extreme fluctuations in value. We have to go back to early times to find a case where they have been so maintained in use except as mere tokens, but a reference to the history of early Roman money may serve to illustrate the point. The first unit and standard of value was the "as," or pound, which, for all purposes of this argument, may be roughly taken at seven-eighths of a pound avoirdupois. The first records (to which Dr. Smith gives ample reference in his *Dictionary of Greek and Roman Antiquities*) would seem to imply an almost incredible cheapness of this metal; 10,000 asses for instance being cited as the sum assigned for the horse (or perhaps the horse and equipments) of an *eques,* and 2,000 for its annual keep. In B.C. 269, shortly after the extension of conquest had led the Romans into close connection with the Greek cities of southern Italy, which had long been familiar with the use of the precious metals—the denarius of about sixty grains weight of silver was introduced as the equivalent of ten asses, or about seventy-two pounds avoirdupois of copper, being in the proportion of one to about 850. But in B.C. 260, the copper "as" was re-reduced to one-sixth of its former weight. This was in the harassing times of the first Punic war, and high authorities differ greatly upon the very obscure part of the question which relates to comparative values; but no such sudden reduction in the weight of current metallic money could have been enforced by law in order to pay off the creditors of the state or of individuals. It is quite credible that a bankrupt should pay only 3s. 4d. in the pound, but it is physically impossible for men to accept payment of all their obligations, including wages, on terms conveying one-sixth only of their former purchasing power, and we have either to suppose a wholly abnormal decline in the value of the necessaries of life, or that the value of the copper had very greatly increased. There seems hardly room to doubt that, owing to its comparative cheapness, it had been largely used for general purposes both of war and of peace :—the bronze so well-known and so much used contained seven eighth-parts of this metal. The opening up of trade may no doubt have expedited the process, but the cheaper and more generally useful metal, once withdrawn, was absorbed for such uses, and soon disappears altogether, except as a subsidiary token, from the monetary system of the country. Whether debtors or creditors got the better in equity of the change may be an open question, but allowing the largest conceivable limit for any wilful degradation of the currency, a rise, not only as compared with silver but in actual purchasing power, must have taken place far beyond that which under any conceivable circumstances could occur in the value of either of the precious metals.

It is far more to the point to show how the precious metals are specially fitted for use as money by the very fact that they do not themselves satisfy directly any of the ordinary wants of mankind; that they are not liable to be consumed on any emergency, or withdrawn to any large extent for such purposes. They remain indestructible and ready to perform over and over again those peculiar functions into which they have grown, and but for which, gold and silver, though possibly valued for their rarity and costliness by the few, could never have been objects of rational desire to the many. Even if it be admitted that the first use of the precious metals, in point of time, was for ornament, that use has been subordinated ages ago to uses of a far more important and general character, which will be clearly perceived if the principles above referred to (§ 3) are fully realized.

CHAP. I.

7. I shall now endeavour to explain, first the primary and general uses of metallic money; then some of the more indirect and localised uses, and the conditions under which it comes to be used inferentially or by means of substitutes. We shall then be better able to see how the great work that money does is to generalise values, and thus to render more secure that continuity of supply, fitly adjusted to the wants of mankind, which is the material basis of all civilization ; and further, that the specific value of the precious metals themselves —which rests chiefly on their utility as money— while serving this function, becomes generalised in

The precious metals have a highly generalised value and serve to generalise all other values.

a pre-eminent degree, though ultimately governed by just the same law of "demand and supply" as any other commodity.

Law of Demand and Supply.

8. This so-called "law" of demand and supply is simply an exposition and recognition of the motives which actually do influence mankind in their mutual dealings, and will continue to do so as long as human nature remains substantially unchanged. On the demand side we have the category of all the reasons why men seek to have the use or enjoyment of any object or services. No limits can be assigned to the intensity of any man's desire to attain such advantages, but imperative considerations will inevitably govern some and influence most, though not always all, of his motives. But the wants of our many-sided nature may be satisfied in many ways. Taking even our most primary needs, man may thrive on wheat or rice or rye or millet, or on all or any of them in any proportion; and his choice will be influenced by what he may have to give up to obtain the one rather than the other. The supply side of the question deals chiefly with the sacrifices which are thus required. In the long run, men no doubt will not work unless they expect to get directly or indirectly that which will recompense them for their toil, but while permanent supply thus strongly tends to be measured by the comparative quantity of labour necessarily expended upon production, casual supply is largely affected by natural accidents. It is sometimes in excess, sometimes in

defect; and the more perishable commodities especially may, for all purposes of exchange, be necessaries or superfluities, invaluable or valueless, according to changing circumstances. So in the ordinary course of nature, which from this point of view is rather rhythmical than constant, we may have demand varying from the direst urgency down to utter neglect, and supply involving present sacrifices ranging through similar extremes. Nothing therefore can be more natural to mankind than the interchange of commodities, unless indeed these reasons are overborne by the instincts, customs, and traditions inseparable from a state of constant warfare. It is not only that the products of neighbouring countries are attractive from their novelty; but each side may have something to gain, and can offer distinct advantages to the other. The notion that in trade one man's gain must be another's loss rests upon a radically false conception of the known order of Nature.

9. It is commonly said that all trade was originally barter. Speaking in the general terms fitted to the present stage of the argument, it may be said with more truth that all trade now and at all times must, for by far the most part, consist of the interchange of consumable commodities, though, for reasons quite other than those just now under consideration, the exchanges are all made in terms of money. But it is convenient to start from this simple notion of trade, and see how the precious metals are naturally fitted to grow into

their special use as money, and are peculiarly adapted to aid in giving effect to some of the first weak promptings of forethought and intelligence.

There are two sides to every bargain. It is not merely giving on one side and receiving on the other. Each must have a want that the other can satisfy. There must be both a surplus and a deficiency on the one side to correspond conversely with a surplus and a deficiency on the other; and these conditions must be continuously maintained and fulfilled if the mutual relations of commerce are to go on and prosper. So even assuming the first difficulties of opening up intercourse to have been conquered and a trade to have begun, a deficiency in one particular may entail not only the direct loss on one side, but an indirect loss on the other; for that which was ready to be exchanged remains in excess, and is not wanted where it is, though those who do want have to go without it. There is a diminished inducement to continue its production, and an increased chance that the same mishap may occur in the future under conditions simply reversed. The continuity of industry is broken for want of its appropriate stimulus, and the material prosperity on both sides suffers accordingly. It is quite premature, at this stage of the question, to say that "capital" set free from one purpose may be devoted to another. Aberrations from ordinary supply are at best probable causes of some immediate waste and loss. How, and how far, such losses can be mitigated or obviated, so as to make such a generalisation as "capital" possible, is just the point now under consideration.

10. Apart from any question of external trade, a supply in excess ˙of apparent wants is a source of danger. An over-abundant harvest, for instance, is, in the measure of its excess, a present burden to the producer if he cannot get rid of the superfluity. He can get nothing for it ; it is liable to deterioration ; it tends to depreciate the value of subsequent harvests if brought into competition with them. It is against the special interests of their own class for cultivators to hold unusually large stores, and they have a double temptation to relax their industry. Even if surplus stocks are distributed in exchange for other commodities, still unusual abundance is always a temptation to lavishness and to idleness. But the precious metals cannot be consumed. They represent the results of a great deal of labour embodied in a "utility" of a singularly indestructible kind. Granted that in very rude and early times they may only have been made into ornaments and merely bartered for other things—probably necessaries of life, under the pressure of actual want— still they remain somewhere ; and wherever they go *to*, it may be presumed they can come *from*. If they are generally held in esteem for any reason whatever, they will on some terms or other get into the hands of those who can afford to hold a reserve of this description.

CHAP. I.

Correla-
tion with
uncertain-
ties of
natural
produc-
tion.

11. If in the order of nature, man's wants and the means of satisfying them had always been coincident, the need to hold such reserves would not have arisen. But chances and changes are constantly happening to individuals and districts and countries, both from their own errors and from causes entirely beyond their own control. Very general or widespread disasters are indeed rare, and a law of average seems to govern all fluctuations which are nevertheless of constant occurrence. Costly ornaments, as such, are merely the luxury of the few whose primary wants are amply supplied and who are not under the apprehension of want; but if they can be usually bartered for such commodities as may in the changing chances of life become indispensable, they become essentially money. Once let them become invested with the notion of general exchangeability, and the rest follows as a matter of course. Consciously or unconsciously, this new kind of utility will be practically recognised; and if experience justify the vague and inchoate confidence first felt, it will grow by its own growth. The precious metals which pre-eminently fulfil the required conditions take up to themselves this special property of representing general exchangeability, and the faith in their general purchasing power, as money, becomes by a natural course of development (extending probably from far back into prehistoric ages) one of the strongest convictions in humanity removed above the lowest stages of barbarism. It is the

one conviction shared by many who differ in race, language, religion, habits, and traditions, and have lost almost every other visible trace of a common origin.

12. And what are these uses? I do not at once refer to metallic money as a medium of exchange, because primarily it is not used as a mere medium. It embodies in itself in substantive form a highly generalised purchasing power, and for certain purposes in the world's economy this power is wanted in such a form. And although it is not possible to express the quantity so required in the terms of weight or value, it may not be in vain to try to indicate what these uses are, so that at the least we may know where to look for the indications of any changes which may affect the use or the supply of the precious metals, whether arising from merely local and temporary causes or from those which are more general and permanent, and form some relative estimate of the magnitude and consequences of any such changes.

13. The adequate reason for holding such a purchasing power in reserve is that we do not immediately know what to do with it, but have a reasonable assurance that it can be turned to some good purpose hereafter. Mere caprice or ostentation, though common enough, are very inadequate motives for holding a costly material which does not increase by natural growth and cannot be used for any of the common purposes of life. The primary use served is simply that

which has already been indicated. The reserve in the form of substantive money is and can only be held in correlation with that natural inequality of production which causes the casual aberrations in the value of other commodities. It is idle to say that the superfluity of one quarter might just as well be lent to supply the deficiency in another. As a matter of fact—speaking of course of the rule, not of the exception—such lending and borrowing has never been carried out in practice without the use of money in some form; and, though giving is an admirable virtue, the lesser blessing of receiving has ever been fraught with the most disastrous consequences—indeed giving, in the mouth of the receiver, very soon comes to mean the unrequited toil and practical slavery of the giver. None can be exempt from the common lot of toil; therefore the abstract purchasing power is rightly vested in a costly substance procured only by much toil. All are subject to inconveniences from the excess or defect of the results yielded to their toil: therefore a substantive representative having a potential value adapted for prospective use is taken by those whose products are in excess, and parted with by those whose more immediate wants have to be satisfied. If there had not been this coincidence between the facts in nature and the qualities and obvious uses of the precious metals, the peculiar functions of money could never have been developed.

Why invested in a costly substance.

14. As far as the adjustments of production and

consumption are simultaneously or directly made, there is no room for the use of money in this primary sense. Even when it has become the common medium of exchange, any one who buys as much as he sells cannot possibly have any money left in his hands. There is no conceivable use for a specific duplicate *representative* of the value of commodities, the utility of which is presently available, and which the owners meantime retain in their own possession. The vague notion that money is in some way co-extensive with wealth, or that, in its specific form and irrespective of the special uses it serves, it constitutes value, arises apparently from some confused idea that because money can usually buy anything at any time—which indeed is, as far as possible, its special function—it could therefore, if only there were enough of it, buy everything at all times: the seller's side of the question being lost sight of altogether. The quantity, or more strictly the value, of money which can be employed, does not in fact bear any direct relation to the wealth of a country in houses, fields, mines, or any such productive property, or to the magnitude of its transactions in commodities interchanged the one against the other for present or proximate use. It depends entirely upon the extent to which the processes of readjustment just referred to are being carried on, the conditions of which are that some members of the community have given up the present possession of the commodities required for the use of others, in exchange for a "purchasing power" vested in a substantive form which may indeed be used at any time, but which it is not reasonable to suppose they will try to use at once to reverse their own act.

If a highly philosophic soul were to urge that gold was useless and valueless, inasmuch as it did not satisfy in any way any of the wants of a reasonable being, the reply might still be urged that it is, at the least, a most effective means of getting credit for such commodities as would sustain him, till he could earn them for himself as the fruits yielded by the natural increase of nature to his own industry, and he may have the added satisfaction of knowing that the receiver of his money, and the receiver from him again and again, will have precisely the same advantage, though no power on earth can so transmute the metal as to make it serve any other purpose more useful to mankind.

Money represents general interests.

15. The distinction must be carefully held between the business of those who are known as money-dealers and the proper functions of money itself. It should be borne in mind that the theorem of "demand and supply" only represents two closely-connected phases of the conditions under which we all live, and it will be well to understand clearly how they severally stand in relation to money. All, without exception, must swell the demand for consumption—that must go on continuously from day to day as a matter of

physical necessity.   All must also be held to make, directly or indirectly, the sacrifices requisite to secure supply.   The first is the general interest common to all : the second is subdivided into innumerable special interests casually opposed to the broader general interest.   It is the general interest common to all that products should be absolutely cheap, that is, yielded to the least possible expenditure of toil—bad work and scamped work, and all such misfeasance, are not in any true sense cheap, but ruinously dear ; while each particular interest naturally desires that its special product should be relatively dear, that is, that its own sacrifices should be more amply recompensed than the sacrifices of others.   Now money can only be *held* by those whose wants and desires are not urgent, and spent by those whose wants, whether necessary or capricious, are more urgent.   For no man spends his money until he gets for it something that he wants more, or for some reason likes more, than anything else that he expects to be able to get for his money.   But by the very act of buying he transfers his *power* of buying to the seller, so that quite irrespective of any wish or intention of the rich—who very much at their option may or may not have wealth in this special form—the possessor of money for the time being is, so far, identified with the general interest just referred to : he is outside of all special interests and the increase which naturally accrues to them.   He is in the most general sense a buyer, and, in common with consumers, desires to get good value for his money.

16. The *holding* of specific money is in fact a burden. There cannot be any usufruct of it, taking the word in its strict primary sense. The cultivator eats the corn grown in his field, trusting that other corn is growing up to supply its place; but the mere money owner who spends to satisfy his wants is rather in the position of one who sells a field which will never come back to him again. There is therefore a very strong and constant stimulus for the holder of money to find out some way of making some use of it which may entitle him to share in the natural increase of production; but though the individual may transfer his general purchasing power, *that* only transfers the difficulty to another. But experience shows—the accumulated experience of ages if you will—that, to use a much-abused phrase, many things can often be "bought cheap and sold dear." But this could hardly afford an adequate reason for the continued use of materials so costly as the precious metals, unless there were some real utility in the operation in which the community at large fully shared; for be it remembered, all operations of the kind are perfectly free from all coercion, except that which arises from natural causes beyond the control of man. Barter affords the most ample scope for the art of mere bargain-driving, and the use of money rather lessens than increases the advantage which craft has over ignorance, for as far as the current

business of buying and selling is concerned, one
man knows what money is just as well as another,
which is by no means always the case as regards
the commodities dealt with. Indeed it should be
observed that though it is the money owner who
tries to buy cheap, it is as the owner of a special
commodity that this buyer hopes to sell dear.
Such a use of money could not have been sustained or tolerated if it were not a fact in nature
that many things are far less useful under some
conditions than under others, and that opportunities constantly arise for adjusting these injurious
inequalities. It is to the purpose in this context
to refer rather to *utility* than to the *cost* of
production, for though commodities required by
others may have been produced with very little
labour, yet the owners are not likely to part with
them unless they have more than they require for
their own wants. Conversely they will readily
part with an excess which they find they cannot
use, although it may have cost them a great deal
of trouble to acquire. Money cannot go beyond
the present urgency of demand, and the first
demand will naturally be that of the producers
themselves to satisfy their own immediate needs.
If under ordinary circumstances any commodity
can be yielded at less cost in one place than in
another, there is an evident reason for attempting
to exchange it habitually for some other consumable product; but the precious metals are not
suited for permanent traffic of the kind, for both

the supply of them, and the uses to which they can be applied, are limited. They circulate with great advantage; they are constantly an object of desire; but experience soon shows that nothing can be gained by unduly accumulating them.

Extended uses of the precious metals.

17. As the precious metals become known and used as money in different communities, a more extended field for, and, to a certain extent, an amplification of their uses is found. It is indeed rather for the convenience of exposition than from any supposed sequence in order of time that I have not hitherto referred to these uses, and do not yet allude to those connected with the division of labour. Different monetary customs and systems have arisen in all ages from differing circumstances, and are to be found in all stages of development in the present day in various parts of the world. My object is not to present an historical sketch, but to deal first with more general principles, and then to proceed to those arising from them which are more liable to casual modification.

All value in exchange is merely relative, and, as far as peoples are isolated in separate countries, whatever may be the quantity of the precious metals seeking employment, the value that can be employed must be determined by the extent to which such uses as I have described can be found for them within these limits. What these limits are, what variety of conditions are comprised within them, whether their boundaries are easy or difficult to pass, are all questions to which a

due reply could be given only by aid of a widely
extended and most searching knowledge of political
and physical geography. But a further special
function of the precious metals as money is to
overrun these barriers and extend the limits of
peaceful intercourse.

18. Given any substance widely recognised, and
as widely appreciated, so portable and indestructible
that it can be carried with the least possible cost
and risk from place to place, and we have a most
potent and subtle agent for extending the sphere of
the beneficial interchanges and adjustments of commerce. Whatever obstacles may be opposed to such
money, by war, by policy, by prejudice, or by
natural barriers, it will be the pioneer best fitted
to baffle, or evade, or overcome such difficulties—
more than all, that unwillingness to act which
results from ignorance and uncertainty. It is a
mere delusion to attribute any peculiar positive or
abstract value to the precious metals. If a given
weight of metal can be exchanged for fifty measures
of corn in one place, and sixty in another, is the
corn cheaper or the metal dearer? If it be merely
a question of getting ornaments, the latter is certainly the more appropriate reply. If we were
regarding corn simply in connection with the well-
being of the inhabitants of the respective regions,
the fact would be of very slight and uncertain
significance either way. But the given weight, say
of silver, affords a means of comparison which is
easily intelligible and sufficiently accurate, though,

as every trader knows, the fact that so many measures are given for his silver to-day is no proof that the same or any greater or less quantity will be given at any future time. Still there is some object, not only definite but tangible, with which anything which can be made the subject of a bargain can be compared. Whether a fixed quantity of commodities is given for a varying weight of silver, or a certain weight of silver for fluctuating quantities of commodities, the comparisons suggested are so simple and obvious, that the silver becomes recognised inevitably as a common standard of comparative value, especially for that surplus of supply which it is desirable to convey from one place to another. The difference between the price in silver at the place of purchase, and the expected price at the place of sale, may be represented as the gradient of effective demand ; the cost and risk of transit, the friction to be overcome : all of which have to be estimated with as much accuracy as may be. There is a certain definiteness thus given, not only to calculations, but still more to the information, often coming from distant quarters and through uncertain channels, upon which action must be taken.

How they specially aid enterprise.

19. Moreover, most commodities are comparatively bulky and perishable, and barter is thus impeded with the friction of heavy charges both ways. It is true, permanent trade must depend upon the ever-recurring demand for consumable articles ; still the precious metals run lightly,

because their friction is so small, and they are thus specially fitted to carry out any one-sided operation which the casual exigencies of any one country may require. Again, at all times, as indeed now also, enterprising men, the born pioneers of commercial intercourse, must have had occasion to reason with themselves somewhat to this effect : " I hear much of the products of this distant region, and am quite satisfied that some of them would suit the wants of my countrymen very well. They are priced cheaply enough in money, but, until I have tried, I cannot tell whether or not they can be obtained in any quantity, nor do I very well know what any one there will buy from me in exchange. If I take merchandise, it will cost me much to carry, and may get spoilt on the road ; and when I get there I may find that I have not brought the right things after all, or they may not like them at first, whatever they may think by and by ; or they may drive a hard bargain with me, knowing very well how much it will cost me to carry my goods back," and so on.   " But gold and silver I can carry secretly, and at very little cost.   They will take that if they will take anything, and if at the worst my venture comes to nought, I can bring back my treasure uninjured."   No doubt precious stones, which to a large extent can serve the same purposes as the precious metals, have, in some stages of society, been largely utilised as money for such reasons as these, and have been more largely in request in consequence ; but while such jewels are only

Jewels.

adapted to the comparatively narrow circle of the wealthy, gold and silver can be divided and sub-divided, and massed again with the greatest ease and no appreciable loss. They can be fitted to great and small wants alike ; a finer edge is thus given to the wedge, and one which can better be applied to any part of the mass which has to be penetrated.

Commerce extended by experiment.

20. Those only who will be at the pains to realize something of the true spirit of commercial enter-prise can appreciate the weight that should be given to considerations of this nature. The boldest soldier, entering upon a new and unknown country, must look well to his means of retreat, or fall under such censure for culpable recklessness as would be quite incompatible with any higher claims to generalship. All commerce—all this work of adaptation and adjustment—has ever depended as much upon experiment as any of the applied sciences. Even at the risk of seeming to carry this side of my argument to an extreme, I would say further, that, but for this spirit of enterprise, prompting "the merchant adventurer" to incur freely the risk of experiments, while judiciously selecting the best means of carrying them out, the use of the precious metals as money would have been altogether inconsiderable. For the demand of the average of mankind is not only capricious, but unintelligent, wanting in forethought to an amazing degree, and lacking the power to realize the advantages or disadvantages which must

inevitably arise from changed conditions until they are actually present to their senses. Instead of the alternations of scarcity and abundance, we should too often have to read of famine and reckless waste, if those to whom the work falls of adjusting supply to demand had not the energy to carry out their work under the heaviest discouragement. They have much need of a wedge to open up ways closed, though closed only by ignorance or apathy. The channel once opened, the stream of products of present utility flows readily, according to its natural gradient. They have to deal the more largely in the material form of money, because the advantages which may be derived from the inter-change of commodities which satisfy real wants are often so tardily perceived. The ignorant many neither know, nor care to know, on what the value of money rests, any more than why the moon rises, or why the tides ebb and flow; equally they care little for future contingencies; but they have become familiar with money, and desire it intensely, though only knowing vaguely, and in a very narrow sense, why it is well with those who have it. The feeling of pride or of security associated with its possession takes off attention from the drawback that they are getting no increase from it, the more so as the burden can be so easily shifted as soon as it is felt. Probably one of the last truths they would be likely to recognise is that in one way or other they are as a body compelled to save, and are thus enabled to recoup the outlay of those who have preserved some needful commodity which they would have wasted. Improvident tribes or nations are poor because they are generally self-indulgent and waste their powers of production, and they have in the aggregate little to offer in exchange with others. But the quantity of actual money used by them is comparatively large, for the most obvious and necessary savings have to be made through its agency. Often it is that the trader's demand, which can be made effective only by the use of such money, takes the place of conscious and intelligent economy, and the trader's supply satisfies the wants or tempts the desires of the former seller by replacing ready prepared in his hand that which his own forethought would never have secured to him.

Indestructibility gives stability to their value.

21. There is yet another property of the precious metals which makes their natural use more certainly beneficial for these special purposes of adjustment. If they were perishable—if the dread of periodical supply were likely to urge holders to get rid of them (that is to buy), on any terms they could, their operations, from the general point of view of those interested in the continuity of the supply of commodities, would frequently be mischievous, and an aggravation of the evils which the primary use of money is calculated to mitigate. Every buyer wishes to purchase cheap, but the very act of buying increases the demand, and is a weight in the scale against himself. Conversely with every seller. Dealings in money reverse the

terms, but do not escape the operation of the rule.
Normally interchanges, whether by purchase and
sale, or by barter, tend towards the equalisation of
supply and of value ; but when made under the
pressure of fear, from whatever cause it may arise,
the aberration from normal values is extreme, and
apt to be in the last degree injurious.   Especially
if the money, which is the specific representative of
general purchasing power, were itself subject to
such a pressure, the terms dear and cheap would
cease to have a specific significance, the whole order
of trade would be inverted and become unintelligible to by far the greater number of those concerned in it.   But the result would be that the
commodities taken in exchange for money would
be sent in different directions, not in accordance
with the relative wants of consumers, but with the
view of forcibly redistributing, not only the burden,
but the prospective loss entailed by holding a form
of money itself liable to depreciation.   Both the
monetary system and that of every industry connected with it would thus be very severely strained.
But the owner of money made of the precious
metals can seldom be under any temptation to
aggravate the inequalities which it is his special
function to adjust.   If his money yield him no
natural increase on the one hand, neither does it
suffer from natural decay on the other.   As the less
of two evils he can afford to wait till a fitting
occasion be found for the use of his treasure.
Obviously he will only make bad worse by entering

into transactions which the natural course of events will not ultimately justify. If he do this by error of judgment the direct loss is his own, and he suffers more promptly and severely than the community to whom he has not rendered suitable service, and who are under no sort of obligation to accept the over-supply he may offer to them of commodities comparatively perishable, the consumption of which can rarely be suddenly increased to any large extent. The fact that money can be held at no appreciable cost gives practically an elasticity to it ; for, though the whole quantity held retains its potential value, only that variable portion for which a suitable use can be found is actively employed. Some serves for ordinary uses, some for more special occasions, while all the hoards are fully drained only on exceptional emergencies.

22. Still the same rule applies throughout, in duly modified degree, to the limits within which the precious metals can be utilised as money. Associating it with the idea of traffic with foreigners and strangers in distant parts, the practical necessity of having the reserve of purchasing power in a specific and tangible form independently recognised by all, is more apparent. The average quantities held will be the greater, as more complicated and indirect adjustments of trade become practicable ; and though the ultimate objects of these operations remain the same, there will be, especially in the earlier stages of civilisation, greater necessity for the use of such money.

But payments in the precious metals cannot be made continuously by one country to another except, indeed, on a comparatively limited scale. The periodical waste is small and slow, and the amounts are steadily cumulative. A State which produces gold or silver in any large quantities has indeed no means of maintaining its value but by exporting it; for the attempt to force an increasing quantity into use, unless there be also a corresponding increase in the special uses for it, can end only in lessening the value of the whole. If we represent the quantity of the commodities parted with for money on the conditions already laid down (§14), by say 100, the treasure which is the equivalent of them must be taken as 100 also. But if the latter be increased to 120, other conditions remaining the same, the only conceivable means of equation is the corresponding reduction of commodities given for each unit of treasure to the proportion of ten-twelfths to one; prices rising apparently in the same ratio inversely. The relative quantities of commodities have to be adjusted in the same way as if they were exchanged in direct barter. The way in which such changes are worked out is clear enough, if only we take care to follow closely the course of the money itself, and not the transaction of the individual. The first holder has more to get rid of, and sooner or later has to give more—that is, according to pre-existing standards, buys less cheaply; but when he comes to sell the commodity bought, the second holders, having already received more, are just in the same position, and the adjustment of the actual weight of money to the value correlated with it is surely effected. And if it be thus impossible for a State producing the precious metals to increase the aggregate value which it can hold, it is equally so for any other country to receive them continuously in excess of its wants, without their experiencing a decrease in value to compensate for the super-abundance of quantity. The abruptness of any such fluctuations is softened by the conditions re-ferred to in the last paragraph, but not the less surely will the result be brought about in the long run.

The converse argument holds good in the event of diminished supply, but in either case the adjust-ments of supply to the demand for commodities—which are the *raison d'être* of money—though perhaps casually somewhat disturbed and confused, are substantially only remotely and indirectly affected. The common standard of comparative value has indeed shifted, but the symptom is that prices, which are never supposed to be fixed, range generally on a higher or lower level, with which all concerned very soon become familiar.

Limit to the trans-mission of metallic money.

23. The value and quantity of money which can be absorbed and held by any one country, and the value and quantity which can, within any short period of time, be transmitted from one country to another, involve very different considerations and give rise to very different consequences. In

the former case any change in value arising from increased or lessened quantity will be in proportion to the whole aggregate held within the country. Gold and silver used as ornaments are of course specially out of the account, and any quantity buried, hoarded, or hidden away entirely, cannot practically be brought into it. But this aggregate may, and in all probability does, consist of the balance of the accumulations of many ages. Its value has been adjusted by the successive operations of internal and external traffic, but the amount that can effectively be transmitted from place to place at any one time for the purposes of exchange is limited by the surplus of products immediately available for sale. Taking this surplus as normally represented by ten, if the attempt is blindly urged to purchase with treasure to the extent of twenty, the only result can be that the prices of products are doubled. But when this excess of treasure goes into the country, and is mingled with the large aggregate there held, its effect may be there represented by one-tenth or one-hundredth, or even may be so quenched by the friction which custom opposes to any change as to become quite inappreciable.

The supply of products will of course be likely to increase when an unusual inducement is offered to bring it forward for sale, but here again the natural law of necessity interposes. Prices must advance in a far greater ratio than the increase of supply thus induced, because the sacrifices entailed by even a rigid parsimony, by the exercise of which some extra supply might be afforded, are no measure of the sufferings which would result from selling that which the owners required for their own urgent needs. Still if a general approximate equation of values has been effected by reference to the precious metals as a common measure, it follows that a change in this standard itself in one place must lead to repeated efforts for a new adjustment until the due balance is restored.

24. It thus appears that the aggregate *value* of the precious metals used as money is not and cannot be enhanced merely by the production of a larger quantity of them. That value can only be augmented with, and by the increase of, the peculiar uses found for it in carrying on the work of the world. A comparatively small supply from mines or other sources is quite sufficient to make good the annual waste of money or ornaments, though with an expanding trade and the growth of wealth generally a large yield may not be more than will suffice to support the continuity of the proportionate value of money.

There is thus a definite, though by no means a fixed, limit to the value which can be held by any country. A certain value is required for its internal uses, and will circulate within it : a certain portion for its external trade will circulate between it and all other countries. There will also be some held in reserve not actively employed, though indirectly associated with the operations of traffic. Thus we hear how in very early times Abraham sought a burying-place in the land of the sons of Heth. The intercourse between these great men of old does not imply any direct adjustments of the nature which has been described. But the 400 shekels of silver paid for the purchase are said to be "current money of the merchant." As the Patriarch received these from "the merchant," so they would be returned by Ephron for those uses in commerce which constituted their value. The convenience of such casual and indirect uses of money is an additional inducement for the rich to keep some part of their wealth in this form, and increases the total quantity, the value of which can be maintained. Only in a highly perfected monetary system is the use of actual money for such purposes superseded, and to the present day, for dealings with nations whose surplus products cannot directly be fitted to exchange with our own surplus products, or those under our control, we are still obliged to have recourse to metallic money, which travels by paths which we cannot follow, and works out adjustments which we cannot ourselves effect.

25. The case of Spain, loaded with the spoils of metallic wealth drawn from her conquests in the New World, is a trite but not the less apposite example of the truth of this theorem. But there was more of real difficulty in her position than is often supposed. Its treasure could have been turned to good account only by the exercise of

an energy, care, and discretion beyond the knowledge of the age. It was positively mischievous, not only because it gave birth to an exaggerated pride of wealth, but because also, when put to the test, there was so little reality in that wealth. Spain, indeed, might without impoverishment have spent the revenue drawn from her gold and silver-producing colonies, and let the treasure go away altogether; but it is a very difficult matter to monetise treasure for the permanent advantage of any single people or country : it flows out, finding its own level and leaving no permanent trace behind. Spending it freely among the population would only lead to a general rise in the price of commodities not beneficial to any one. On the contrary, this tends only to attract supply from abroad not required for home consumption, but designed merely to obtain the superabundant gold, which would thus be drawn out, leaving the country to fall back on its own interrupted and weakened sources of supply. Or suppose a more extended effort. Gold is sent abroad to buy food for the support of labourers engaged upon works not immediately productive, but, when these are completed, if they are to be made permanently self-supporting, the supply of hoarded gold must cease, and the new product has to get into consumption. It is only a small part of the task to make something which *would* be useful *if* it were wanted by those who could give an acceptable equivalent for it. The real factors of production are the "labour"

that can work, and " capital " consisting of the
aggregate of things necessary to support labour,
and the attempt to promote it by mere force of
money is very apt not to coincide with the natural
development of industries mutually supporting
each other, and tending to increase together.
Those who have hitherto supplied food for gold
are not, as might hastily be supposed, so dependent
as to be forced to take this new product instead of
it, for they cannot in the nature of things have
sold more than their surplus. New conditions for
free adjustments have arisen with only a somewhat
weak presumption, *a priori*, that they can now be
effected between the same parties. Heroic attempts
to fit and graft on the industries started with such
money, upon the permanent natural conditions of
industrial life, require also a most heroic capacity
for combination and adjustment.

26. Gold and silver are not names to conjure **The law of**
with : as far as they constitute money nothing else **average.**
can be made of them. Yet are their uses such as
have been described of a most real and practical
kind, fully adequate to account for the high and
universal appreciation in which they have ever
been held, for by their aid man is better able to
provide against those aberrations from the ordinary
course of Nature which from time to time threaten
to beat him down or bear him backwards in the
struggle for life. These are often said to be
governed by a " law of average," vaguely conceived as a sort of mitigating influence which, if

left to itself, will somehow or other prevent any one from suffering too cruelly. But the security which a knowledge of this "law" affords is attained only by exertions and sacrifices of the same kind as those required to attain the fruits yielded to toil under any other natural laws. The beneficence is shown rather in the power with which man is endowed to see in that law reason to temper confidence with forethought, and dread with hope. Self-adjusting the law may indeed be said to be in the sense that the work required is done with marvellous efficiency by the half-conscious exertions of the many engaged in it, controlled and guided by the experience of generations, and any rash attempt to set aside the methods so ruled and developed may be productive of incalculable mischief. But self-adjusting it is not in any other sense, and though a wise government will be slow to interfere with the functions of trade which, if it rightly gauges them, will be found infinitely too great, complex, and minutely subdivided for it to assume, yet it should be its study to watch over and recognise the due scope of its operations ; to use rather than to supersede its action, if need be, for the public service ; above all, to relieve it from needless restraints or artificial monopolies, and as far as the action of the law or authority can subserve such ends, to purify it from the canker of false dealing, which is the worst foe to its prosperity. Further, it must be kept in mind that though trade and productive industries are closely allied, the range of the former must be within the conditions under which the law of average operates —in other words, no skill in distribution can compensate for absolute deficiency in production, however much it may do to mitigate its most direful effects. And herein the "Law" of Demand and Supply, as rightly understood and limited, is justified. It is propounded subject to the obvious postulate that the demand must be "effective," that is, its scope is confined to those who have money or money's worth as a means of interchange. It affords no excuse for the misapplication of the *laissez faire* doctrine to those who may be made destitute by a widespread calamity. On the contrary, it clearly indicates the true nature of the remedy which should be applied. Bring them, if possible, within the range of distributive organisation by making their demand *effective*, rather than thwart or weaken that organisation at a time when all its energies are overtaxed. Money in such emergencies works, in many ways more widely, cheaply, quickly, and effectively than any other agent, but the hard fact must be clearly recognised that only by means outside of the equitable laws of mutual interchange can it flow to the destitute.

27. The mere fact of material production is often so completely taken for granted, that the effects of open traffic are directly misjudged. Thus, in a time of famine the population of an Indian village is found to be in danger of starvation. The stores are empty, for not long since the grain in them

High degree of stability attained under it.

was sold. Silver, and with equal discrimination roads also, are at once set down as the cause of the destitution. It is not considered that had not the grower by these very means been made sure of a market, the grain in all probability would never have been grown at all. The difficulty in all these cases is from the extreme poverty of a large portion of the people who are living from hand to mouth. It is not so much that a trader has taken away grain and left rupees, but that the seller of the grain has not *kept* any adequate reserve of the money given, either in specie or in any other form of permanent value. Mere money is not, and never can be, the cure for poverty of this sort. Let us further follow this case as affording fair illustrations of the principles involved. The notion of keeping separate and adequate stocks of grain in every village is doubly irrational. In the first place, scarcity comes at uncertain, often at distant periods : there is the strongest tendency both in men and in governments to forget an oft-deferred evil. Stores are sure to be neglected, or to dete-

(§ 14.) riorate, and the burden of the duty, often not fairly distributed at the beginning, is done in a per- functory and inefficient manner. Then again. All perturbations within the memory of man are com- paratively of short duration and extended over limited areas. If, therefore, we submit ourselves intelligently to this "law of average," a far higher order of security is attained ; and more than this : Let the necessary conditions be developed ; that is,

let there be sufficient production spread over sufficiently wide and dispersed areas ; let the means of
communication between them be safe and easy, and
an adequate motive for holding the needful reserves
of supply comes within the influence of ordinary
experience. They are wanted now here, now there ;
and the holder's patience is not worn out or suffered to sleep from interminable delays. Money
too is kept ready to do its part, and is especially
useful in lightening exceptionally urgent transactions which are in excess of the ordinary means
of traffic. It helps to spread the cost of hasty
adjustment over more adequate periods. Nor can
I forbear a passing word on the moral aspects of
the contrasted systems. The segregation on the
one side tends to foster suspicion. Every stranger
is a rival, and in a time of apprehended scarcity
the wild desire of every one to make himself safe
is a strong temptation to untimely secret hoarding,
which greatly aggravates the evil. On the other,
the habit of mutual intercourse and interdependence assuages these fears and mitigates these
tendencies, so perilous in a time of danger. A
more intelligent apprehension of natural law and
higher feelings of social morality go hand in hand.

28. The practical nature of the benefits of
adjustments under the law of average is well
exemplified by the common practice of insurance.
That a very high degree of security is attained by
generalising a large number of riskful items is well
known to all, but that is not quite the point

Illustra-
tion.
"Loading"
on the pre-
mium of
insurance.

CHAP. I.

referred to. The premium paid is considerably in excess of the calculated equivalent of the risks incurred. It is "loaded" to cover the costs of management and afford a fair profit to the under-writers. Shrewd men of business pay down this addition to the calculated equivalent of their losses at sea, for the compensating advantage of adjusting these payments to their ordinary incomings, rather than have to meet them in heavy amounts which would throw out the continuity of their ordinary arrangements. Metallic money used in trade answers very closely in some respects to this "loading" of the premiums of insurance. It is a necessary outlay, and though costly, is amply worth the cost.

The "limit of perfect recovery."

29. It may perhaps still be objected that such facilities for distribution after all only spread the evils of scarcity over a wider area, but do not afford any complete remedy for them. It is an inconvenience, no doubt, for any one district to be disturbed by an unexpected demand from a distant quarter, and though the seller, say of grain, may directly gain as much as his local customers lose, the indirect disturbance occasioned may ·be of much more consequence. To this specific argument it is no reply to say that all give and take in turn. Still, though it were shown arithmetically that the evil had only been diffused, and perhaps increased, by the process, it by no means follows that important benefits are not secured to all. As has been before observed,

there can be no comparison made between the several degrees of scarcity. The argument, after all, is of much the same weight as a calculation that a hundred men, deprived of a single meal, suffer as much in the aggregate as three or four starved to death. Even in mechanics we do not find that a certain weight makes a "breaking strain," and every less weight merely causes a less injury. A "limit of perfect recovery" is soon reached. Just as it is with a chain which would be wrenched and broken with a strain of two tons applied at once, but will raise many thousands of single tons, and decay at last from other causes altogether,—so it is with men and countries. If only in the vicissitudes of life the extremity of pressure can be mitigated, no permanent injury is suffered. Imperfectly as the work of production and distribution is carried out, the power of treasure as money has often done this much for suffering humanity, and the traditions of its efficacy form a part of the long accumulated teachings of practical experience.

30. The uses of the precious metals have grown up for the most part entirely without the aid of laws ordained by any sovereign power. Authority has sometimes recognised, but far more often failed to recognise, the true bases of their value, or the conditions under which they could be beneficially employed as money. In either case its influence was only remote and indirect, and helpful only in so far as it was confined strictly within such

limits as may fitly be ascribed to jurisprudence. If, for example, the scale of current market weights had got into confusion, or, what is very much the same thing, if it were a matter of doubt and uncertainty what proportion of pure metal (which is all that is accounted of value) should be given in any weight delivered, the law may, indeed cannot refuse to, discharge its special function of deciding on the disputed points of any formal or informal contract which may be brought before it. Its decision is a nullity, and settles nothing, if it do not define peremptorily and exactly what is to be done in satisfaction of its decree ; and this, for the most part, will form an authoritative precedent for the ruling of all subsequent cases. Or if customs are so conflicting as to entail constant litigation and public inconvenience, the legislature may venture to ordain that such and such definitions apply to such and such terms of weight or capacity ; but even regulations of this kind must be carried out with much patience and discrimination, for when they are broken through ignorance, or still more by those who take advantage of the ignorance of others, it is hard to inflict so extreme a penalty as a denial of justice to the suitor. Arbitrary power may indeed decide on such points unjustly for its own benefit, or unwisely from mistaken policy, and terrify or deceive its subjects into accepting new terms for all existing obligations ; but no power on earth can restrain men from being guided by the practical experiences and by the pressing necessities of life.   The estimate of any future comparative values cannot be controlled by a change in the terms in which they are expressed. Trade may indeed be driven away and industry crushed by the attempt, or more probably driven to subterfuges and concealment, ending generally in some tacit compromise, much to the discouragement of open dealing, and serving only to perpetuate some pedantic absurdity of form required to save the dignity of baffled authority.

Money is indeed most essentially the agent of free interchange.   Even if turned to the purposes of international war it can only work on the free will of the individual.   It may appeal to motives which are well matched by a traitor's perfidy.   Gold is neither moral nor immoral ; it simply conveys a most potent and unqualified power of choice. It may be made the agent of the most subtle temptation, but cannot be used for direct coercion either in war or in peace.   But these, after all, are but accidental and perverted uses of it as a medium of exchange which by no means contribute to the productive utility which constitutes its value.   It may elude the grasp of legally constituted authority, but its work cannot be done unless a high standard of integrity is maintained among those who deal with it.   It may be said to be the most efficient agent of fraud against force ; but when force and fraud are thus put into opposition, the term "*unjust*" applies equally to both, and each has a claim equally good, or bad, to fall back upon, the ethics of a state of warfare. The power of money and the privileges derived from *status* are often in conflict; but these topics will be more fittingly treated hereafter. Meanwhile we shall often have to look for realities beneath the surface, to "read between the lines," often feeling our way rather by careful induction than by the direct light of testimony.

CHAPTER II.

(*Money.*)

EXTENDED USES OF METALLIC MONEY AND OF
SUBSTITUTES FOR IT.

1. My argument has not been drawn out merely to
prove the utility of the precious metals as money.
I might well take the verdict of common experience
unquestioned upon that point; but my object has
rather been from the first to indicate the nature
and the measure of the uses to which they can be
so applied, because, on going further into the
question, we shall soon come face to face with the
appearances which have given rise to the most
opposite and contradictory theories regarding
metallic money. It has been treated of as though
it were the source and basis of all wealth. It has
been disparaged as though its use were a mere
figment and delusion which should be rejected
altogether as a relic of the barbarous past. We
have thus not merely to inquire what monetary
system is ideally the best, but must endeavour to
see how it is that "money," admittedly of a very
imperfect character, works at all, to what extent it
may be trusted, and under what circumstances it is

of uncertain and shifting value, or wholly inefficient. In this relation we must take human nature as we find it in all parts of the world, neither forgetting its essential points of unity, nor overlooking the casual differences, which, though comparatively superficial, are still perhaps the outcome of the circumstances of many generations, neither imputing to it qualities which it does not possess, nor assuming that whatever is, is right and incapable of reformation. Moreover, the practical necessity must ever be kept in mind of preserving the continuity of all the multifarious transactions which are, as a matter of fact, carried on by means of money. Changes in its form or in its terms can only be made operative subject to this necessity; but still under the pressure of necessity, or supposed necessity, they will be made in a very irregular and arbitrary way. It is idle to say that the use of such a medium might be dispensed with altogether, for we have nothing to do at present with such notions of an ideally perfect system of interchange. The same causes which have led to the division of men into separate countries, kindreds and classes, required still more strongly the use of a measure and reserve common to all, but the value of which was not under the control of any, for the limited and restricted intercourse which, in spite of wars and jealousies innumerable, they have contrived to maintain. But the direct influence of money has not been in any way to supersede the confidence which may naturally grow up between man and man. The earliest records afford indications that trust without any tangible security has always been a feature of commercial polity. If the direct mutual transactions of A and B are not equal in value within any particular period, the balance may remain over as a matter of account stated in any terms which may be agreed upon. Debts may be expressed in corn or oil just as well as in silver. But this implies the expectation that occasions for the further adjustment of supply to demand will shortly arise between the communities with which A and B are severally concerned. Otherwise, and in the ever-recurring case that under constantly changing circumstances, the occasion for new transactions will next arise in quite different quarters, substantive money will be required. For though B may trust A, it does not follow that B, who has no visible sign of wealth to show, will be trusted by C D and E, and so on. A far-reaching and general purchasing power is, therefore, required in cases to which personal confidence does not extend. When a perfectly intelligent sense of fraternity pervades the whole world, money may be converted into silver walls or golden gates, or applied to such other uses as a transformed society may find for it. Meanwhile its highest employment is to be a common link between the sundered tribes of humanity as far as it can be made to serve that purpose.

2. Although the precious metals are the common measures of value which can be applied with the greatest certitude and exactness, and under the

Permanence of weights used for money.

greatest variety of circumstances throughout the whole civilized world, yet the actual standards of money value which currently obtain in different countries are strangely diverse. And the source of these discrepancies will be found in the vain attempts which have repeatedly been made to assign a transcendental fixity of value to money itself, over and above that which arises from the working of natural causes, as will appear more clearly hereafter. But where the simple and rational notion of a weight of the precious metal as a practical common measure of exchange value has been preserved, there are singular indications of the tenacity with which the units thus adopted have been recognised for ages. Thus at the present day, for the external trade of the greater part of Southern Asia, we have the Mexican dollar coming from the most prolific sources of production in the New World, which maintains with singular precision the weight of the old Roman *ounce*. In the north and more ancient part of China, the only unit of value is a fixed weight of silver, circulating on the credit of private bankers as to its purity, which we find to be in the somewhat strange proportion of $\frac{37}{40}$ths or $92\frac{1}{2}$ per cent. fine, being the same as that of the old Tower pound of silver which was the original standard recognised by Charlemagne, and introduced into England before the time of the Conquest. The full weight of the pound troy then was 11 oz. 5 dwt., and it would therefore contain as nearly as may be an old Roman pound weight of pure metal.

Again there seems some reason to think that this Roman ounce, the name of which certainly was received (οὐγκια) among the various systems current among the maritime Greeks, was just one sixteenth of the *Attic* mina. Now this Attic system had been adjusted by Solon in the sixth century B.C., in the proportion of 72 : 100, to the Euboïc scale, which latter also remained current in other parts of Greece, and was certainly one of those used by the Babylonians. The Mexican dollar bears just this proportion to the *tael* weight of China, which, it may be reasonably conjectured, was in correspondence from a very remote period with the scale established in Central Asia.[1]

[1] Two systems of weights came to Greece in early days from the older civilizations of Asia, the first origin of which is lost in the still earlier history of the Chaldæans: the Æginetan and the Euboïc. They were related to each other respectively in the proportion of 12 to 10, thus early indicating the conflict between the decimal and duodecimal modes of notation. About B.C. 600 Solon, in carrying out certain great social reforms, including a scheme for the general relief of debtors, to which it is needless here to allude further, introduced the Solonian or Attic system, which, as is commonly said, reduced their indebtedness in the proportion of 100 to 73. But there seems good reason for believing that, at all events, the new scale of weights was adjusted in the proportion of 100 to 72.

I am indebted to Dr. Smith's *Dictionary of Greek and Roman Antiquities* for the summary of the very various evidences upon this moot point, and my argument upon them is based chiefly upon considerations of monetary exigencies.

The quotation cited from Priscian (art. "Pondera")

It is not probable that these are mere coincidences, nor is the accordance and perpetuity of the weights used for the precious metals at all

explicitly states the small Attic talent to be 60 minæ, and the large talent 83⅓ minæ, which is equivalent to 100 to 138⅔, or 72 to 100. If further it be established that the Æginetan standard was to the Euboïc as 6 to 5, and the same Æginetan to the Attic as 5 to 3, the relation of the Attic to the Euboïc must be 72 : 100, and no other; and this evidence is precise, exact, and to the point, as to the difference of scale. References to the terms on which debts were satisfied are not necessarily so. The debtors had no claim, as of right, to relief in any exact proportion, and though 100 new talents were equal in weight to 72 old, it does *not* follow that neither more nor less than 100 had to be paid in satisfaction of existing debts. Now, though it is very poor work to explain away little differences in order to make figures agree, it may be equally misleading to ignore the fact that certain expenses *must* be incurred in carrying out any such composition as that referred to. If such a difference as that between 72 and 73 were appropriated to be set against the necessary charges of the operation, just that was done which might be done to-day under similar circumstances. It is needless to inquire in what form such charges were paid. Assuming, as inherently highly probable, that something had to be paid, it is perfectly natural that the popular account of the matter should be that the end of all the trouble was that, for the weight of 73 old talents, debtors got rid of crushing claims against them for 100. The exact adjustment of the old and new scale of weight was a technical question, and fractions never have been popular.

It is indeed vain to look for exactitude in any casual references to money. Just the same kind of discrepancies which perplex an archæologist would meet an inquirer

incredible, though, as will have been seen, the old
weights may appear disguised under new combinations.   The substances dealt with are singularly

into a matter apparently so simple as the relative weights
and value of English and French standard gold coins.   In
any book of the day, written perhaps by a banker, a
casual reference might be found to the fact that 20
sovereigns had been changed for 25 napoleons.   This is
just what any one would have to do in London who had
to go to a money changer.   Nothing apparently can be
more explicit or satisfactory to the casual observer.   We
are so much accustomed to find that money can be changed
without any special charge, that not one in a thousand
will reflect that *if* a money changer is employed at all,
he must make his living out of some difference in the
transaction.   A Cambist, however, finds the respective
weights of the 20 sovereigns and the 25 napoleons, instead
of being equal, are 2,465·5 grains for the former and 2,489
for the latter; but if further he assay the coins and bring
French gold to the English standard, he will find the
difference to be on the other side, the 25 napoleons giving
only 2,443·75 grains of the English standard of purity,
making the 20 sovereigns worth very nearly 25¼ of the
French coins.   And this is as far as a numismatist can go.
But if the investigator should happen to light upon the
accounts of a bullion dealer, he would again be thrown
into confusion by finding small differences between the
weight of the coins and the weight of metal transmitted
as equivalents for them, and might have considerable
difficulty in finding out the fact that a specific charge—
under ¼ per cent.—was made in the French mint for the
expenses of coinage, and that a corresponding charge was
made in another form in England.   Expenses of this kind
may very well vary in far larger proportion, and yet be
quite as obscure to all, except those engaged in dealing in
coin and bullion.

imperishable, and there have ever been, in bye-gone
ages just as much as now, strong reasons for keeping up some intelligible parity between the systems

The fact in this case is that the "par" between French
and English coin is not as 25 to 20, but as 25·225 to 20.
Now if we were to adopt the French monetary system,
and declare 25 napoleons were full value and legal tender
for 20 sovereigns, either all debtors might gain by paying
25 napoleons, when they should (taking weight for weight
of equal purity) have paid 25·225, or the state might
retain this fractional ·225 (less than 1 per cent.) if it provided the supply of new coin. It would serve to go
against the costs of coinage—the small loss on taking in
slightly-worn sovereigns, and so on. Charges of this kind
must be incurred for such work in all times and places.
The change made as between debtor and creditor would
thus—without any straining—not be in the same ratio as
that permanently established between the old and new
coinage. If, to carry the analogy a step further, we were
to accept the napoleon as our unit of value instead of the
sovereign, debtors would be greatly relieved by being
permitted to pay 21 of these instead of 20 sovereigns,
although a strict conformity with the new monetary scale,
arbitrarily established, gives 20·18 only as the equivalent.

I do not mistake an argument of this kind for a proof
as to the special point raised, but the discrepancies between the popular, or even the social and political
estimates of money, may be very much accounted for
by such considerations, while evidence as to consistent
weight and scales is not affected by them.

I have not had the advantage of seeing the argument
of Böckh, to which Dr. Smith refers, and my support of
his conclusion is probably derived from considerations
very different from those which have influenced that
erudite scholar. Be that as it may, I cannot but think
that the balance of probability is very strongly in favour

which were brought into commercial connection
with each other. A simple and accurate comparison
of actual weights was sufficient for international

of the assumption that the Attic scale was adjusted,
to the Euboïc in the exact proportion of 72, not 73 or 75,
to 100.

The weight of the Roman libra at very nearly 5000
grains seems also fairly established; this gives 416 or
417 grains for the uncia, which certainly is the weight
of the Spanish Mexican dollar. The relation of this
weight to the several scales used in Greek trade is not
so clear.   One identification suggested is with the
Æginetan *half mina* of about 5550 grains, which gives
a difference as 9 : 10. The Roman weight, however, is
as nearly as may be three-fourths of the Attic mina, and
the uncia therefore is one-sixteenth, a fraction which is
not in direct accordance with either the decimal or duodecimal scheme of notation.   But the binary system,
preserved in our avoirdupois weight, expresses most
directly the *half-half-quarter*, which is a fraction so frequently arising in the natural experiences of daily life,
that it may well claim to have an exponent of its own,
which it in fact has had from time immemorial throughout India, where the anna is not only the sixteenth of a
rupee, but is commonly used to express that fraction, just
as the *uncia* expressed one-twelfth. We thus have the
Roman ounce and Spanish Mexican dollar (equal to one-
sixteenth of the Attic mina) and the Chinese tael
(equal to one-sixteenth of the Euboïc mina) standing to
each other in the proportion of 72 to 100, and the Euboïc
(the decimal) scale was certainly in use in Central Asia
when riches and civilization there were at their highest
point and the Chinese already a distinct people whose
national continuity has remained unbroken to the present
day.   The links of connection are not quite clear, still
we may with comparative safety infer the immutability

intercourse ; and those who were practically concerned in this work would be in no danger of falling into the error of supposing they could by any

of the Chinese weight, not only from the conservative
character of the race which looks back to antiquity with
such peculiar veneration, but also from the fact that the
State there has never coined the precious metals, and has
not therefore fallen under the usual temptations to tamper
with its standard of weight. The tendency to confound
weight and value together is however found even here,
where a local tael of silver as delivered by bankers may
differ from the standard tael; such difference being a
compensation for costs of exchange : but as these local
weights are expressed as a fractional difference of a
decimal scale, the connection with the common unit is
clearly maintained.

Nor need any peculiar virtue be attributed to the
Spanish and Mexican governments for keeping up with
comparative fidelity the full weight of the *uncia* as far as
their coinage is concerned. They had not to deal with a
local and domestic currency, where debasements under one
pretext or another might have passed under the authority
of the royal prerogative. As acting for a silver-producing
country, they had to sell largely and constantly to the
free markets of the world, and a check was thus kept
generally upon attempts to reduce their coins, though
signs of the natural tendency to do so are not wanting;
indeed the proportion T717 instead of T720 per 1000
dollars fixed specially for transactions in silver at the time
when the East India Company first traded at Canton,
corresponds with a slight debasement in the old Spanish
imperial dollar.

On the other hand any mere investigation into existing
metallic currencies will quickly show how hopelessly the
notions of weight and value have been confused and confounded when once local money and coinage have been

artificial means give any additional stability to the value which had become inherent in the precious metals.

3. On coming, on the other hand, to local systems which have been made the subject of many profound theories and much very paternal legislation, we meet with infinite perplexity and confusion. Monetary troubles have found their way into the

made the subject of formal legislation. Indeed the works of professed Cambists, however trustworthy as to the actual coins described, and interesting to numismatists, usually ignore altogether points most necessary to determine any monetary problem. Even among the generally well-selected extracts of the work referred to (though the true theory is elsewhere recognised) I find one in which a comparison is made between the weight of ancient silver coins and the present British shilling, which is in fact a mere token of the aliquot part of the gold sovereign, and as far as the principle upon which any rational comparison can be instituted is concerned, might just as well be made of tin or copper.

I am far from disparaging the work of those laborious investigators who have often thrown perhaps all the light that could be thrown upon a very obscure subject. It is not that their evidence is to be discredited, but a due regard to the necessary limitations of the functions of money must correct the conclusions drawn even by the witnesses cited. As will be shown more fully in the text, the very object of authority in tampering with the currency is, as a rule, to make changes which it does not wish to avow, or to remedy evils, or worse, imagined evils, the nature of which has been altogether misunderstood.

My main argument in no way depends upon the concurrence suggested, but the point appears to me of sufficient interest to deserve notice.

uncongenial pages both of ancient and modern history. Greece and Rome have had to grapple again and again with the currency question, the ages of faith were familiar with the debasement of the coinage, and modern credulity has witnessed the collapse of paper circulations. I do not refer to direct tyranny or overt injustice. If a rich man be condemned on a false accusation in order to confiscate his wealth, if a strong-handed robber plunders a town or a caravan, if a greedy king pulls out the teeth of an unhappy Jew till he ransoms his person with solid gold, grievous as are the wrongs suffered, they do not entail the bewildering mystification which so much aggravates the evils of an arbitrary maladjustment of monetary values. They are, in fact, a more subtle form of disease to which the more complex forms of civilization are liable, but the hopelessly contradictory obscurity of the evidence regarding such changes as these irresistibly suggests the inference that the dicta of authority ordained one value, while the stronger law of necessity enforced another. Custom, tradition, superstition, precedents more or less completely misinterpreted, fraud subtle and forceful, sheer ignorance, poverty, greed, necessity have all exercised their influence on at least the external forms of money. All kinds of substitutes have been tried, and even some of the most worthless have for a while served some purpose. Strongly as we may be disposed to assert, that the precious metals are the best common measure of value all over the world, and that therefore they will and must as a matter of fact be recognised as pre-eminently money, still it is also a fact that even mere intrinsically worthless tokens, in no fixed and assignable relation to gold or silver do, under certain circumstances and within certain limitations, form a common measure of value, and constitute money with which comparatively highly organised systems of industry can be carried on. Our own past experience has proved that a nation can both fight and thrive with a paper currency. Yet in all cases, popular instincts and sound theory alike cry out for *real* money. I trust therefore that I shall be held justified in having attempted to determine independently the primary basis of the nature and value of the precious metals as money before entering upon the complications arising from abortive attempts to establish artificial systems in connection with the higher and more elaborate subdivisions of labour, the more so as we shall have to come back to these first principles again and again in the course of our further investigation. There have been error and exaggeration in many theories held to be sound, and the germ of neglected truths in many which have been rightly rejected as fallacious. As a closer analysis will show, functions of money which are radically distinct have been confounded together.

4. Danger evidently begins with the introduction of artificial substitutes for money, and the question next arises :—Into what further and secondary uses

Secondary uses of metallic money.

have the precious metals grown, and how, how far, and under what conditions can their use be safely superseded by tokens or by other forms of money?

Reference has already been made to their use as forming a world-wide common measure or standard of value, inasmuch as they are not only universally known, but their exchangeability can be practically tested, owing to the ease with which they can be transported from one place to another. But this test will not needlessly be applied. They furnish, even more readily, a means of speculative comparison between the value of all and sundry commodities, and a given weight of metal, if only a sufficiently accurate identification of the true weight of such a costly substance in different regions can be afforded. Hence it is that while we cannot but suppose that the hand, or foot, or pace suggested the first rough measures of length, the earliest historical traces of any exact metrical system show a reference to weights rather than to measures, and these weights first come to us in connection with the precious metals. And this use is not the less important because it is merely inferential. They thus afford the best basis for determining whether the actual transport of commodities should be attempted or avoided. The conclusion may show an opportunity for barter—although the goods virtually exchanged might be bought and sold with money already on the spot—or for the actual transport of treasure one way or the other. We have thus an ideal as well as a material practical utility.

Again, as far as transactions were comparatively infrequent, and of considerable importance, the metal used no doubt was (as it is now) carefully scrutinised by those who were competent to judge of its weight and purity. But as this money came to be employed more freely among the many who were familiar with it only as something with which they could buy with one hand and sell with the other for their daily needs, no such scrutiny was natural or indeed possible, and money had to be taken very much on trust. Hence would arise the practice of coining, in some form or other, either under the authority of sovereign power, or by men of repute whose mark or stamp inspired confidence. Naturally such coins would be in the first instance the simple multiples or fractions of some known unit of weight, and so far coined and uncoined money would remain in perfect accordance. But this important change is begun; people soon cease to look so closely for themselves to the weight and quality of their money, and gradually come to associate value and purchasing power with the authority of the mere marks impressed upon their coins, and as these are worn light by use, the agreement with the original weights becomes more and more imperfect. But still in many cases the worn coin will pass more currently than the full weight in metal, because the receivers are familiar with the former and are unused to and know nothing about the exact value of the latter.

This "general *recognisability*," as far as it

Recognisability.

extends, is a new element of convenience and consequently of value, which however is evidently confined within narrow and arbitrary limits, though within those limits it may become a very prominent and important factor of purchasing power.

Modified use for subdivided labour.

5. The want of money which will circulate in this way is more and more felt as the divisions of labour become more complex. In a certain sense there is a division of labour even in the lowest stages of society, but a broad general distinction may be drawn between the mere difference of employment which results in the production of various commodities, each completed and made ready for use by one set of labourers ; and the division into distinct stages of the work necessary to fit any one commodity to the purposes for which it is ultimately required. In the first case there will be little use for metallic money except in the way and to the extent which have already been described. In the second, new conditions, differing both in kind and in degree, are introduced. The transfer of such sub-sections of work does not depend, or depends only remotely and indirectly, upon the natural inequalities of production. A work once begun must go through all its stages to completion, or all the labour spent upon it will be thrown away, and as each stage is completed, specific remuneration will be required. But the man who has done the special piece of work he has engaged to do earns his share of such other products as his needs require,

and naturally desires to get that unfettered power of choice which money conveys, rather than direct payment in particular commodities; and moreover, payment in kind is, in such cases, for the most part out of the question. The practice of making payments in money tends to become general simply from considerations of mutual convenience, and because the greater variety of productions, and the difference in the quality of the products themselves, make the power of choice more to be desired [I. 4]. Still there is no necessary increase in the aggregate of commodities held for consumption— or, to use words which more closely represent the changing circumstances—increased production is balanced by increased consumption with no new necessity for an increase in the proportionate balance which has in the aggregate to be held in reserve. The work in any given community is just as much as ever an interchange of consumable commodities, and men's necessities compel them to use their money quickly. It gives them a power of choice, but it does not relieve them from the pressure of wants which can only be satisfied by parting immediately with it. There is more work for money than ever, but it has to be done so promptly that the quantity kept in use cannot possibly be augmented in anything like the same proportion as the transactions which are carried on by means of its activity. The greater this activity, the more rapid the circulation ; money may be more seen, but there is not more of it required. Nevertheless all these adjustments cannot be carried out without some friction. In a vast multiplicity of cases small amounts of money—of purchasing power—must be held in reserve for short periods, so that in the aggregate there will be a certain additional value of money constantly held in circulation, and chiefly employed, it must be observed, *within* the limit of transactions in commodities which are in course of preparation for their final use. There is a special social circulation in aid of the subdivision of labour. The money however still in its degree represents a *purchasing power held in suspense*, and so far its utility is of the same kind as before, but not only is the power of holding it in reserve more cogently limited, but its use hardly extends beyond facilitating selection and adapting merely personal demand to supply. It does not aid in adjusting the excess and deficiency of production which is the primary utility of the precious metals as money.

If the material substance of the money used for both these purposes is the same, of course no line can be drawn between, what may be called, these two funds : but if otherwise, the primary uses will be served by bullion—as I may now call uncoined gold and silver—while the secondary uses may be served more or less perfectly by money which is only fitted for local purposes, and which is subject to chances and vicissitudes which cannot appreciably affect the general value of the precious metals.

6. In regarding local currencies, therefore, we find that the notion of weight may become gradually lost, and a notion of value substituted for it, vaguely based upon custom and authority, but maintained unconsciously by the fact of mere continuity of use. Well recognised symbols of little or no intrinsic value will pass more currently than any substance, however costly, which is not generally known as money. Hence it is that a mere tally or token serves equally well as the metal itself as long as it is not required to go out of its proper sphere, and many a paradox in questions of currency may be explained by the fact that the apparently most anomalous "money" is nothing more than a tally. Tallies or substitutes will serve just as far as, in point of fact and by common consent, they do circulate freely. That they have practically a value cannot be denied, but what is measure of the value of these substitutes, and what is the nature of the basis on which it rests?

It has already been shown (I. § 22) that the value of metallic money which can be used for primary purposes and · international trade is strictly limited ; and that the quantity or number of units tends to increase as long as the supply can be afforded. But the mere consideration of cost does not affect their value, except through its effect upon supply. Precisely the same reasoning applies to the use of any substitutes for metallic money, but it must needs be rigorously applied, or an insidious confusion between weight and value may lead to

CHAP. II.

Value of "tallies" depends solely on local conditions.

very erroneous conclusions. The value which depends upon any actually existing relation between supply and demand is imperative. A certain quantity of money is required to meet certain definite wants and represent a certain amount of value held in suspense. People on the average will keep very much the same quantity in their actual possession unless there is some adequate reason to the contrary, and a reason adequate to cause any change must be one which appreciably affects the whole community. And this "law of average" resolves itself very much into this simple and undeniable proposition : that, without some change in the causes which affect society in this particular way, there can be no change in the resulting effects. Any uncertainty in the operation or continuity of such a "law" would indeed be a reason for dread and surprise. An average demand, therefore, is by no means a fitful or inadequate basis of value. On the contrary, none more certain and absolute could be devised. Substitutes of inferior intrinsic value may be at first received with doubt and hesitation into circulation, but, once established, the difficulty is not to retain, but to get rid of them again ; for quite irrespective of the cost of the material of which it may be made, each unit of current money becomes absolutely vested with its proportionate share of purchasing power, which is definitely owned by some one whose rights cannot be ignored. It is received for so much, and paid away for so much, as long as the balance of demand and supply for that which, as a matter of fact, does the special work of money, remains the same. Its want of intrinsic value does not directly affect either the magnitude of the transactions. measured by it, or the aggregate value of the money held. Its value is not only governed, but governed exclusively, by this concurrence of circumstance, which may be termed a natural law.

Any one holding money of this kind must keep it very much under the same conditions as treasure. It gives no increase, nor does it waste by natural decay. No one will retain more than he can make use of, nor, as far as he has an option, will do with less. However small its intrinsic worth, each unit represents an aliquot part of the total of money of all kinds indifferently, which may make up the circulation ; and though no one may know what that total is, the value of the part held is proved and tested by what it will buy, just as the value of true metallic money is proved and tested. The fluctuations which arise from altered conditions of demand—to keep still to this side of the question —are the same, whether the currency is composed of the metals common to the world as money, or of tokens of local value only ; but the liability to violent changes will be, *cæteris paribus*, greater when confined within the limits of a single country, than where the effects of a casual perturbation can be diffused over many.

7. Now if the substitues for money are kept clearly

within the value required for local uses, while, side by side with them, the metallic originals remain in circulation, any excess which may arise in the aggregate quantity of the home currency flows naturally out. Even if not specially required for external trade, the increase which would cause a very detrimental aberration in local value is lost ere long in the vast ocean of the circulation of the world. Equally the same great source supplies any deficiency as long as a place is kept open for the influx of the metallic portion of the currency which thus comes and goes as required, and the same standard or common measure of value is preserved throughout. As long as the "tally" can be freely exchanged for (say) gold at the option of the holder, there can be no doubt that the value, howsoever it may be based, is practically guarded and supported on all sides, not only by the costliness of gold, but also by the universality of demand for it ; and with it retains that degree of stability which results from the most widely-extended average of demand and supply. As long as these conditions are fulfilled, the use of tallies or substitutes has not been carried so far as to throw local currency out of due and exact accordance with the general standard. The aggregate value of money used to facilitate the local current interchange of consumable commodities, including all transfers of incomplete work required to carry out all the multiform sub-divisions of labour, may safely be carried on by such tallies. A certain number will always be thus kept in useful employment; and there is no reason whatever to seek to withdraw them from it. They are not designed or adapted to fulfil, nor are they required to fulfil, other more general purposes of money.

The connection between the local and general currency thus secured is something like that maintained by joining a small tank to a large reservoir. If only the connection be not altogether obstructed, the excess or deficiency of the smaller supply is constantly made good. Any variation between the corresponding levels above the line of connection on either side is met by a proportionate increase of pressure on one side or the other. Below that level there is no such pressure, and it matters not from what independent sources the inferior supplies may be drawn.

For the ultimate readjustment of the larger aberrations of production the precious metals are not the less required : and, as the integrity of local money should not merely be maintained but amply secured by adequate reserves, some further value may be advantageously employed to make up the casual ebb and flow of such local currencies. Still the aggregate use of the precious metals as money is not necessarily very much increased.

8. The precious metals may, however, flow out of a country from the exigencies of external traffic : a reduction in the quantity of money will evidently be the result ; and this contingency deserves some special consideration, for very similar appearances

Undue
export
quickly
readjusted.

arise from remoter causes which may be very different. An export of money implies an effective demand for the foreign commodities taken in exchange for it, and may equally arise from a comparatively urgent want of the latter or a superfluity of the former. The first effect of the consequent scarcity will be to raise the value of any given quantity or unit of money, in relation to all disposable commodities in the region specially affected : that is, they will be cheaper with reference to the general scale of monetary value. A re-adjustment naturally follows, *unless* the exigencies of demand for local consumption counteract the tendency. In that case prices will not fall, but the presumption afforded of an actual decrease in wealth is a very strong one. For the measure of value common to all the world, and which is not likely to be appreciably affected by merely local causes, shows that a less value of money measures the total balance of disposable commodities. No change in the mere form of money can meet such a case as this. It is a question of the right employment of capital and industry, which will assuredly lead to an effective demand for a certain proportion of metallic money as soon as they have again created new uses for it. But the export of money has not been the cause of the poverty, but the recognition of the legitimate effect of it : for there is no *use* to be found for the excess of metallic money at home, and nothing whatever can be gained by hoarding it. A congestion of money,

arising from diminished circulation, has been relieved, and an undue fall of relative prices is
prevented by the natural export. A poor country
is *pro tanto* the better, not the worse off, from
having got rid of a superfluity; though if the
causes, whether moral or physical, of its penury are
persistent, the advantage gained is very small and
transitory.

The normal effect of a reduction in the quantity
of money is, of course, a rise in its value leading
to a fall in relative prices which will quickly draw
back the required supply. Bearing in mind that
the value of money which can be utilised is very
greatly less than the total value of commodities
which can be made available for international
exchange, a comparatively small effect upon prices
is quite adequate to bring about this result. Low
relative prices provoke both buyers and sellers to
reciprocal action, and as a change in the value of
money casually affects the vastly larger aggregate
of all commodities generally, the field over which
this inducement may exceptionally operate is indefinitely extended. Moreover, a relative scarcity of
metallic money and consequent low range of prices
in one place necessarily implies in some degree the
reversed conditions elsewhere. Given the condition
of wealth in such commodities as can generally be
made serviceable directly or indirectly to the world
at large, and the adjustment of their value to
the common standard will follow in due course of
time without any undue strain. The process of

adjustment, however, being ever like the movement of a pendulum—always in relation to a mean, but never resting in it.

9. Before proceeding further to consider the use or abuse of substitutes, it will be well to refer briefly to the effect of marked changes in the more permanent value of the precious metals themselves. It is liable to be affected not only by increase or reduction of current supply, but by the increase of wealth during times of general peace, or by widespread desolation in times of war, or new international relations may be opened up with countries previously isolated. It is quite possible that a local scarcity or redundancy of money may arise from circumstances quite independent of the immediate relations of the country affected, and the consequent perturbations may be of sufficient strength and duration to make it evident that the common measure of value has been itself the subject of change. The operations of interchange involving chiefly the primary use of money are nevertheless adjusted without difficulty. Different prices, that is, different weights of metal, are constantly being given for commodities as circumstances may require, and nothing suggests the idea of fixity on one side or the other. But as regards the more popular and social uses of current money, the notion of value tends to predominate; and because the precious metals have been found to be the best common measure and standard of value

for all the purposes of industry at any one time, it is very readily taken for granted that they will continue to be so at *all* times. Though this notion may very naturally arise, it is not the less in excess of the truth, and is the evident source of many of the fallacies which have beset successive theories of money. When a scarcity of metallic money arises, inconvenience is chiefly felt where contracts extending over long periods have been entered into, or certain money payments have become fixed by use or custom rather than by adjustment according to the varying conditions which govern relative value. The stability of the value of money being unduly exaggerated, a sense of wrong is apt to arise when this confidence is disturbed, which often vaguely and blindly seeks remedies which serve only to aggravate the evil. Money is scarce and harder to get than it used to be. Prices of commodities are lower, but this does not attract so much attention because they have always been subject to fluctuations. It is more difficult to keep fixed debts down; they accumulate year by year. Customary wages may remain the same, but with this pressure it appears that fewer can afford to pay them. The weight of the burdens of life is not distributed as before, but falls with increasingly intolerable severity upon some classes. If the sentiment of even-handed justice and perfect " altruism" prevailed; if every man could appraise his neighbour's work on the same scale as his own, the readjustment of prices to the changed value of money would very soon be found. If even "enlightened views of self-interest" induced a general willingness to consent to the expression of something like the old range of value in the new terms required, the difficulty would be reduced to a mere matter of troublesome estimate and calculation. All the material essentials of prosperity remain the same. But as the world goes, producers see only that they are wronged by continued low prices, and creditors who hold obligations expressed in appreciated money insist on the strict letter of their "rights," and the pressure may thus well come to a breaking strain.

The reductions of the weight of metallic money recorded in ancient history, which have been already referred to, must in all probability have taken place under such circumstances as these. For the reduction of the weight of money implies a corresponding reduction in the rate of all payments to poor and rich alike, which is hardly conceivable except on the supposition that there had previously been a corresponding fall in the money price of commodities. The changes indeed appear to have been a settlement by compromise after a long period of pressure and uncertainty. The impossibility of getting payment in full from debtors would incline creditors to accept a modification of their claims, who indeed, for reasons which will be sufficiently obvious, might prefer a reduction in the value of the money in which they were to be paid, rather than a change in the formal terms of their contracts.

Vulgar needs may have been met by expedients beneath the notice of the historian, nor can any close analogy be drawn between the requirements of a society comprising a large numerical majority of slaves, receiving their means of subsistence in kind, and those of a free population receiving wages in money, as a matter more or less of contract or of customary right.

The same considerations should be kept in mind when judging of our own early coinages. During the five centuries down to the beginning of the sixteenth, the weight of the silver standard pound was gradually reduced in the proportion of a hundred to fifty-three. Looking to the condition of the nations of Europe and of Asia during the period, an enhancement in the value of the metal in a somewhat similar ratio is by no means improbable; and if this were so, the changes which seem to have worked smoothly were probably not on the whole injurious. Then follows a short period of palpable debasement and consequent confusion. The reduction of the French livre (originally the same as the English pound) to less than one-twentieth of that weight, and of the Scotch to one-twelfth of the English "pound," are at best outrageous exaggerations of any conceivable appreciation of the metal, and the evils consequent on these debasements are notorious.

It would be a dangerous error to suppose that all reductions in the weight of metallic money were palpable and unmitigated frauds. There always have

MONEY AND VALUE.

been and ever will be very specious reasons in favour of such changes, though the desired ends might be obtained by other means. It is rather against fallacies, and the one-sided, partial, and inequitable action taken upon them, that we have to be on our guard, especially the tendency to throw off as unjust any burden merely because it is unforeseen and unexceptional; and this is very apt to be the case when theories, unduly extended, break down under the pressure of natural conditions which have not been duly anticipated.

The known or reputed success of any such expedients as those which have just been referred to would in any event greatly favour the notion that money could be created or its value controlled by the authority of the State, and the traditions of them, however imperfectly understood, would be sure to be quoted as a precedent in times of financial embarrassment in favour of attempts to regulate the currency by legal enactments. Such cases at least afford some illustration of the principles involved, and will serve as a contrast to show the different effect of measures which, under the specious guise of avoiding all change, are in reality of a far more subversive tendency.

Supposed change in a measure of length.

10. Further to illustrate the working of such a change in the correspondence between the quantity and the value of money, let us suppose the case of a clothier whose measuring-tape had gradually stretched by use. It will not be to the point to assume a dealer's weights reduced by wear, for, in

money, value and quantity change inversely, and an *increasing* "purchasing power" must be given to the clothier's ell. As far as he both bought and sold with the same measure there would be very little difference in the result. The weaver if paid in kind would give cloth and receive back his coat, leaving a remnant for the clothier's recompence as before. Only the man's coat would be too big for him, and, if the measure remained unchallenged, the general deterioration of the race might be inferred on such grounds, much to the concern of the statisticians of the period. But as weavers have other wants than coats and clothiers other customers than weavers, their dealings would be carried on by the common medium of money, which, as we cannot well deal with two shifting measure at once, we must (simply inverting the terms of the case) assume to be a fixed value. The weaver then, gradually finding out that he had to do more work for his pay and consequently could earn less, would stand out for more money. The clothier would naturally appeal to his accustomed measure, possibly ask whether it had changed last week, or last year, or on any day in particular, and his view of the question would probably be that weavers were growing idle and luxurious. Still sooner or later he must give way, and has then no choice but to make a corresponding increase in his charges to his customers; or he would be squeezed out of life altogether, and they—notwithstanding their alleged attenuation—would have to pay just as much for their coats as their fathers before them, and, perhaps, might regret generally that they had not had the good luck to be born clothiers themselves. But in truth the *friction* has been working against both these industries, though, allowing for that, the interchange of commodities for the satisfaction of actual wants has gone on throughout substantially on the same terms.

But if we may suppose a weaver to be under a long contract to supply cloth—or to have to pay rent for his looms in it—or to have gone struggling on for years always with a balance against him carried on and on in the lengthening ell without correction—the burden in course of time becomes intolerable. No opportunities have been afforded of gradually readjusting natural values to the changing measure, and the unfortunate debtor in the last case loses virtually not only on the balance, but on every delivery which he makes by way of payment. What is the remedy? We who know all about the clothier's expanding measure can say at once, " Call the old debtors together and arbitrate their accounts as nearly as possible according to the original ell, and take care that the standard measure of the trade is not exposed to any such aberrations in future."

Peremptorily to order the interpretation of recent contracts by an obsolete scale, on the ground that that was the only true and proper ell, would be a manifest injustice. If the old measure is restored, means must be provided for readily translating all recent agreements into the terms re-ordained.

\\ 11. The weak point of the simile is, of course, the change supposed in a measure of length, which evidently could have been tested and corrected in so many ways. But, reverting to the case of money, we have to deal with the fact that the standard of value is not in any such manner open to verification, while we are so used to refer to money as a common standard that it requires a very considerable effort of mind to conceive of money itself as measured by all commodities. Practically it is useless to try to reduce deductions, drawn from any such generalizations, into terms which at once recognise this undoubted truth, and yet can be so commonly understood as to be fitted for practical use. In popular apprehension relief is to be found for prices too high or too low: money may be scarce or abundant, but that (in any such sense as we are now considering) it should be cheap or dear is not a notion readily entertained. Nor is this reluctance altogether unreasonable. Money generally is, and always may and ought to be, the best measure of "value in exchange" which the world can afford, and it is an infinite convenience to take this nearest practical approximation to stability as an accepted datum. Just as the supposed weaver would say, "When I made my contract to give so many ells of cloth, the price of it was much lower," so a man owing money which had become scarcer would say,

CHAP. II.

Difficulty of determining the value of money itself.

"Times were easier when I signed my bond, and I could then get more for my produce ;" and each of them would be totally unable to express the state of his altered relations except in these, inverted, terms.

12. It is one thing to recognise as a fact that the stability of the value of the precious metals rests only on a world-wide average conditioned by their natural costliness, and quite another to devise any remedies for its aberrations, which shall not cause perturbations infinitely greater and more pernicious than those which they are intended to counteract. It is safe to say, that, whether the reduction of the weight of current metallic money did or did not restore a former standard of value as measured in commodities, the local currency so dealt with would certainly remain in accordance with the general standard of the world, for a mere change in the weight of the unit could never impede the influx or efflux of the precious metals. Relative values remain unchanged, and would quickly be reduced to the new scale by a simple process of arithmetic. In dealing also with an ideal case it was easy to show how directly special cases could be met where what may be called an equitable claim for relief could be made out. But in actual experience any such cases as these are extremely difficult to identify and separate. The effects arising from a scarcity of money cannot be by any means striking in any single instance. Other commodities are constantly fluctuating, actually as well as

ostensibly. Men grow rich by good fortune and industry, or grow poor by thriftlessness and misadventure. Who is to decide which out of many possible causes are those which have led to individual failure? One noticeable feature, however, when money is becoming really scarce, is sure to be the friction imposed by custom to the natural readjustment of prices. Considering how keen is the struggle for life and wealth in all ages—how often custom will interpose to mitigate the excessive strain on hardly-pressed classes—how indeed there must be some approved utility in a custom, or it would never be established at all—it is no wonder that those in whose favour a custom may operate should hold fast to their "rights," and be supported in them by general sympathy. There is no evident cause, such as the failure of an annual crop, to account for and justify a change. What tells in the long run is that a weight so small as not to attract attention is constantly thrown into one scale. Money does not come to hand so readily as it used to do. To recognise the fact that the same weight of metal may go further as money, requires a change in the association of ideas which is not easy, and requires a very uncongenial exercise of thought. Experience indeed would prove to demonstration the more recondite truth, but that it is not always permitted to do. At first sight it often seems as if it would be much more easy for us to change circumstances than to adapt ourselves to them. All admit that prices must rise

and fall, but the cry as of suffering comes from the
side of those who, with no abstract idea of value,
only want, and think they "ought" to have, the
same quantity of money as before. The logic is
one-sided and not consistent, but it brings the
fact of the reduced *quantity* of money into prominence. Here is the apparent cause of the evil :
and if it is supposed that money can be made by
the dictum of authority, the short way out of it is
evidently to make good the deficiency by the issue
of substitutes.

Direct
effect of
over-issue. 13. But have we not got to this point before ?
Yes ; but under very different conditions. I then
showed (I. 37) the place in the circulation which
substitutes for metallic money might safely hold,
and that as long as they were convertible into it
and in fact representatives of the precious metals,
they were suitable for all purposes of local currency.
Now, however, we have lost sight of this basis for
a common measure of value. It is, in fact, though
perhaps not consciously, discarded as inadequate
and inconsistent, and the attempt is made to fix
and maintain a local standard of value, instead of
conforming (not real values but) the terms in which
value is expressed to the world-wide standard.

The case will probably be made most clear by
stating it in direct and converse terms :—

Money, meaning metallic money, has become
scarcer and consequently dearer ; therefore every
unit of it has a proportionate large "purchasing
power:" that is, commodities are relatively cheap.

Notwithstanding this, the influence of custom induces men generally to look for as large a *quantity* of money as before, which it is, *ex hypothesi*, impossible for them to get.

To supply this want substitutes for money are issued with the result that the desired *quantity* of money is afforded :—but the "purchasing power" divided among a larger number of units, falls proportionably for each of them, and current local prices rise accordingly.

But the purchasing power of metallic money is supported by the world-wide demand and cannot therefore so fall in relation to commodities generally.

Being thus artificially disparaged locally, it will tend strongly to flow out, or be drawn out, to those places where it maintains the higher value in exchange for commodities.

The influx of commodities, thus artificially stimulated, tends to depress local prices casually, owing to excessive supply ; and further, the outflow of metallic money again reduces the total quantity in circulation, and tends still more, and more permanently, to depress the relative value of all commodities.

If the issue of substitutes should be now arrested when the aggregate of the money in circulation is on the same scale of value as that of metallic money, no further export of that money will follow, but in this case the first object of the operations will be abandoned.

But the apparent necessity has arisen more strongly than ever for a further issue of substitutes to restore the desired number of units of money. If they are so issued the same effects as before must follow till by degrees all metallic money is eliminated from the local circulation.

A new and isolated measure of value is thus established, the quantity of which may be indefinitely increased. The precious metals will still be required for external commercial intercourse and held accordingly, but will not be in any definite and determinate relation to the local currency.

The respective bases of the two currencies may be thus contrasted :—

Substitutes for money represent an aggregate of purchasing power held in suspense, within the limited area in which they circulate, the number of units of which can be increased at a merely nominal cost at the discretion of the sovereign power.

Gold and silver used as money represent the same power generalised with a very high degree of efficiency throughout the whole world, the number of units of which cannot be increased at will, but is subject to a high natural cost of production.

14. I have put forward the case of the over-issue of (inconvertible) substitutes under the most favourable circumstances. The fact of an appreciation of metallic money has been conceded, though it is practically a very difficult matter to prove until

after the change has made so much progress that the new standard has been practically adopted for a large proportion of current transactions. For the sake of argument, the increase in the quantity of money of all kinds may further be assumed merely to have kept the value down to its former level. Does this warrant the inference that the stability of money as a persistent measure of value may be secured by a judicious issue of money-tokens without any regard to gold and silver? If they are required as commodities for foreign trade, why should they not be bought and sold in local money like any other commodities? This form of the question is open to the fatal objection that it covertly assumes the very point to be determined. No one denies that the precious metals can be so bought and sold, nor can there be any doubt that value is secured to token-money by the natural law of demand and supply, just as peremptorily as it is to metallic money. But this is not the issue. What we want to ascertain is whether the precious metals, under the conditions which actually do govern their value throughout the world, are or are not a more equable measure of value than any substitutes which can be used as money under the control and direction of individual skill and foresight; or to come, perhaps, still more closely to the point, whether by any artificial scheme which can be devised and carried out, a yet higher degree of equability can be secured than that which the precious metals naturally afford.

I have already shown how, speaking generally, the precious metals are set apart specially for use as money. No gain can be made out of them unless actively employed, while there is on the other hand no inducement to force them into circulation apart from the advantages to be found by making them available as money. They work as it were automatically because they are pre-eminently fitted for this use, and, for the most part, for no other. The " sanctions " of this great natural law of adaptation are far stronger and more subtle than any which could be imposed by authority, the weakness of which latter becomes apparent when put to the test of what it really can effect. Granting that it may so happen that a local issue may maintain for a time a previous standard of value better than the common measure of value, if that should have been exposed to extraordinary perturbations, it is totally against all experience to suppose that any one country can itself be for any long time exempt from natural changes. Sometimes more money will be required, sometimes less, and, to preserve a fixity of value, money must be withdrawn from, as well as put into, circulation. Here is the crucial test. Metallic money when not wanted in the currency would naturally flow in or out on any variation from the general level, but local tokens cannot dispose of themselves in this way. There cannot be a greater mistake than to suppose in a vague way that if good money flows in, it will take the place of bad ; the latter if depreciated retains, locally, a value which is definitely owned by some one whose right as an individual cannot be ignored, but must be bought out if the token is to be withdrawn.

15. But it may be said tokens cost little or
nothing, and so can be hoarded without expense. Why not issue and withdraw them as they may be wanted ? It is true they cost nothing and have no intrinsic value of their own, but not the less every unit is intended to represent *pro tanto* a certain purchasing power, and the authority which issues them has to deal with substantive values not the less because it deals with them indirectly. Say that the State pays its debts or current obligations by the issue of tokens instead of by money drawn to its coffers by direct taxation. Every holder has in some shape given value for them, and they can be repaid ultimately only by specially increased taxation. If such tokens are paid in for taxes in due course of collection of the revenue, the Government cannot afford to hoard or destroy them because they happen to be made of paper. It has received them as value from the taxpayer, and must pay them out for the requirements of the State, unless an actual surplus of income has been provided to withdraw them. It is at best money borrowed in the face of rising prices and repaid in the face of falling prices. Or suppose that, by way of keeping a reserve, the State buys property by the sale of which such tokens can be redeemed at discretion. Half-theory may say, what better can be done than buy when

money is scarce and prices low, and sell it when money has been made plentiful and prices are high? But the very doing of the thing required reverses the terms. How can a Government buy with money tokens when by its own action it is (increasing the number, and) lessening the value of its own issues, —or sell on the reverse conditions? The attempt to do so covertly would be "not only a crime but a blunder," which would utterly destroy the confidence of all who had to deal with it. If done at all for the public benefit such operations must be done openly. Bear in mind that we are not treating of borrowing and repaying according to the necessities of the State, but of dealing solely for the object of acting upon the quantity and value of money. Now the very action of any one as a buyer tends to raise prices and as a seller to depress them, against himself, and unless there be a countervailing difference in the actual value of the thing dealt in owing to a greater or less demand for it for actual use, the mere buying and selling again is a waste of trouble and expense and a loss to the dealer. These supposed dealings of the Government do not serve any such purpose of adjusting supply and demand, and consequently in the natural course of events will result in a direct loss. Moreover it has to deal largely also with property and commodities required for the current needs of the public service, and must use money for the purpose like any other agent. To require it to "regulate" the medium of exchange by means of which these operations are to be carried out is to impose upon it a duplicity of functions which are radically incompatible. Nor is the difficulty avoided by delegating its authority to any separate body. It will still be called upon directly or indirectly to buy and sell freely, and also to regulate the common terms in which the agreements are expressed.

In fact, on this hypothesis the weight of the balance wheel is to be saved, but the work has to be done by constant interference to adjust artificially the balance of a most complex machine. Schemes of this kind are the mere result of an overactive ingenuity which has lost sight of, but has not gone far enough to regain, its hold on the primary conditions which govern the work of adjustment. The argument drawn from the small cost of substitutes when their use is extended to such objects falls to the ground : the employment of them is at best difficult and probably costly : probably also fluctuations will be induced quite as serious as those which it was intended to prevent; and these, moreover, will be liable to operate with all the more pernicious severity from being confined within the comparatively narrow limits of a single country.

16. Practically the results of a resort to such expedients is likely to be infinitely worse. If once a Government undertakes the regulation of values, every opposing interest has a one-sided claim to urge. Money which in fact indicates, if not with absolute accuracy, at least with rigid impartiality,

Liability of optional issues to abuse.

every failure in the due adjustment of supply to demand, is put down as the cause of the evils which it detects. Hasty and selfish ignorance constantly attacks the symptom instead of the disease. Debtors suffer : the cry is for more money, that they may the more easily pay off their debts. Prices rise, and the poor suffer: again more money is asked for, that wages may rise. Pensioners, and all who have commuted present claims for prospective payment, suffer : again more money is wanted, for it becomes constantly more difficult to reverse the policy of applying palliatives to all pressing evils. The country, as regards its local currency, has no real reserve to fall back upon, and further forced and arbitrary distributions become necessary remedies for former abortive attempts to evade mere transitory inconveniences. In fact, the true functions of money are over-ridden and reversed (I. § 15), and every special interest in turn makes good a claim against the general interests of all. But no possible shiftings of the measure of value can be a true remedy for misadjusted or deficient production, while the uncertainty engendered renders the higher work of organised industry well-nigh impracticable.

The attempt to "regulate the currency" artificially is not only peculiarly liable to the gravest abuses, but, even under circumstances far more favourable than can reasonably be assumed, is of very doubtful advantage, and this without any imputation of intentional fraud or specially corrupt motives. The bitter lessons of experience will, sooner or later, teach any capable or solvent Government the suicidal folly of the attempt to contravene the laws of value and to "make money" by this summary process. One of the strongest reasons against entering upon such a course is the extreme difficulty of retracing the false steps made in it. When a metallic standard is once lost, the attempt to revert to a former standard would often cause more injustice and hardship than it would remedy, for the vast majority of current agreements are made on the existing value of the currency unit. It is a question for compromise and arbitration : the best interpretation possible must be put upon the actual value of the current money, and that, expressed in a weight of the precious metals, will subsequently retain on the new scale the highest degree of stability which it is practically possible to secure.

17. There is in some respects more to be apprehended from an increase and consequent depreciation of money than from the decrease already referred to. The more immediate effects are very much the reverse of those supposed in the case of the clothier's lengthening ell (II. § 10); but, as regards more protracted obligations, while the appreciation of money may end in a strain severe enough to break all contracts expressed in it, its depreciation does not entail evils of so overt and palpable a character. A debtor cannot pay more than the value of all he has, but it is always within

Rising and falling prices contrasted.

the limits of possibility for a creditor to do with less. He has at least his labour free, while that of the debtor is forestalled. Debts may be more easily paid, the weaver's task more easily wrought; but as the (ostensibly) larger quantity of cloth is required for a coat, it is the wearer of coats who would have to beat *down* prices, and in this he would be likely to succeed, because, notwithstanding the delivery of the usual number of (nominal) ells, an unsold stock would remain over on the weaver's hands. Still the friction is against the consumer, and, materially speaking, in favour of the workers. Whether this is any real benefit or not is quite a different question. A hard bargain or an unduly hard enforcement of it is injurious, but undue laxity may lead to still worse consequences, at all events in the vast majority of comparatively short transactions in which mankind are most urgently concerned. There are always many and subtle compensations in practice for any exaggerated pressure in legal or customary requirements. The over-exacting rule not only tends to induce caution in undertaking engagements, but a specific margin is allowed on a vague estimate of anticipated shortcomings which current experience shows to be necessary, and prudence dictates an ample performance of the work required to conform to a standard which is *felt* to be rigid, and is in fact somewhat more than rigid. The easier rule of rising prices not only engenders confidence, but condones rashness; close and careful calculations are disparaged, for, somehow or other, things come out right in the long run better than any one could have expected. The harsher rule again applied to those spoilt by "good fortune" of this kind puts a strain upon them which they are ill prepared to bear, and "no favour" is perhaps as necessary as "a fair field" for permanent success. In a certain material sense it may be very true in such cases that what one man loses another gains, and thus readjustments very readily come about ere long. Still, so much suffering is entailed by any extreme fluctuations, that no rational means of mitigating their effects should be neglected, nor any rash experiments tried at the risk of aggravating their severity. The poorest and weakest suffer most perhaps from changes which, in terms, are in their favour, for those who are driven by necessity must accept the conditions which the strong and rich, who can wait, may require for their future security. Sharp and sudden changes are felt by this class in all countries as a peculiar hardship, and a sound currency is perhaps of the most importance to those who have the least money in their possession. But very gradual changes can have hardly any appreciable effect upon the masses of the population, whose specific engagements are short, and, though habitually renewed, are always liable to revision, while the mere casual and temporary fluctuations which arise during the process of readjustment in the value of metallic money have hardly time to reach them directly.

Still, the effect of a scale rising or falling, even by slow and imperceptible degrees, may be recognised by a certain difference in the prevailing tone and spirit of enterprise and industry, but the mischievous consequences will be slight and manageable if the question be rightly understood. No harm will come of trusting to the "elasticity of the revenue" in the one case, or to the "practicability of economy" (which in fact implies elasticity in another direction) in the other, provided that such terms are not blindly used in place of an intelligent effort to inquire fully into the reasons upon which these confidences may be severally based.

Fluctuations of an isolated standard.   18. The nature and degree of the stability of the value of the precious metals, and the conditions upon which it depends, must constantly be kept in mind. There is no security whatever against the accident of an excess or deficiency of them at any one time or place, though there is infinitely less likelihood of an extreme severity of pressure affecting these than any other commodities (I. § 21); like water, they quickly find their own level with wonderful facility. A local currency, however, when out of direct connection with them, does not give or take its share of the common stock; these casual variations are therefore more abruptly marked in local money, and the temporary effects of such fluctuations, as regards foreign intercourse, are more severely felt. It has, in addition, its own fluctuations, independently and without help from the outside world. So the *relative* changes between

the scales for internal and external trade are liable
to be unusually frequent, and may also be extreme.

It is worth while to trace how these merely
relative discrepancies are calculated to affect injuriously the most remote ramifications of local
industry. The work of production is sometimes
held to be completed as soon as the product receives
its final form, and is placed, ready for consumption,
in the hands of the wholesale dealer. I should say
rather that it embraces all workers, from the first
labourer in the field or mine to the last who places
the product in the hands of the consumer. I should
care little to insist upon so small a distinction, did
I not desire to show how completely the work of
distribution and adaptation permeates all production. The category is ill-reasoned which excludes
the distributors or retailers of bread or clothes,
while it must of necessity include the cost of those
who have done precisely the same work for the
several items which have gone to make up these
finished articles. Materials crude or partly fitted
for use may be brought from all parts ; tools
wanted for future work must be kept in stock. The
artisan could ill afford to leave his own special
work to do that of the distributor of the commodities which he requires for his own daily support.
An item of cost must no doubt be added for each
distribution ; but the object and effect of it in
every case must be held to be a better and more
economical adjustment than would otherwise be
practicable, and the wider and more unrestrained

H 2

the range of choice the greater the probability of carrying out this work to the advantage of all concerned. There may be useless, ill-judged, luxurious and extravagant distribution ; the same may be said of production ; the stringency of the utilitarian test can be applied with just as much or little rigour in one case as in the other. There is nothing gained by making a distinction which cannot be consistently observed, and which, as far as any question of value is concerned, implies no difference. Even accepting the definition that the result of economic production is to be expressed as " utilities fixed and embodied in material objects," it is not the less true that, though the material form may not be changed by the act of the final distribution, the utility at last, as at any former period, depends upon an exactly suitable adjustment in quantity to the wants of consumers.

Their ill effects on local industry.

And as this work of distribution and redistribution so permeates all production in all its stages, it follows that, as the intercourse between countries increases, various sections and sub-sections of production will be facilitated by the interchange of inchoate and incomplete utilities, if I may so call materials partly fitted and prepared for use ; and thus the uniformity of a common measure of value becomes of importance even for those industries which may appear to be of purely local interest, especially where such industries are active, enterprising, and highly organised. Home and foreign trade and industry are thus inextricably united ;

and as foreign trade will inevitably be carried on by means of bullion as a common measure, it must of necessity be adopted throughout to secure the manifold advantages of preserving, in its most plain and simple form, the same measure of value for the whole circle of productive energy. This may not be very evident to those who have never given a thought to the innumerable ways in which ingenuity has to be exercised in fitting production to the various wants of mankind; but it is obvious enough to those who know how precise are the adjustments required, and how fatal a seemingly small obstacle or uncertainty may be to their practical accomplishment. A good or a bad monetary system may be enough in itself to turn the scale between the national success or decay of industrial enterprise.

19. Nevertheless it should be clearly understood that the precious metals do not in any sense *govern* the cost of production, but serve only to *measure* the relative common value of the products. The cost which will be devoted to local production must depend upon physical and natural conditions; upon the proportion which the population available for labour bears to the means of employing it, and the nature of the objects or "natural agents" upon which it can be employed; upon customs, habits, and all other accidents which influence the decision of the members of any one community, among themselves, as to the way in which it suits them best to employ themselves under their existing

circumstances, or, more strictly, according to the opinion they may form upon their actual knowledge and comprehension of them.

If any commodity is produced expressly for a foreign market its price in gold or silver depends upon that market, and its value, as compared with similar commodities produced elsewhere, is estimated, most readily and exactly, with reference to that common measure by the consumer; but whether it is or is not worth the while of the several producers to continue their production on the terms offered does not depend upon the comparison so made in a foreign market, but upon the conditions which actually obtain in each of the producing countries severally. A knowledge of the different conditions under which commodities can be afforded no doubt tends remotely to the equalization of the total costs of their production. It may lead to immigration or emigration, to the borrowing or lending of capital, and the adoption of other means by which such conditions may be really changed and developed in various producing countries. But the function of gold or silver as current money is mainly that of a trustworthy measure—the application of it depends upon the intelligent discrimination of the user. It shows comparative values in one proportion in one country and in other proportions in other countries, according to the sum of the varying conditions and influences under which their work is carried on. The exchange value of the completed product is also easily compared by all the world according to the same common measure, and thus the small beginnings of international trade are more readily brought about and the practicability of further interchanges suggested ; but of the motive powers which can bring about the changes in local conditions which make such interchanges feasible, money, in the substantive form of gold or silver, plays a very subordinate part. It serves to indicate differences, to test, and, perhaps, ultimately, to regulate them, but it can do little further either to create or to remove the causes of these differences.

20. It is needless to enlarge upon the manifold abuses of which a reckless and corrupt issue of bad money may be made the instrument. One weakness, error, and fraud naturally leads to another ; and if it be asked, How can all laws of value be broken and set at naught ?—how can people live at all under such conditions ? I can make no better reply than to ask in return, How does an unpaid army live in an enemy's—or for that matter in its own—country ? There is no law of justice in interchange observed. So far as money is used, it is a mitigation—or possibly only a prolongation —of the misery suffered. But short of these extremities it must be admitted that the issue of debased or inconvertible tokens, or of paper-money, is a most effective way of getting value which could not be obtained by any ordinary means of taxation ; and it is too much to say that even this expedient cannot be justified by any emergency to

The potency of forced issues.

which a State may be subjected. The operation comes very much to this. The State pays its creditors, including its soldiers, servants, artificers, contractors, and others, in mere tokens which cost them little or nothing and represent a very vague and indefinite right to substantive repayment, but they are declared to be a legal payment and satisfaction for all debts incurred. The receivers have a right to pass them as lawful money, and under the circumstances the right to withhold any property or commodities which the alleged exigencies of the State require is practically over-ridden. The loss is not directly ruinous, for the quantity of actual money which any one need hold at any one time is comparatively small. Every time he passes the money it may be at a loss, but the loss is so graduated as to be supportable, and in compensation for it higher nominal prices have to be accorded. No man can do without money, and thus no one can evade the share of loss which falls to him. He gets less for his money, and money's worth is subtly drawn from those whom no tax-gatherer could reach. The impost actually falls on the holders successively of substantive money during the time when its depreciation is going on. It is the over-supply, not the low cost of the base or paper money, which brings about the fall in value, but it is the low cost which makes the operation remunerative. If the whole quantity of good money at first in circulation be taken at 1,000, and the over-issue at as much more, every man's specific money is worth half what it was before, and the Government has gained the other half. But this is all that it gains : for the rest, higher (nominal) prices require higher (nominal) taxation. Not that this result could ever be precisely shown, even if the value of the original money could . be . ascertained. For an infinite variety of new causes, affecting with more or less stringency the demand for such money as can be had, will inevitably have come into operation. Still the proportion of excess is assuredly an efficient cause of an equivalent depreciation, and the State will assuredly be paid in its own coin : though it may be impossible to assign precise figures to this cause, or to many other of the causes which govern the ultimate value of the currency.

It is true moreover that some of the paper issue may take the place of metallic money taken out of circulation, and to this extent the new issue as a substitute for money previously current does not exaggerate the total supply. If the metallic standard were restored by bringing up and cancelling the excessive issue, this portion might still remain in local circulation (II. § 7) though made convertible into metallic money at the option of the holder.

Nevertheless tampering with the currency is one of those expedients which, looking to the ultimate cost, can hardly be called otherwise than desperate, though it is idle to deny its immediate efficacy and that there may be emergencies so imminent that the question of future cost sinks into comparative insignificance. It is enough to show that such a policy is shortsighted and extravagant in the last degree, and the monetary science of modern civilization can make all the resources of a country available for its utmost needs without resorting to any such reckless methods.

Dislocating effects of sudden changes.

21. Some further illustration may be given of the way in which the terms of all contracts are thrown into confusion by extreme changes in the value of current money, and how the whole machinery of productive industry is strained and crippled by such fluctuations. Thus : a property worth 100, charged with a debt of 80, may become worth 200 in depreciated money ; but the debt is payable in "lawful" money at the option of the debtor, and is discharged at the same figure of 80. So the owner has a balance of 120 instead of 20, and is nominally richer by 100, and actually so by 40 (that is $\frac{120}{2} - 20$), and the creditor is so much the poorer. Practically, however, in times of national emergency and distress the sale price of property tends naturally to fall. The direct law and intention, however, in such agreements is that the owner of the property retains the right to all prospective advantages, and bears the corresponding risk of its decline in value ; while the holder of the debt against it has nothing to do with these contingencies. But a rough idea of equity is

gratified by making him take his share in the losses arising from widely-spread and unexpected pressure. If the actual value of property falls as much as the value of money has declined, the debt, though expressed in the same figures, would be virtually halved, and both debtor and creditor would suffer in the same proportion. But if the price of property, though actually lessened, had not fallen so much as money had become depreciated, the results are even more anomalous than those first quoted. For the sake of simplicity I will use the term *gold* to distinguish prices according to the original standard and *currency* to signify the depreciated money. The first value of the property was 100; the debt on it 80, and the balance, clear to the owner, 20, all in gold. Say that it is sold at a decline of $\frac{1}{4}$th, or 25 per cent., we get the price of 75 in gold, which is equal to . . . 150 in currency.

The debt, though originally due in gold, is still payable as . . . 80 „ „

leaving a balance to the owner of . . . 70 „ „

and this 70 in currency is equal to 35 in gold: so that notwithstanding the fall in actual value of 25 per cent. the owner gains 15, the margin at the first being only 20 in gold. The creditor not only bears the loss of 25 on the value of the property, but also of 15 more, both estimated in gold, which last remains in the pocket of the owner. In all such cases the holders of property of any kind would be not only relatively, but actually, enriched by the fall in the value of money: and this kind of confusion reigns throughout the whole social and industrial system. The proportion of change cited is rather high, but taking the original figures it will be found, that money depreciated 20 per cent. and property at nominal rates only 10 per cent. higher, gives a positive gain of 5 in gold to the owner.

Money actually depreciated by 20 per cent. and property by 25 per cent. would still throw a loss of 16 on the creditor and 9 only on the owner, both taken in gold.

Conversely, when obligations are made in a depreciated currency which subsequently recovers its normal value, the claims of creditors, enhanced in most unequal and arbitrary proportions, are likely to absorb all or more than all the value of their debtor's property. In both cases the machinery of industry is thrown into dire confusion and subjected to strains which it is not fitted to withstand. And the reflex effects of such aberrations may be even more pernicious than the direct and more obvious consequences. In the first case there may not only be a reasonable desire to possess real property, rather than money which is of doubtful value, but this desire may very easily be recklessly exaggerated. In the second case there will be a strong inducement, equally liable to exaggeration, to lend money in order to secure, not merely the usual share of the gains of production, but also the increased purchasing power of the money in which the principal sum lent must be returned.

The inevitable result of such complications is that capital, which for such purposes can hardly be expressed otherwise than in the terms of current money, shows alternately the extremes of timidity or of recklessness. The tendency of all which is that the true work of production is disparaged and slighted, for personal profit or loss does not depend so much upon its actual success, as upon skilful manœuvring to secure the advantage in the abnormal fluctuations in the common measure of value.

The notice of such disorders as these is advisedly made in connection with the forced issue of paper money, and serves to show the great difference that there is between the slow and gradual changes which are consequent upon a decline in the natural value of metallic money, and the more violent perturbations which may be artificially *caused* by sudden inflation and contraction of the currency.

22. It is beyond the scope of this treatise to enter into any detailed notice of the recent financial history of the two great countries which have so recently suffered the heavy calamity of war upon their own territory. I desire here to refer only to general principles which, under varying forms, must operate equally in all ages. The Government of the United States in its emergency made heavy

CHAP. II.

Recent experiences.

United States.

issues of paper money, and thus drew very largely upon the actual value of their existing currency.[1] The patient determination with which this great country has set itself to reduce its public debt has deservedly maintained and raised its national credit. The great staple industry of cotton-growing quickly recovered, and extended to even larger dimensions than before the war. No doubt has ever been felt regarding the substantial wealth of the country or the unabated energy and enterprise of its people. Yet the collapse of industrial credit in 1873 was no mere panic or failure of exceptionally reckless or unfortunate individuals. Its effects have been of unparalleled duration, and the disastrous results disclosed show how complete must been the misconstruction of the relations between property and money values upon which that credit was raised. Visible effects do not always follow at once upon their radical causes, and very powerful influences other than those to which reference has been made have no doubt been at work to aggravate the evils suffered. But the amount of dislocation and failure is astounding. In the railway system alone, in addition to the result of two previous calamitous years, we still find in 1876 property aggregating no less than one hundred and sixty to one hundred and seventy millions of pounds sterling has come or is coming under foreclosure for mortgage bond

[1] The *Economist* gives the export of gold *coin* up to 1876 as £122,000,000, of which £54,000,000 was in the seven years from A.D. 1860 to 1865. Over £7,000,000 of silver *coin* were also extruded. There has, however, been a considerable re-import.

debts or other similar obligations, and, without any falling off in the natural resources of the country, the depression of industry is protracted beyond all precedent. It is not that changes in the value of the currency could alone have caused such widespread disaster, but the whole unstable fabric of enterprise has been raised with the greater facility on a basis itself shifting and untrustworthy.[1]

France, on the contrary, though from motives of precaution compelled to suspend nominally the convertibility of its notes, has always maintained practically the full value and integrity of its circulation. The fine machinery of credit was in no way impaired or confused, and, by means of it, not only was the enormous weight of the national burdens borne, but value to the extent of over two hundred million pounds sterling as indemnity to Germany was actually transmitted out of the country ; yet neither then, nor since, have any signs been shown of distress arising from dislocation or strain of its financial system. One

CHAP. II.

France.

---

[1] It is true that one of the accidents of the civil war in the United States was that it destroyed to a very great extent the production of cotton, which was their great staple for export, and a special need thus arose for some other article of value to supply its place in foreign commerce. ‐ But though this is a valid reason for the export of gold and the issue of paper to supply its place, it does not justify the policy of so great an over-issue as to have depressed the value of the currency dollar to an extent which, apart from speculative movements, cannot be estimated at less than 50 to 30 per cent. The extreme rates (quoting $100 gold in currency $) being, in July 1864, 222 to 285 ; in December of the same year, 213 to 243 ; in May 1865, just after the end of the war, 129 to 145 ; while as far on as 1868 prices ranged from 133 to 150 : which clearly indicates not the use of gold, but the abuse of paper.

great cause of the strength and the success of France is no doubt the fact that the great mass of her population could and did subscribe to the national loans, and thus, without any disturbance of the currency, put their property and credit effectually at the disposal of their country. If the wealth and the will so to use it had not been there, no monetary contrivances would have been of any avail. Not the less, but the more should the lesson be taken to heart ; for it shows how much more effective a direct appeal to the resources of a country can be, than any financial expedients which obscure and disguise the nature of the obligation imposed.

Comparison of values at different epochs.

23. It may sound like a paradox, but it is not the less true, that the very fact that gold and silver are not themselves perfectly equable and permanent measures of value makes it all the more imperative to keep to them as the common measures of value. If the idea of a definite and perfectly equable standard of value could be realised, any community might adopt any measure of value it chose according to its own notions of convenience or economy, and it could be rectified from time time by comparison with the ideal with no greater difficulty than is now felt when dealing with different scales of weight or measure. But the only way of getting at any estimate of positive value in any sense is by the double comparison between the quantity (weight) of money, having

a general and intrinsic value of its own, which
purchases commodities, and the quantity of commodities and utilities which purchase such money.
When, however, the money has only a shifting
reflex value from local commodities and conditions,
the problem becomes so utterly vague and involved
as to render any approximation to its solution
utterly hopeless. Thus if in an inquiry into
relative values in ancient times or in foreign
lands we can get at the true weight—the question
of purity is resolved into weight—of a standard
coin or unit of value, there is some definite clue
to go upon which is a very appreciable aid in the
investigation, but if we find only a token for interchange bearing a reflected value, any attempt to
base comparisons upon it is altogether vain and
delusive.

24. So now if there be any reason to apprehend
any change in the purchasing power of the precious
metals, any attempt to interfere in any way with
the free action of the "law" of demand and supply
would be peculiarly mischievous, and serve only to
obscure the abstruse and complicated calculations
required to estimate the extent to which such
changes may have permanent effect, while only
upon such an estimate could any remedial measure
—should any such ever be required—be based for
a readjustment of the terms in which value should
be expressed. There is no danger of too sudden a
change in the world-wide value of the precious
metals, and the whole machinery of commercial

CHAP. II.

Appre-
hended in-
crease in
supplies.

I

credit is calculated to bear much greater strains from fluctuations in the value of property and commodities than can ever come upon it from any change in metallic money. The attempt to force an undue quantity too rapidly into local circulation (I. § 23) may, indeed, produce serious perturbations in casual value; but a moment's reflection will show that any direct tampering with money in such cases could only weaken and delay the natural action of the forces ever at work to bring about an equilibrium. The prices of commodities will adjust themselves to the common standard; and even if the pound should fall in value to 16s., the only remedy and way of preserving both the "standard" and the "common measure" would be to recognise the fact that 25s. must be paid instead of a pound: which is, in fact, precisely what we have to do when corn, for example, rises from 32s. to 40s., or from 40s. to 50s. per quarter. Neither capital nor labour nor the natural productiveness of Nature are touched by such changes. The vast extent of the world-wide interests concerned in the precious metals is the best security that no permanent change in their value can be sudden or capricious, but any attempt to transcend, artificially, the high degree of stability which this wide average affords would surely be most ill-advised and presumptuous. For the rest, if cases of undue hardship or injustice can be proved, it will be within the power of special legislation to provide a remedy.

25. Hitherto I have referred to the precious
metals as costly, but have treated only of the
nature of their uses and of the demand which has
consequently grown up for them.   It has still to be
seen what security there is for their continued costliness and due scarcity.   The value of all commodities no doubt tends ultimately to be measured by
the necessary costs of production under the most
unfavourable circumstances to which the necessities of consumers compel a resort.   The difference
between that and all lower rates of cost does not
decrease the "value in exchange," but constitutes
a "rent" for the clear profit of the owner.   The
rational application of this theorem is commonly
sufficiently apparent, but is perhaps not so obvious
in the case of the precious metals.   Gold especially
is transmitted to us with undiminished lustre from
every age and from every clime.   It comes indiscriminately from the earliest civilisations of Central
Asia, from India and China, from well-nigh forgotten nations who have left but a dim tradition of
their wealth, from regions where the early Scythians
may have gleaned and the Russian princes of the
house of Demidorf now work their mines; from
Egypt of the Pharaohs and the Ptolemies; from all
lands and peoples known in classic history.   The
rude ornaments of the aboriginal tribes of Africa
of unknown antiquity which excited their wonder
still come to us, mixed with recent washings from
golden sands owning European lordship, and, it
may be, with the *doubloons* coined by Spaniards

I 2

from Montezuma's gold, taken by *his* ancestors from the Toltecs whom they displaced, and by them from yet earlier inhabitants whose traces are a wonder and a mystery to the new world. Europe ever has been, and still is, a contributor, and not long since the too scanty yield from the river Ullie deluded the fond hopes of the people of Sutherland-shire. The few grains of the luckless digger in Australia are melted down with the big nuggets and the yield of the last "bonanza" in Nevada, paying fabulous profits to its owners. In one sense gold is the cheapest of all products. Its perfect durability is wonderful. It is used and reused, and suffers no waste except from actual mechanical attrition, and its cost may be distributed over a hundred generations. Silver, also, though less durable than gold, has come down to us through many cycles of years and from all parts of the world ; the memory of those who have raised it has long since passed away, and the fruits of their toil are for the most part lost in the ever-recurring round of growth and use and decay.

But though it is evident that the attempt to estimate the cost of bygone production must be altogether futile, and the yield of any one, or of many years, can bear but a small proportion to the accumulated stores diffused throughout the world, the working of all existing mines depends upon the law common to all commodities, and the necessary expenses of those carried on at a minimum of profit are as good a measure as can be applied to the stability of their "value in exchange." The greater or less supply of any one mine can have little effect on the general range of prices, and if these are not remunerative under existing conditions, the inference is plain that the wants of the world will not afford the cost and labour required for this additional supply.

26. From time to time the world is startled by accounts of vast discoveries of metallic wealth, and it is by no means beyond the limits of probability that excessive supply may cause some change both in the general and in the relative value of the precious metals. Each of them is found in different districts and in different parts of the world separately, or with such small traces only of the other as to be of no monetary importance, but they are also found associated together, and the great feature in some of the recent discoveries in the Western States of America, which lately attracted so much attention, is the immense mass of ore yielding apparently about 40 oz. of silver, which silver contains about 1½ to 2 oz. of gold, to the ton. The shafts and levels are sunk to a depth of about 1,700 feet, and the deeper workings are said to be richer especially in gold. Great expenses have no doubt been incurred, but these do not tell very heavily on cost when the aggregate yield is very large, and the report of Dr. H. R. Linderman, of the United States Mint, in 1875, estimated the mass of ore to be worth 30,000,000l. to 60,000,000l. sterling. But similar events are no new feature in

CHAP. II.

Augmented supplies

the history of mining, and his remarks on mining generally, in the face of this great "bonanza," are worth quoting in this context. "Notwithstanding the improvements which have been made in mining and in the reduction of ores, the business is one of uncertainty and hazard, and taking one year with another the expenses equal if they do not exceed the production"—"the first capital which follows these (the first) prospectors is generally sunk, and but a small proportion of mines are continuously worked and many totally abandoned after considerable expenditure has been made." Natural mitigations of their effects. It must again be borne in mind that the yield of any one year or cycle of years can bear but a small proportion to the accumulated stores of all the world, and the ability ultimately to absorb and adjust the value of new supplies of the precious metals is a totally different question from that of the circumstances which may arise from time to time to retard or to facilitate the introduction of unusually large quantities of bullion into other countries for value to be received by some course or other from them. It is easy to sell the metal in many places, but value in a suitable form for returns as payment for it cannot so readily be found. There will thus be a check to over-rapid supply from the direct difficulty of getting the increase into circulation, and though a pressure on the part of the producing countries may cause frequent local perturbations, the effect of these will have to be very widely dispersed before any great

fall in general value can be established, and the
notion that either of these metals can be displaced
by a mere vulgar panic from the position they hold
by the custom and tradition of ages is altogether
extravagant: the more so as the fact which is
palpable to popular apprehension is not that
the money is falling, but that prices are rising
continuously.

27. As regards gold especially, the nature of the
operations required under ordinary conditions to
procure it is particularly simple; and methods are
still used with success which must have been
practised in the very earliest ages. It is found
comparatively pure : it resists the action of almost
all substances and does not enter into chemical
combination with them. Its high specific gravity
renders it easy to distinguish and to separate it
by comparatively rude mechanical contrivances, so
that present experiences may be taken as throwing
some adequate light upon the past. The splendid
nature of the prizes occasionally secured with little
toil, and the glamour which surrounds the subject,
have ever made the search exceptionally and inordinately attractive, but the broad teaching of
experience proves that it is too often in the long
run a very sorry quest. The larger part of the
yield of gold is still found in alluvial drift, and
where nature has been at work for ages upon the
exposed rocks in which it is contained, very rich
accretions will naturally be found in the first
instance among the *debris* washed down. Thus

The pro-
duction of
gold.

some of the earlier diggings in Australia gave at first as much as $1\frac{1}{4}$ to $3\frac{3}{4}$ oz. of metal to the ton of earth washed, but this average was on a comparatively small scale ; and after the first gleanings have been secured, 10 dwts. ($\frac{1}{2}$ an ounce) per ton seems a very full estimate of the average production permanently afforded on any large scale.[1] Nor do more modern methods of mining affect this general conclusion. Organised labour and better appliances requiring a largely increased outlay of capital overcome greater difficulties, and thus only make good their competition with ruder kinds of labour under easier conditions. There is a marked similarity in the manner in which gold has been deposited and worked in all quarters of the globe, and indications from the old world and the new

[1] See the elaborate returns annually published by the Government of Victoria. These, of course, *prove* nothing as to the cost or conditions of production in other quarters, but there seems no reason to doubt the commonly received opinion that gold mining in Australia is carried on under comparatively favourable circumstances as regards the *quantity yielded*, while many other occupations are open to labour which keep up the rate of wages to a relatively high level.

The following particulars from the Report published last year are suggestive. Dividing value of gold exported and received at the Mint among mean numbers of miners employed we have:—

AVERAGE EARNINGS PER MAN PER ANNUM.

	Alluvial mining.	Quartz mining.	General average.
1871 ...	£65 17 11½ ...	£164 10 4 ...	£93 6 0 ·62
1872 ...	65 0 6¾ ...	159 0 6¼ ...	93 17 1 ·47
1873 ...	59 15 9½ ...	164 15 9¾ ...	93 16 2 ·62
1874 ...	58 9 2¼ ...	183 0 9 ...	99 8 3 ·07
1875 ...	63 5 5 ...	182 17 8 ...	104 4 4 ·02

These averages include, especially in the case of quartz mining, the proportion required to recompense previous outlay on works of a permanent character, and to replace the cost of expensive machinery.

point to similar results. A large proportion of our supply, some of it procured with the aid of very costly machinery, is yielded at or under the rate of $\frac{1}{2}$ oz. (10 dwts.) per ton of material crushed or washed. Work by the Chinese is certainly often done at less than half that rate. Now these figures give a proportion of 1 part to 65,000 up to 130,000 or over in weight, and in *bulk* brings us up to millionth parts which have to be recovered, and this is taking into account only the drift actually raised and washed, or quartz rock crushed, without allowing for shafts sunk or earth removed for preliminary operations. If one were to file down a sovereign into 10 or 12 barrowloads of earth and mix them well up together, the task of recovering the metal would be by no means an unfavourable specimen of the easiest kind of gold-finding.

Although it is not possible on any such data as these to frame a precise estimate of the purchasing power of gold, yet it is evident that a substance yielded only in such very small quantities to so much labour cannot be otherwise than costly. Labour no doubt is of unequal efficiency, but it is very fairly established as a general truth, that however much wages may vary the real cost of manual labour does not very widely differ in any part of the world. Any serious reduction in exchange value cannot fail materially to curtail the sources of supply, while a slight advance will ensure increased production, under these conditions. A reference to the records of modern gold mining strongly confirms these deductions. The first yield of new diggings is large but gradually decreases as the accidentally rich accumulations of *debris* are worked out, but the deep quartz mining is carried far down without a falling off from the moderate scale of return here indicated.

The production of silver.

28. The supply of silver does not rest upon the same conditions. There are serious practical difficulties in the way of getting at it by merely mechanical means, and though from a scientific point of view as much may have been done by modern discovery for one metal as for the other, it by no means follows that the relative effect on their economic value will be similar. The gross value of the yield appears to be much larger.[1] Thus an average is given of the most important Spanish mines near Guadalagara of $4\frac{1}{2}$ oz. per quintal or 90 oz. per ton of ore. The average richness of ores treated in Mexico is given at $2\frac{1}{2}$ to 3 oz. per quintal or 50 oz. per ton, and an average assay from Guanaxuato shows 49 to 65 oz. per ton, while a yield of 29 oz. was not, *in 1843*, thought worth working in that place. The successive reductions in the royalty paid to Spain during the last century, which was decreased

[1] I take these figures chiefly from the work of Mr. J. A. Phillips on *Mining and Metallurgy* (Spon), and purposely avoid any assumption of exactitude in the text. There are no data on which to warrant any conclusions of the kind, but the figures cited afford tests which may fairly be relied upon for general conclusions.

The extensive collection and generalisation of the facts bearing upon this important question is well worthy of the consideration of the Government.

from 50 down to 5 per cent. on the value of the
produce, confirm the general reports that mining
was not then a profitable undertaking; but if,
as seems highly probable, some such gross products
are the rule, it is clear enough that there is a very
large margin upon which more modern skill and
machinery can be brought to bear. It is a metal
too which enters into a very great variety of
natural combinations; it is found under very
widely different geological conditions, and in very
many different parts of the globe, though the
command of the supply has been practically with
the new world since its discovery. It is commonly
found with gold, yet not, it must be remarked,
combined according to laws of atomic proportion,
but commingled with it, as alloy, in very various
quantities.

Nevertheless, though the exchange value of
silver does not seem to rest so closely upon the
necessary cost of production as that of gold, it is
yet relatively very high as compared with all the
baser metals, and none of them can come into competition with it as a medium of exchange or common measure of value. Roughly speaking a comparison in avoirdupois weight would give as equivalents : 1 oz. gold, 1 lb. silver, 1 cwt. copper or tin,
$3\frac{1}{2}$ to 4 cwt. of lead or zinc, and 1 ton of rough
iron. The mere dust and waste of our iron would
counterbalance all our gold. Its price in silver
would hardly turn the scales in which it is weighed.
There is a large difference between the relative

CHAP. II.

values of gold and silver, yet there is so much larger a gap between the latter and copper or tin, that the two precious metals stand altogether apart for all practical considerations.

The yield in the mine will govern their relative value.

29. New conditions may no doubt arise as portions of the world's surface now little known are opened out and occupied. The cost of conveying any commodity to a market enters into its exchange value just as imperatively as the cost of material production, though in the case of substances so portable as the precious metals the corollary of the proposition is applicable with far greater weight, and it is the diminished cost of transmission of the supplies necessary to support the labourers employed in mines which tends in a much greater degree to lessen the necessary outlay. All these circumstances must be well considered as accidents bearing upon the question of current production of both metals alike; but the relative richness of the auriferous and argentiferous mines respectively, which will have to be worked to supply the world's demand, is fundamentally the factor which, duly corrected for the cost of extracting them from the rough material in which they may be contained, must govern ultimately the relative value of the precious metals.

Gold and silver have no fixed ratio of value.

30. Both gold and silver, as has just been observed, stand distinctly apart, and, as far as my argument has hitherto been carried, have been treated together, as severally and independently capable of satisfying the special conditions of utility

which pre-eminently constitute money. This much they have in common. But neither on historic, nor geological, nor economic, nor any other grounds is there any reason to suppose that they are or can be related in any definite proportion of value the one to the other. Gold is indeed rather suited for current circulation in the richer, and silver in the poorer countries, though by no civilised nation is the one metal only used exclusively for external commercial interchanges. The one may to a certain extent be substituted for the other for the purposes common to both, just as copper might be used more largely than usual in proportion to tin, or the reverse, according as either of them might be deemed relatively cheap. All articles are in this way affected by others which thus come into competition with them, but not the less is the value of each one of them specially determined. Previous to the discovery of the new world however, the proportionate value appears to have very generally ranged at about 10 to 12 parts silver to 1 gold. A mere comparison of ancient coins often leads to very uncertain and contradictory conclusions, but it seems clear enough that in the time of Alexander the Great, the ratio of silver to gold was as 10 to 1, and three centuries later in the age of Augustus, as about 12 or 12½ to 1, and these figures may fairly be taken to indicate the proximate proportions in other civilised countries including those only indirectly connected with the great powers of the Mediterranean, which indeed were not pre-eminent for mere wealth as measured in money. For if intercourse be not entirely cut off, very small differences in the relative value of the two metals used as money form a most efficient inducement constantly at work, to bring about for each severally the true equation of its general value. That which is relatively cheaper will always be preferred for transmission to any place where it is relatively dearer, and the smallest fraction of difference will determine the choice of the sender whenever the necessities of commerce require that metallic money should be sent in either direction ; or if the difference be sufficiently large the metals respectively will be brought and sent for the special purpose of exchange the one against the other. The difference in relative value in countries however indirectly connected with each other tends strongly to be equalised, but no such process tends to increase or lessen any difference which may arise in the general appreciation of the one rather than the other. These interchanges only work out more surely and inevitably the respective values of the two metals according to the conditions of demand and supply which may affect them severally.

These streams run constantly if only the *gradient* be sufficient, and very small gradients which can be so readily and precisely estimated will cause the flow of innumerable little rills which will tell very perceptibly in the long run. Kings and potentates may make war, but it does not follow that their subjects will forego their natural pursuits, and only when war and anarchy desolate a land does such commerce cease.

The same causes must ever have been as much at work between Carthage and Tyre and Babylon, or between Byzantium and Bagdad, as between London and Calcutta or Canton. The vast increase in the facilities of transit and in the extent of traffic expedite the adjustment of greater values, but do not change the principles involved.

The range of intercourse between different nations was unusually extended about the two epochs just referred to. Subsequently at Byzantium gold appears to have been as high as 1 to 14 or 15 parts of silver; but it was a more troublous world in those days. Our own gold coinage began when the ratio was about 1 to 12½ in the fourteenth century; it appears at one time to have been under 10½ in the fifteenth, and about 1 to 11½ in the sixteenth;[1] but these fluctuations to some extent at all events were most probably rather local than general. After this period, the effect of the South American discoveries began to be felt, and the ratio steadily rose to about 1 to 14½ in the seventeenth century, and to a very little over 15 in the eighteenth; Sir Isaac Newton's valuation of 1 to 15·21 proving too low by about 1½ per cent. Adam Smith gives the ratio of 1 to 12 as subsisting even in his own time in China, and considering not only the isolation but the vast wealth and extent

---

[1] Taken from J. R. MacCulloch's article on Money in the *Encyclopædia Britannica*.

CHAP. II.

of that empire, it is easy to believe that the readjustment there came about tardily. It is moreover known to be itself a producing country. Japan entirely isolated for two centuries worked out exceptional ratios altogether, but, on the reopening of that country to the world, the differences were at once merged in the general average without any appreciable effect upon it. During the latter half of this century the further discoveries of gold and more recently of silver, and silver and gold together, have worked further changes, and the present (1877) proportion of gold to silver is very unstable at about 1 to 17½. It is at present premature to draw any general conclusions from recent occurrences, but the subject will be further discussed hereafter.

Meantime it is sufficient to add, that every argument urged against the attempt to assign an artificial value to the precious metals together, tells with equal force against any attempt so to fix a value on either of them, or by consequence, the ratio of value as between the two. Calculations of relative value expressed in the terms of one can easily be translated into the terms of the other, and the price of either one as measured in the other, shows exactly the extent of their divergence or convergence within any given period, which can thus readily be ascertained, though it cannot be controlled.

Special and "intrinsic" value.

31. For the nicer adjustments of currency the distinction must be carefully kept in mind between

the cost properly required for production, and the charges subsequently incurred incidentally for the use of the precious metals as money. It is perfectly true that the cost of the last labour required to transport the metal to any place, is just as much a part of its cost in that place, as that of the first employed in the mine. So also the labour used for making a coin enters into its cost just as much as any labour previously expended upon the metal, and just the same may be said of plate or jewels or any other work of art. The difference is that while these serve only local or special, or perhaps both local and special, uses, the bullion of which they are made serves a far wider and more general range of uses, and so is, as it were, a certain datum line above which casual value may go and to which it can again return. When the intrinsic value of a coin or of plate is spoken of, it is in reference to this highly generalised and equable value, and the term is significant as founded on the fact that while in most cases materials deteriorate much in use, silver with very little, and gold with no appreciable, loss, can be melted down whenever they may be required to serve their primary and most general uses.

Now although there is no change made in the outward form, there is much the same change in the value of metallic money taken from one place to another to serve as a purchasing power specially applied. It is used only as a means to an end, and the attainment of that end adds nothing to its permanent value. In the ordinary fluctuations of interchange, the gold which now goes from west to east may come from east to west at some future time, and by these means only the general average equation of value is approached. The way in which different relative quantities of metallic money and of commodities act and react upon prices has already been explained, but a certain cost or friction attends these operations which must be borne as part of the charges incidental to the course of each and every completed operation of interchange. Thus: if A buy any commodity of B and send treasure to pay for it, he does so only in expectation that that which is bought will repay not only the cost of its own transit from B to A, but also that of the money which has been sent from A to B only because it is the least costly way of conveying purchasing power to a distance in the substantive form required. Undoubtedly the money when it reached B was more costly by the amount of charges incurred upon it than when it left A, but the special act of utility for which it was designed being accomplished, this accidental element of value is lost, and when, in the course of events, treasure has to be sent in the reverse direction from B to A—or indeed in any other direction—the mere weight of metal is the only point regarded. Assuming the costs of transit to be 2 per cent. at a time when a speculative financier were regulating the currency, he might assume weights in the proportion of 102 to 100 to be equivalents, and even take great pains to find out the exact amount of difference at the time. But this 2 per cent. is really plus *or* minus, as casual exigencies may require an influx or efflux of bullion.

In the same way we might perhaps very truly say that a yard of cloth in England was worth 33 inches of cloth in China. If we were to make 33 inches there equal to a yard, putting the costs of transit out of sight, the yard in both places might be sold at the same price. But this simplicity is merely fictitious and ends in exaggerated confusion, for when Chinese cloth has to be sent to England, taking costs in the same proportion, the 33 inches has to be raised not to 36 but to $35\frac{3}{4}$ inches.

This is a further reason for keeping as closely as possible to the simple notion of a definite weight of metal as the unit of value. Dealers in bullion have always had to do this, and any authoritative declaration that different fixed weights are the same value, is simply reversed by arithmetical calculation, and casual charges on one side or the other are taken into account according to the varying facts of every actual transaction.

The value of all metallic money as measured by all commodities fluctuates only according to the ultimate conditions of the widest range of average. Local variations are continuously in progress in numerous and irregular smaller divisions not determined merely by proximity, but according to the changing exigencies of commerce. A certain

K 2

amount of friction constantly obstructs all movement, and this item must by no means be ignored.
Local differences in value supply the motive power
by which this friction is overcome and the work of
adjustment carried on. Any attempt by misguided
authority to thwart or disguise these differences,
or to try to indicate equivalent values by different
weights of the same metal, is futile, not only
because it assumes a degree of stability which does
not exist in fact, but because also it opposes the
very work of adjustment which it is the special
function of money to bring about. And the same
reasoning applies as against any attempt to affix
different relative proportions to the two precious
metals in different countries. The permanent and
more casual elements of value must by no means
be confounded.

Friction.   The theorem of the general equation of demand
and of supply as affecting the precious metals having
been stated as a problem in pure mechanics, it
is well before leaving this branch of the subject,
to bring thus prominently forward the practical
truth that there is a certain amount of friction
which has to be overcome in all the processes of
adjustment of comparative value carried on by
their aid. They are not ideally perfect measures
of value, though for very many purposes they are
by far the best which can be devised, or rather
they are far better than any which could have been
devised by the conscious efforts of human skill.
Every departure from simplicity not only mars

their present utility, but renders it more difficult to estimate and to deal with any imperfection they may show as permanent standards and common measures of value.

32. The conclusions drawn in these two chapters may be thus summarised :—

(1). During time immemorial the precious metals have grown into use as a generally diffused and most widely recognised purchasing power, which is thus vested in imperishable substances, the quantities of which cannot be increased except to a limited extent and at a high rate of cost.

(2). Their primary use as money is to aid in that redistribution of commodities rendered needful by the inequality and uncertainty of natural production : a higher degree of security for the due continuity of supply is thus worked out according to a general law of average.

(3). The quantity of commodities which can be so distributed is the surplus as against the defective production of different regions.

(4). The natural traffic that springs up between different nations is for the most part virtually barter, or the interchange of commodities directly required for use or enjoyment. Metallic money therefore can be employed primarily only for the purchase of the excess for which suitable commodities cannot be offered in exchange.

(5). The total value of money that can be

employed cannot exceed the total (surplus) value of commodities thus available for exchange with it. An increased quantity offered can only be disposed of on the terms of a decrease in the value : or conversely by an increase in the weight of every supposed unit of the aggregate weight of metal :— or, more familiarly speaking, by a general rise in money prices.

(6). Metallic money is a purchasing power held constantly in reserve. It does not itself yield any increase, nor does it waste by keeping ; there is therefore a constant, but not an excessive, inducement for the successive holders of it to spend or turn it to the uses for which it is fitted, as opportunities may arise. But as a reserve it ever remains in one hand or another.

(7). The monetary unit of value must be conceived of as a specific weight of metal : different units in different countries are rectified by simple arithmetical calculation : alloy in the precious metals has ever been rejected as of no value : pure metal only is virtually taken into the equation : they can be approximately tested by simple methods : divided or massed as occasion may require, and moved from place to place at a very small expense.

(8). Metallic money thus comes also to be generally referred to as a common measure of comparative value in widely separated regions, and is used inferentially without changing hands in substance. It thus greatly facilitates, without cost, the calculations required to estimate the differences in the relative value of commodities, which it is the object of commerce to adjust.

(9). As subdivisions of labour become more specialised and complicated, money is more extensively required. The use of a general purchasing power gives each worker an effective means of choice as to the way in which he will receive his equivalent remuneration in the completed products of other workers.

(10). This buying and selling, however, represents for the most part the current interchange of consumable commodities *within* the ordinary range of production. The only use of money in this case is to serve as a common measure and medium of exchange for immediate use ; the units of it are used over and over again within short periods, and thus the whole (say) annual production will be measured by a comparatively very small value of money in actual circulation.

(11). Still a certain limited amount will constantly remain in circulation applied to this purpose only and not required for any other. To this extent mere tallies, as far as they are currently received, may serve all the purposes of money.

(12). The value of the total money in circulation must conform to the total amount required directly or indirectly to carry on the current transactions needed to satisfy the wants of any community :

the greater or less number of units into which this total is divided must correspond with a less or greater value of each unit.

(13). The value of a metallic unit is in correspondence with the value which obtains throughout the world at large, and which is sustained by the scarcity and high cost of production of the precious metals. Metallic units unduly depreciated locally by reason of excess will therefore flow out; or, if unduly appreciated from local scarcity, an inflow will make good the deficiency.

(14). Tallies or local substitutes for money which can be exchanged at will into the metallic equivalents which they represent, and which consequently circulate side by side with them, are so far guarded from any great fluctuation, because any part of the excessive aggregate which is composed of metallic money will still flow in or out, thus adjusting the balance required for local use. The *value* of the unit being thus fixed the number of the units is adequately restricted.

15. But such tallies having only a local value can never go out of local circulation, but will there fill the place of metallic money.

As there is no natural limit to the issue of inconvertible substitutes of no intrinsic value, so there is no limit to the extent to which they may become depreciated.

(16). Tallies or substitutes issued in excess, become depreciated in proportion to such excess, but subject to that proportionate reduction are vested with an actual purchasing power and (though of no intrinsic value) cannot be withdrawn from circulation, without rateable compensation to the holder.

(17). Metallic money will always be required for external trade, and will be (apparently) of a variable value, as measured in a purely local currency. Such variations in the measures of value applied to external and local commerce respectively, are a serious hindrance to the accurate adjustment of supply and demand, especially where labour is highly subdivided and organised.

(18). The general equation of the value of the precious metals, and of commodities, is brought about by the constant transfers by which local excess is distributed and local deficiency supplied.

(19). Differences thus constantly arise in the local value of the precious metals, within the limits of the cost of transit from one place to another, but subject to these changes, the value in every place tends always to the mean value worked out according to the general law of average.

(20). The value of the precious metals themselves also tends towards a general mean equating the total average supply to the total average demand according to the general conditions affecting such demand and supply throughout all the world open to commercial intercourse.

(21). No greater stability can be secured artificially than this world-wide average is calculated to insure.

(22). Gold and silver stand apart from all other metals by a very wide difference in value, and are severally or jointly available as money.

(23). But these two metals stand in no definite ratio of value the one towards the other. They are produced generally under different conditions, are each more specially suited for different purposes and conditions of society, and have in fact varied considerably in relative value during historic times —and especially since the discovery of the New World.

(24). The gross amount of production in gold-mines seems to be disproportionably lower in value than that in silver mines. Should this be established as a general fact, it follows that its present cost is nearer to the minimum cost at which production can be carried on, and therefore that gold is for all future considerations unquestionably the more trustworthy standard of value.

It will further be seen hereafter that the quantity of tangible money, and *à fortiori* of metallic money, tends to become reduced to the minimum. In some of the intermediate states of society the quantity of the precious metals used as money is disproportionably and needlessly increased ; but as industry becomes more highly organised it is used rather inferentially, and in its specific form is required only for those uses which I have termed primary.

33. This theorem regarding money and the precious metals is put forward simply as an exposition of the working of motives common to humanity in all ages. The adaptability of such money to certain ends has ever been obvious, in the most literal sense, to some active sections of society, and its use has been accepted generally as the result of the experience of many generations. But the so-called "laws" of value, or of money, are nothing more than this. Like other economic "laws" they have a claim to be accepted as true only so far as they throw adequate light upon the reasons why certain correlations of cause and effect have very widely obtained. It is a mere confusion of sense (perhaps accounted for but not excused by the unfortunate similarity of terms), to argue as though any direct penalty would or should follow the breach of them, as in the case of legislative enactments. Still more so, to treat them as the connoted relation of antecedent and consequent which is termed "natural law," wherein to prove an exception in any one case is to disprove the validity of the law itself. If the term is used at all in such economic questions as the present, it must be in a very different sense, not indeed less true, but less exclusive. In quoting the "law" of demand and supply for instance, I do but recognise the fact on the one hand that numerous things may excite in

men a desire to possess them, and that no one can say how much or how little any one may be disposed to sacrifice in order to gratify his desire. But on the other hand there is an equally prevalent desire to gratify such wants at the least possible sacrifice, or, what a very limited amount of reflection will show to be very much the same thing, to gratify as many of them as possible. As far as these natural and perfectly legitimate influences operate on both sides, they tend to bring about the interchange of all commodities for which there is an effective demand at all, for equal sacrifices of energy. But I commit myself to no theory whatever as to what men will or will not, should or should not desire, nor as to what sacrifices they may or may not be able or willing to make. The "law" is an assertion of certain tendencies, not an assumption of the result to which they tend, and is no more disproved by any number of cases of inequality than the universal natural law that water will find its own level is controverted by the existence of a wet hill-side or of a lake at the top of a mountain. So with money. No one is obliged to use it, except indeed in so far as any individual is practically obliged to conform to the usages of the society of which he is a member; but where neither ignorance nor artificial limits have restricted its employment, its effects may not inaptly be compared to those of fluid pressure for subtlety and power. Further, if men, great or small, choose to hoard untold amounts of treasure, there is nothing to prevent their doing so ; only the reasons stated for the opposite course have ever been found strong enough to make this the rare exception and not the rule of action.

Regarding money as essentially conveying a power of free choice, its use is evidently in some degree anomalous in a state of society based on the principle that the great mass of the people had no right to exercise any volition at all. The lord, receiving the whole surplus of all production, or, indeed, considering that even the labourers lived on the fruit of his bounty, though perhaps liberal in the disposal of a superfluity which cost him nothing, was not likely to form an estimate of value which would satisfy any independent test, though by no means slow to take money when he could get it on his own terms. And this is the root of the strife between privilege and gold. To compare a great productive natural agent like land with mere money is out of all reason. It is the system of exclusive rights of ownership, as against the rights of free interchange, which were, and, in some degree still are, in conflict, and the results of the one cannot fairly be measured in the terms of the other. The defect common to both is that neither have ever been able to include all who had wants to be satisfied within their systems. But the pauper or the man out of work is certainly not worse off than the lordless serf with neither rights nor claims against any one, while the free workman will hardly change places with the serf well or ill cared for at the will of another. Adam Smith showed us a century ago how the old order passed away, leaving, however, some anomalous traces, especially in matters of opinion. But the system which is dead here, is in more or less force in other countries and modifies the power and uses of money accordingly.

Commercial monopoly. Commerce also, so far as it has been a monopoly, has not indeed refrained from the employment of so powerful an agent as money, but has constantly striven to restrain its full use ; and the fallacies of the mercantile systems which so long afflicted industry are closely connected with the attempts of exclusive commercial guilds to thwart and obstruct the rational circulation of the precious metals. Gold meant freedom of choice, therefore it was to be kept jealously under their own control, or at least within the limits of their own nation. They had no adequate idea of the laws which underlie freedom and no trust in it; no perception that the actual uses and conditions of trade were to distribute and equalise, not only the value but the utility of the products of the earth and of labour ; and no knowledge of the truth that all natural instincts and interests tend to bring gold enough to those who could do this service as surely as the shadow will follow the substance. They lost the substance of value by grasping at the shadow.

Commercial wars. Commercial wars also followed, but these were rather for the restriction than for the extension of trade. It is true that as between open plunder and exclusion, and the qualified sufferance secured by treaty, there is some advantage gained in favour of the latter, but as long as exclusive rights were ordained by special law, so long would money, in obedience to the broader natural law, tend to escape restrictions and work out results widely different from those which "ought" to have followed according to the theory promulgated. But it is altogether an error to suppose that trade can be forced upon an unwilling people by war. It is a contradiction of terms to say any one is *forced* to buy or sell. It would be infinitely simpler for all parties to steal the profit at once. The so-called commercial wars in which this country has been recently engaged have been to restrain the injurious interference of hostile governments with the free intercourse into which the mass of the people were only too ready to enter. To take as an extreme case the wars connected with the opium trade in China. The charge popularly made is that the East India Company "forced" the use of the drug upon an unwilling people. It is difficult to realise any process by which this could possibly have been done ; but as a matter of fact, from the very first, the one thing for which the Chinese would under any difficulties manage to bring their silver, was opium. Demand from their side could not have been more urgent or more effective. It is not the place here to enter into the question whether this country ought or ought not to have aided the

Government of China in enforcing the sumptuary laws which, as was alleged, it desired to enforce, but it is much to be regretted that questions involving grave moral considerations should be argued on assumptions which are at variance with any possible conditions of free intercourse. The economic effect of the restriction was, for long, an abnormal use of silver for the traffic, while profitable native industries did not receive the stimulus which a naturally extended trade was calculated to afford.

It is needless to multiply instances of the way in which the uses of money which may appear obvious in one country are ignored in another; these exceptions do not invalidate the weight of the rule that the free uses of money constantly escape the control of artificial bounds. Money dealers may perhaps make use of complications in current money to get a base gain from the unskilled or unwary; but for their own purposes these entanglements are unravelled. Whatever money may be said to be, gold and silver, solely and simply, are established as such by the usage of all ages and countries. Least of all things is such money under the control of any government regulations, or of merely conventional morality. It is used for better or worse according to the demand which is practically made effective.

Money, in short, supplies a test, but not a principle, of action. Men's wills and desires must either be radically changed, or their persons most effectually coerced, to effect any change in the way in which they will use it.

The more subtle forms of fraud and over-reaching will ever be associated with mystifications about money, and changes in the currency have always been a favourite panacea with those who have most reason to dislike the results shown by its impartial disclosures.

The apprehended disturbance in the value of the precious metals may give unusual speciousness to attempts to tamper with the simplicity of the indications they afford; and those who, with the best intentions, desire to avoid the recognition of changes which, if they come about at all, will come with inevitable force, may be found in concert with those who would be willing enough to make the currency itself the subject of licentious speculation.

It is on such occasions as these that a reference to first principles is peculiarly needful, and these I have endeavoured to elucidate.

CHAPTER III.

ON THE NATURE OF EXCHANGE VALUES : PROPERTY AND CAPITAL.

CHAP. III.

1. THE validity of the principles which have been advanced can best be tested by applying them to existing monetary systems. In this country we have a most complex and efficient commercial and industrial organisation, to which I shall refer more especially, as showing the operation of principles common to all systems, though points of difference as between systems more or less advanced will also come under observation.

The British pound.

Little need now be said about our own unit of value. It is a definite weight of gold. Had the so-called price of the sovereign been 4*l.* per oz. this would have been more easily recognised ; for the fraction of a quarter of an ounce is thus plainly indicated ; but the more cumbrous expression, 3*l.* 17*s.* 10½*d.* per oz., is resolved just as inevitably into a fractional weight. As 3*l.* 17*s.* 10½*d.* is to 1 oz., or 480 grains troy, so is 1*l.* to the sovereign —that is, to itself—and can be nothing else than 123·274, &c., grains of standard gold ; and our subsidiary coinage, whether of shillings and pence representing aliquot parts of this pound, or our paper Bank of England notes representing multiples of it, are not merely referable to, but at all times convertible into, this metallic unit, which may therefore for the present be assumed to be throughout our common measure and standard of value. Some questions on minor points of the form of a portion of the money which obtains currency will be referred to hereafter; but this is pre-eminently called *the currency*—that which, under the authority of the State, is made compulsorily a legal tender, in the terms of which the great majority of our obligations are, directly or indirectly, expressed, and in which every member of our society is necessarily concerned.

2. It has at different times been urged—"Why should gold (or silver) only be represented by paper? Other commodities, undeniably, have value. Why should there not be a land note or a commodity note as well as a bank note?" And the reply has too often been given in a somewhat blind spirit of direct contradiction. But in simple truth they are so represented in every possible way that convenience can fairly require. There are innumerable instruments and documents which represent value, such as cheques, bills of exchange, and promissory notes, which circulate and pass from hand to hand; but, voluntarily only, and, speaking generally, only among those whose position is such that they can form a reasonable judgment as to

how far such instruments are worth the value
expressed upon the face of them : that is just as
far as they can circulate on their own intrinsic
merits. So also bonds and shares of all kinds
representing real property and obligations based
upon it circulate to a certain extent, and it is most
desirable that they should freely do so, with no
other restriction than that dictated by a common
sense of rectitude, viz., the *nature* of the value they
bear should not be concealed, but apparent by the
form of the instrument put into circulation. These
and many other means by which value is expressed
and transferred from one to another may represent
either separate class interests in their interior relations, as, for instance, the bills of exchange current
between wholesale and retail dealers : or more distinct interests in their relation to each other, as a
manufacturer's bills given to an importer for the
cost of raw produce, equally in both cases representing the voluntary dealings of those who to this
extent are associated, and more or less directly
co-operating, with each other. But for the perfection of a highly-organised system of industry, both
the manifold association and the perfect division
of labour are essential. Not only such related
interests as these, but many others, are temporary :
rigidly so as regards the several transactions
entered into, though similar dealings may, in the
ordinary course of affairs, be repeated over and over
again. Still, even in this class of operations, it is
of great importance that means of readily agreeing

upon an exact and definite line of severance of such mutual interests should be provided, and so indeed with all men regarded as consumers, with each and all regarded as producers, throughout the innumerable articulations of society. To a very great extent, no doubt, interests so related must stand or fall together, and there cannot be a more wholesome truth inculcated than that the increased specialisation and division of labour of all kinds implies and requires a higher order of mutual interdependence. Still personal inter-responsibility of the kind referred to should not be needlessly extended beyond the limits within which personal co-operation is desirable. Money should have a basis of its own, and be the common standing-ground on which any one may rest, and from which any one may start afresh, especially when, in troublous times, existing relations of value, or, in other words, prices generally, have been unusually disturbed. The question very much resolves itself into this simple issue : Whether the currency shall have an independent *intrinsic* value of its own, and whether that intrinsic value shall depend on that commodity which, as a matter of fact, possesses the most convenient and widely-recognised purchasing power in the world. There is no limit to the freedom of interchange of commodities, securities, or property of any kind, or to the modes in which they themselves may be represented, but none of these have a general purchasing power in anything like the same degree as gold, and what they have not in themselves cannot, by any occult art, be put into paper representing them. Moreover, the question is not, in the present day, what forms of currency can be got to work tolerably well, but what afford the best security attainable as the basis of a highly complex, and, upon the whole, wonderfully efficient, system of social and industrial organisation requiring coherence. and unity in all its parts, while preserving to all full security and liberty of action. No doubt whatever should be suffered to exist as to the universality of the "purchasing power" of that one form of value which any man is compelled to receive as "legal tender" from another.

Fallacies
arising
from con-
founding
the two.
3. But the general aim of those who desire an extended and variable currency based on securities, seems rather to be that when commodities or securities of any kind do not pass currently among those conversant with them, that, indirectly, the State should make them practically current by issuing notes based upon them, and thus the sacrifices necessary to insure a real adjustment of value are to be avoided. Schemes of the kind are constantly found either to involve some transcendental notion of a fixity of value not warranted by the changing conditions of the order of Nature with which we must conform, or are empirical remedies not calculated to amend the cause, but to disguise and avoid the effects, of popular delusions regarding the comparative exchange value of some special description of property. Thus, if there be

a "mania" regarding the worth of land in particular places, or of mines in any country, or indeed of any new modes of applying industry, prices rise far above the range which the results obtained will ultimately confirm.   Meantime the possessors of such fictitious sources of wealth will have borrowed money on the security of them, and the securities in whatever form they may have been expressed will (as experience has often shown) pass from one to another, or may be the basis of other borrowings in other forms, till a very considerable section of a community may be involved in a vicious circle of fictitious value without any special personal fault or greed or recklessness of their own.   If within this circle only the value of the pound could be reduced by a half or even a larger proportion, whether by over-issue of notes, or in any other way, substantial rough justice might be done to a special class of sufferers, and it is natural enough that they and those whose sympathies are strongly excited by special cases of distress, should desire to adapt the common measure of value more nearly to their own particular emergency, and ignore the immeasurably greater interests of the world at large whose dealings have been conducted on a normal and rational basis.   " When I said a yard I ought to have meant a foot " is virtually their plea, *and so* feet are to be taken for yards by the great mass of people who have been careful to say what they meant throughout

CHAP. III. in the ordinary dealings of productive industry. Any such plain statement of the issue in question is of course denied, and the enhanced value though only purely nominal, is loudly asserted to be a real element of wealth. That necessary condition of value, so easily assumed in an *a priori* theory, viz., the adaptability of the utility promised or produced to any presently felt want in the community —is most commonly vehemently alleged and the fitting test of experience as vehemently decried. But as far as a remedy can be found for such misapprehensions it must be special and not general. Such unfortunate debtors may perhaps be excused for paying 5s. or 10s. only in the £, but it is too much to ask that 5s. or 10s. should be declared to be a pound in order to meet their self-imposed difficulty. In fact no money can do more than facilitate the comparisons which will be well or ill made according to the intelligence brought to bear upon the subject. Well based money affords a good and practically exact means of making such comparisons: ill based money one which is more or less shifting, partial and uncertain :—but this is all. If any one is urged to pay money for a share in a Company to extract Moonbeams from Cucumbers, he must not look to the currency for any direct help in forming his judgment on the feasibility of the project ; but it does afford him a ready means of comparing this offered share with commodities and property of many various kinds. He has it equally in his power to buy so many pounds of cotton, or tons of iron, so many yards of town land, or acres of fields in the country, or square miles of virgin soil in fresh regions. He may buy a share in a business, contribute to a school or an hospital or an almshouse ; spend it in personal luxury or pension a deserving relative. He may if he will, without any very great difficulty, estimate the comparative attractions of these and many other courses open to him and give effect to his rational decision. Or, he may buy the share in the hope that some one more reckless and foolish than himself may give him more than he paid for it, and find to his sorrow that there is a limit even to human folly. In any case a sound currency can no more be to blame than the inexorable rules of simple arithmetic, for the falsity or exaggeration of his conclusions. The unqualified purchasing power parted with in ex-change for the share might, at the mere will of the owner, have procured him any other of the objects or gratifications indicated. As far as a man is owner of money in this sense, he has the choice of all vendible articles that the world affords, and, as far as the conditions of the present argument are concerned, is free from all anterior obligations and at liberty to shape any course he chooses for the future.

4. Real and personal property, securities, and obligations of all kinds, commodities, and even

services, all come into the market to be exchanged the one for the other in the common terms of money, and we should know something of the nature of all these and what severally it is that can be bought and sold, in order fairly to understand under what conditions these exchanges can be effected.

Let us try to trace therefore, from a monetary point of view, what is done when property and securities of different kinds are bought and sold.

Land, for instance, may in this country be said to be always worth more than it could possibly be made to produce in one or even in twenty or thirty years' time. Its price is said to be at "so many years' purchase" on the income of one year. It is simply absurd for any one who willingly pays forty years' purchase for a coveted property to complain he only gets $2\frac{1}{2}$ per cent. for his money. How could it be otherwise? And quite as much so to expect that low interest and a low value of property can be secured together.

So also as regards the National Funded Debt: the money received by the State has long ago been spent and its sole obligation is to pay an annuity at the rate of 3 per cent. per annum on every 100*l.* nominal stock, until it may be redeemed. If Consols go up from 95 to par, the nominal value of this stock is increased by over 35,000,000*l.*, but the country is not one penny the richer or poorer, nor can it even be predicated that we are in any way in a worse or better position at one

time than at the other. It is simply a question
between buyers and sellers.

Again the figures representing money on a share
in a Railway, Dock, or any such Joint Stock Company, serve only to indicate as far as the share
has been paid up, the money which *has been* spent;
the share itself represents an aliquot part of the
present good-will, property, and whatsoever else
may constitute the value of the undertaking.
Neither the corporate body issuing the share nor
any one else is bound to refund the sum so expended, and an owner who desires to sell must
find some one who, in exchange for his portion of
and interest in the concern, will restore to him,
probably not the exact " purchasing power " with
which he parted in buying or paying up his share,
but some greater or less sum as may be agreed
upon between them. The original capital, in this
case also, represented on the share in the terms
of currency, is probably consumed altogether for
the support of labour expended on the work; but
the same currency equally measures, and will
measure and represent over and over again, the
capital presently in existence, which in its turn
passes away and will over and over again be replaced
by production. Here also the year's income bears
a small proportion to the total expenditure or to
the prices paid on the transfer of shares. A good
or bad dividend is a fair indication as to whether
the undertaking is adapted to supply existing
effective demand, but the price of the shares is a

mere matter of adjustment between individual buyers and sellers which does not in any way directly affect either the interests of the corporation or the national wealth.

Securities based upon such property are subject of necessity to very similar conditions. A mortgage from a monetary point of view is a conditional payment as for purchase, which, if certain stipulations are carried out, will not be completed; meantime the holder is only in qualified possession of his property and of the income derived from it. Railway debentures not many years back were commonly regarded simply as mortgages of land, but when it came to the crucial point of entering into possession, it was evident that a slip of land perhaps a hundred miles long by ten yards or so broad, much encumbered with ballast, here shut out from the sun, and there exposed to the elements, was not the kind of property into which an ordinary creditor could enter with advantage. Adapting the form to the facts of the case, debenture *stock* is now a first charge on all the rights and properties of the corporation which issues it. Speaking generally it is merely a case of divided ownership as between debenture and other stockholders; and so it is generally with debentures and debenture stocks secured on productive property of other kinds.

5. Land, Government stocks, railway and other such shares, have this in common. Many years' income is sold for a value expressed in

money paid down at once, and setting aside mere exchanges of property, this necessarily implies that there is on the other side a similar amount of accumulations made during former years which can be paid for this prospective advantage. The owner has a right as against all the world to his property, and to all that in the course of nature he can derive from it ; but he has no right whatever against any one for the price he has paid for it. Subsequent sales are a matter of subsequent adjustment with other parties altogether. The relatively high prices given for income to be received hereafter not only indicate a confidence in the stability of the annual resources upon which it depends, but a more general faith also that the same or some larger proportion of accumulated earnings will at any time hereafter be forthcoming should the buyer desire to reverse his position and sell again. And as long as the country remains fairly prosperous this expectation is likely to be fully realised.

But it will be seen that the nature of the security afforded is of a very different kind from that which is vested in the precious metals, and can never be an appropriate basis for the issue of money. A period of pressure is just the time when all desire to keep their accumulations in hand, while on the other hand there is every probability that a more than ordinary number of sellers of income would be driven into market. The value of such property is, in the long run, comparatively stable, depending as it does on the average product of a range of years ;

but though it is thus removed from the ordinary chances and fluctuations of more active enterprise, it does not form an independent reserve of value generally and widely available. It is essentially a local and not a general security, and can be sold only by taking value in large proportion out from the general fund which, in the case of any sudden emergency, it is desired to increase. Before the seller of such property can return the value he has received he must first get a buyer who is able and willing to withdraw it. The security for such a purpose is wholly illusory, and if paper money has to be issued at all, it is far better to make it on the direct responsibility of the State, than with any pretence of a security which could only be used when it was not wanted.

The imposing notion of money based on real productive property has certainly captivated the imagination of some skilful advocates, but the substance eludes the grasp of those who attempt to realise it.

Property yielding a periodical income.

6. To return, however, to the main argument. Similar conditions attach to all property which is sold on any estimate of its annual production. Whether the phrase "so many years' purchase" is used or not, an investor is sure to look most directly to the income or dividend which he may expect. If a direct and certain answer can be returned to his inquiry, a price can be fixed upon with comparative ease and certainty. But other considerations of future hopes and fears may also

come into play : the sum given for uncertain results is more a matter of individual opinion which must stand or fall by the test of time. But whether we are considering real property: ships, mines, factories, the securities based on any of them, or partly even the capital embarked in commercial undertakings, the estimate formed of a *future* periodical income is the chief factor in the calculation formed of their *present* value. There may be many other exceptional "·unearned increments" besides that of the economic rent of land, but nevertheless the great rule of production is that this income has to be continuously earned by adapting supply to more or less variable conditions of demand. It is a question of tense, but the time when is of the very essence of the question.

The corollary is inevitable, opposed as it may be to many vague popular ideas of wealth. If the income and all reasonable expectation of income ceases, the so-called value of the property *has* already ceased and determined. Its very *raison d'être* has passed away. But the capital which has been sunk is that of bygone days: the present and prospective loss is of income only. Losses are made for the most part, not when, but long before, they are discovered and acknowledged. A burden has already been more or less consciously borne, which can be lightened in the future only by fully recognising the changed conditions under which our industry can be effectively reorganised. A nominal item of capital based on the expectation of earnings which can never be realised has to be struck out of the account. But on these premises only it is impossible to predicate whether the nation has suffered or will suffer any detriment, or whether it is only that obsolete modes of working or sources of supply have been superseded by those which are better.

Let us take the case of any undertaking on which capital has been expended, but which cannot or does not yield any income. I am far from urging that such an enterprise should be hastily abandoned; on the contrary, the ultimate success of many good schemes depends upon the patience and strength of their conductors to endure unexpected and often undeserved losses. Temporary difficulties may at the outset beset the best laid plans. It may even be within the limits of sound —though certainly somewhat dangerous—policy to grant some special support or immunities to a branch of industry struggling to make good or to maintain its position as a fairly productive and self-supporting agency. But if this cannot be done, it is idle to suppose that capital can be saved by artificial protection. The owners of the property may by this means be enabled to sell—or to live upon—what is nominally their undertaking; but the true working of the operation is best explained thus :—A has " sunk " his money and has no hope of getting any return from it which can be sold to bring him in an income. Artificial aid being afforded to A's undertaking, he sells " it " to B, who, under any circumstances, would have to bring in quite new capital to pay to A ; but what A really sells to B is his right to get indirectly from the taxpayer, or from whatever may be the source from which artificial support is drawn, an income which must in some way or other be earned by some one year by year. A, no doubt, is personally recompensed. *He* is saved, but the loss which is not and cannot be retrieved, is merely thrown upon others ;—and in all probability is greatly aggravated by the surreptitious and indirect way in which such compensations are usually afforded. If the interest represented by A has any claim to compensation, by all means let it be fairly adjudicated, but do not let us be under any delusion as to the effect of the award.

7. Lastly, it must be observed that as the price of all income-yielding properties must be an equation of their aggregate value with the total sum of accumulations which, at any one corresponding time, is held applicable to their purchase, such (actual) price will fluctuate irrespectively of the purchasing power of any given unit of money, or of any fluctuation in that purchasing power. No change in the common measure of value can change either the proportion which the income bears to the "principal" paid, or the proportion which one aggregate of value bears to the other. But these several elements of relative value will themselves be liable to variations—as when income rises or falls, or property of different kinds comes into more

Several risks of property and securities.

or less demand—from causes which lie quite outside the question of the stability of the exchange value of money itself.

Securities, or obligations based upon such properties, the value of which is expressed in a fixed sum of money, are secured, to the extent of the full value of the property upon which they are issued, against all fluctuations in value from these causes (except in so far as the owners may desire to sell them before the time when they become payable), and, in all cases, from the first brunt of the risks and uncertainties which attend upon all undertakings in a greater or less degree. But they are directly liable to fluctuations from any change in the value of money itself. It is within the limits of possibility that if this were very largely to increase, the income as fixed in money might absorb the whole revenue derived from the property assigned. On the other hand, if money were to depreciate, the *value* of the security would fall with it, though its *safety* could not be adversely affected, but rather the reverse. Taking all contingencies into account, there is one class of risks to be set against another ; as between property, which, having no fixed value in money, will sell for more or less money as that money is worth less or more, but subject always to the risks and conditions of production, and of the market, just referred to ;—and the obligations based upon it, which are secured from all risks except that from which property is exempt. And it must not be forgotten in the estimate that gold possesses elements of stability which do not attach to any other kind of property whatever. The value, or more strictly speaking, the *balance* of value—of property charged with obligations expressed in fixed sums of money, is exposed to fluctuations from all the causes referred to.[1]

Money in any substantive form is seldom required at all for any such transactions, though concurrent values,—*i.e.*, the exchange values at the moment of interchange—of so different a nature, are all expressed in the terms of it.

It is further evident that the value of all properties and securities of the kind referred to, must

---

[1] Here, however, a further word of warning may be appropriate. No doubt, if the common measure of value is likely to decline a new element of risk is introduced into all securities which are specifically made payable in it. But it would be a very one-sided conclusion that therefore securities generally should be sold or avoided and real property bought in preference. For the prices of both kinds of possessions are not fixed, but based upon an ever-varying estimate of the prospective advantages of all kinds to be derived respectively from them. If such a rule as this were popularly accepted we should certainly have real property unduly enhanced in price, and securities expressed in money as unduly depreciated. In dealing with values it is never safe to assume any fixed datum, as is so often unconsciously done. The necessity of a rational comparison between relative values cannot be evaded. The best remedy for the risk incurred is to save a "sinking fund" out of the income received, which may be set against the apprehended depreciation, and a compensating reduction in comparative value of securities is all that is required for the purpose. This precaution no doubt would often be neglected. Still securities are not so named without some very real significance, and are preferable for many reasons for all those investors who have not the capacity or opportunity to maintain that supervision over real property which its interests usually require.

be some multiple of the anticipated increase which may gradually be derived from them, and the next step is to see what these accretions are, how they may be used, and how and in what sense they can be said to be accumulated. The further application of the test of money will throw yet more light upon the nature of its own value, and of the value of all things measured by it.

Value and capital.

8. As the terms "value" and "capital" will be frequently used in this enquiry, I must explain as briefly as I can the meaning to be here attached to them ; not only because these words are often very inconsistently apprehended, but also because I wish specially to bring into prominence the view of utility and its correlated value as dependent upon continuous adaptation and adjustment. Though the word *price* is commonly used to represent the terms of interchange as expressed in money at any one time, and *value* the purchasing power based on more permanent considerations, both are subject to the same conditions, which however affect them somewhat differently ; so we must understand the nature of value in order rightly to interpret the meaning of fluctuations in price expressed in money. *Capital* also, as consisting of certain aggregates of commodities, must be duly considered in the same context.

9. The *value in exchange* of all things the production of which can be indefinitely increased is no

doubt referable ultimately to the quantity of labour requisite for such production, as Adam Smith and Ricardo pointed out long ago—but of course only the quantity necessarily or usefully employed can be taken into account. Mr. J. S. Mill, however, by some of his definitions, appears to imply that the question of value is fundamental only in an industrial system founded on purchase and sale, and writes (*Prin. of Polit. Econ.*, Book iii. c. 1) : "The conditions and laws of production would be the same as they are, if the arrangements of society did not depend on exchange, or did not admit of it." But though exchange would not be aptly described as "the fundamental law of the distribution of the produce," it is surely a necessary condition alike of that division, and that association of labour upon which all civilization depends. It is difficult even to conceive of any state of society, especially any in which population and natural resources stand in anything like the same proportions as they do in the more prosperous countries of the world, where such interchange was not a condition of their very existence. Production itself, as it must be understood in all such cases, is conditioned not merely casually, but necessarily, by the practice of reciprocation and interchange, so that if labour is to be organised at all, the fundamental laws of exchange value must obtain, even under a system of purely equal communism, which is only conceivable under the condition of assuming an ideal state, which should not only redistribute the inequalities in the results yielded to equal quantities of labour, but also require that these unequal results should be fairly yielded *by* such equal quantities of labour employed under different natural conditions. And if this be the case, a knowledge of the laws of relative value and of interchange is not only necessary for rightly understanding the working of any existing system of social organisation, but should be equally the basis of any and every theory for its amendment or regeneration.

Economic rent.

Thus the economic rent of land under culture, as far as it represents a fact in nature, must as inevitably accrue as the difference in value between rich and poor metalliferous ores which can be worked at the same outlay. Land and ore are both "natural agents," and if in the same sense they are unequal in value, the inequality can be identified as soon as the fact of the difference becomes known, and exists not the less because the overt expression of it may be suppressed by custom, or overlooked from ignorance. If a division be essayed on the basis of an equality of production, an unequal balance of human energy, or potentially productive labour, is thrown out. If on the basis of an equality of human exertion, a difference in the quantity of products is the necessary result. These differences may be wasted, or they may be neglected, but not the less are they in reality of that kind which can equitably be represented by money and brought—it matters not to the argument under

what conditions—within the system of social interchange of value. Beyond this there are differences
in productive power between labour aided and un-
aided by tools or machinery, or aided in different
degrees ;—or which can be more or less efficiently
organised. Risk, health, social convenience, and
many other considerations have all to be weighed,
and the somewhat abstract notion of a " quantity"
of labour implies the necessary sacrifice directly and
indirectly of energy, rather than mere exertion of
either brain or muscle. The range within which
any comparison can be made is of course limited
by natural conditions of race and country, nor is
there any formula by which to estimate the relative
outlay of energy by a watchmaker or a navvy, a
hack writer or a scientist ; but in all such cases,
though the centres of difference, if I may so speak,
are widely separated, the margins touch and over-
lap, so that while the total value of labour in each
circle must be equated separately with the total
demand existing for it, and in daily practice will be
equated in the terms of money, the different results
so presented by this equation show cause more or
less adequate why a transfer of labour from one
industry to another should be considered or attempted, and "quantities" of labour are thus
experimentally tested and estimated.

One qualification however must be made with
regard to labourers in a highly organised state of
industrial society. Work is subdivided into many
different sections with incalculable advantage to the

power of production ; but this condition is involved: —each one who takes up, and carries on, a section of the whole task to be done before any commodity can be adapted for use, has to deal with materials which have already acquired exchange value in virtue of labour already bestowed upon them. A bad workman therefore may very readily waste more value than any exertion of his own can give to the object upon which he is engaged, and he thus may become rather a spoiler than a producer of utilities. Hardly any form of labour is so ignobly "independent" as to be exempt from this condition, and the quantity of it, which can be accepted as imparting value is limited inexorably by the very necessities of civilization.

No limits can be assigned to the exchange value of those things the supply of which is absolutely limited, whether permanently or casually only, by the conditions under which any one act of interchange may be effected. And it may be remarked that the value of things appreciated only or chiefly for their rarity will depend rather upon the means, judgment, or caprice of the buyer than on the estimation of the owner.

Value "in use" and in exchange.

10. The elementary conditions of free association imply a free interchange of services. It follows that those who receive services, or, more adequately to express the inter-relation, all men as receivers of services, will exercise their own discretion as far as they can, in the choice of those services—whether directly rendered or ultimately yielded in the form

of commodities—which they will accept; and all as rendering services will reasonably prefer to afford those which they can most readily perform.   This is the fundamental principle of free trade in its broadest sense.   The contrary implication involved in a system of exclusive privilege or monopoly is altogether untenable as affording any rational basis for reciprocity.   A right to render service without regard to the preference of those who are supposed to be served is so obvious a contradiction that the desire to impose conditions so anomalous has been constantly disguised under some specious pretext. Hence it is that value *in use* has been so perversely confounded with value in exchange, or value of that kind which is in correlation with the free interchange of services.   Long ago the first principle upon which the latter is based was partially seen, but this did not suit the pretensions of those who desired to secure to themselves an absolute right to all surplus products, or to the services of all those supported by such products:—in other words, to all they could possibly obtain.   And their justification was appropriately found in "a truth which is half a truth."   The natural increase of the harvest or of the flock was considered as the "gift of God," which was appropriated by those who were strong enough to keep possession of it.   But such exclusive possession can only be maintained either by force as a right of war, or as a political institution, subject absolutely to such conditions and changes as the higher welfare of the State may require.   The doctrine, however, was, and still is, most admirably suited to monopolists of all kinds, aristocratic, commercial, or democratic, and a system of exclusive privilege rendered physically tolerable by almsgiving will always be in favour with those to whose class-interests the impartial application of equal principles of justice is obnoxious. But the properties inherent in all materials whatsoever upon which human care and skill can be beneficially employed are in the same sense equally a "gift" to all mankind, and the mysteries of these gifts in organic and inorganic matter are alike absolutely inscrutable and beyond our powers of production. The great principle in the economy of the industry of a free people, is that the labour bestowed in rendering these "gifts" available for use, and not the "gifts" themselves, is the ultimate basis of that kind of value which can be rightly brought into question between man and man, though the relative serviceableness of the labour bestowed cannot be left out of consideration.

The theorem does not traverse the relative duties of classes or of individuals to the State or to each other, but affords an equitable basis upon which mutual obligations can be determined and regulated.

Producers may not directly or indirectly force on their own terms their products upon others : nor may consumers dictate the terms upon which products shall be rendered to them. The choice of what is most acceptable to himself must rest with

the consumer. The best, or rather the most suitable, services will command a preference. Every
"producer," on his side, must have an equal
freedom of choice as to the way in which he
may strive to make his services acceptable. The
"quantity" of labour required and which will
willingly be accorded thus becomes the ultimate
measure of reciprocal value.

11. Underlying all are the great laws of physical   The physical bases
necessity. There is no possible escape from the   of value.
stringency of the law that men are kept alive by
the continuous consumption of things which can
be replaced only by the continuous application of
labour. But under favourable conditions, where
abundant natural agents are at command, where
labour is skilled, organised, aided by art and by
science,—all the primary wants of the whole can
be fully satisfied by the results—direct or indirect
—of a part only of the labour of the community.
Utility among other conditions depends upon a
right adaptation of quantity, and a superabundance
is valueless because it is in fact useless. When
the prices of any commodity are forced down,
owing to casually excessive supply, it is merely
an indication that the holders of it are striving
to escape the natural penalty of a misadaptation.
They are glad to get it applied to some use on
any terms, though it may not be that to which it
is naturally fitted, but the permanent conditions
of value are not thereby materially altered. The

surplus of labour—the primary wants of which are provided for—can only come into the great common field of co-operation by supplying utilities —things or services—which though of greater or less—perhaps very much less—importance than the due supply of the necessaries referred to, are still infinitely more useful and valuable than an excess of them: and as far as there is free intercourse between the different occupations thus arising, the value of equal quantities of labour will not be very diverse. Still the process of equation always going on is a double one: *viz.* that of the "utilities" which the workman may receive on the one side for his own satisfaction, and, on the other, of the relative quantity, bearing value, which each workman may render for the satisfaction of others: the former represented in money as "wages" and the latter as the "cost of production." Whoever may be the owner of the products of the surplus labour indicated—or even if it be not applied to material production at all— it is equally clear that a strictly fair comparison between "wages" and "the cost of production" is essential under any just system whatever of organised industry. The higher cost of different utilities is no exception to the rule, for it will be found to resolve itself into the duplication and reduplication of laborious processes. Rough iron may thus be worked into fine and costly steel implements by successive quantities of labour ex- pended upon it, and so bear a very high value, though the remuneration given throughout may have sufficed to procure for all alike only the common necessaries of life.

The existence of such a surplus is clear in every case where agricultural rent is paid for land. The accretion of it arises under conditions over which the rent-owner has no control, and it is incontestable that the necessities which give rise to the charge, and not the charge itself, govern the cost of production. Still it is equally true that on all rent-paying land, the total value produced must equal all rent as well as all costs, direct or indirect, expended upon it. A less production would pay all costs of production, *i.e.* provide, at the least, all necessaries according to the scale of usage actually obtaining, for all workers employed. The rent therefore must represent a surplus of production not required for those workers, and which can only be reasonably employed to support other workers engaged in other ways than in the production of such necessaries as are already, *ex hypothesi*, supplied for them. What value of utilities "all cost" may represent it is impossible to say. It may be enough barely to provide scanty food and clothing, or suffice to provide a large share of the comforts of life. A very small proprietor might indeed not have enough to support himself; but in no case could the labour of a rent-owner as such be required to produce the value of the share he receives. The same cannot be said of the profit of a farmer or trader, whose work is necessary although it may

CHAP. III.

afford him only a meagre livelihood. It needs no proof that remuneration under whatever name it may be acquired is often much in excess of this, but profits—using the term as indicating one of many ways in which services are recompensed—are often earned under arduous conditions and associated with peculiar risks : they must not be confounded with the profit in a more general sense, which accrues to the nation or individuals by the excess of production over consumption. This point will be referred to more fully in the next chapter.

Aggregate money value made up of manifold interchanges.

12. Statisticians who have attempted to estimate in the terms of money the total income of the country have sooner or later found that they were counting incomes over and over again, and have therefore sometimes set very arbitrary limits to their investigations. But the fact should be accepted from the very first and be no bar to carrying on the calculation to the very last. A general idea of the condition of every one in a country is more intelligibly conveyed by stating his income in the common terms of money than it could be in any other way, and, rightly understood, the sum of incomes duly classified, gives a very fair impression of the material condition of the whole community. But no idea can be properly realised of *any* income which does not follow it as being spent. Directly or indirectly it must go to make up other incomes, and the result is necessarily distribution, though it may be distribution in very uneven proportions. Thus a wealthy man spends so much on plate : the

silversmith has his profit, a portion of which he may spend on plate too, or on any other superfluity : so with his foremen and skilled workmen ; so on to the worst paid productive labourer, who must at the least have wages enough to supply him with the necessaries of life. There are innumerable ramifications and interlacings of industry, but this much is certain ; that however intrinsically worthless the thing produced or service rendered may be, if accepted at all, the first necessaries of life are earned in exchange for it ; and as a matter of fact many of the most evanescent and trifling of luxuries are so highly paid for, that the producers are themselves large consumers of mere superfluities under the same conditions, *viz.*, all who contribute to their production earn a certain minimum wage.

13. So it is nothing less than a hard fact that merely to lessen expenses, even on the most worthless trifles, in order to give the money away in alms, may be only putting the bread into one mouth by taking it out of another. Well-to-do workmen, if their trade partially leaves them, may save, but they cannot do so except on the same condition of withholding their outlay in some direction. It is this half of a truth that gives rise to the popular notion that the mere spending of money is good for the country. Very much in accordance with it I have heard a landlord, of whose personal beneficence there is no doubt, argue that it would be a good thing if land were exempt from all rates, as then the owners would have more

to spend in wages. A certain section of shopkeepers urge that they pay taxes which support the national expenditure, and if their profits are lessened they cannot continue to do so. Extravagantly-managed corporations boast of the support they give to various tradesmen who live by supplying them with luxuries. The bare facts cited are true, but as an argument they are utterly worthless : any one may retort that if he also has less to pay in one direction he will have more to spend in another. If the butcher gets 3d. per lb. less for his meat, his customer has just so much the more to spend elsewhere. The argument is a purely personal one as to who is to have the preference. No doubt labour is supported by all existing industries, and they are supported by all that is actually spent upon them, but that is a totally different thing from admitting that all existing forms of industry are necessary for its support, or are the best adapted to embrace all capable of labour within their limits. Forcibly to destroy any industrial organization on the ground that its products were intrinsically worthless, would in all probability throw out many labourers from the circle of industry, which, as far as they are concerned, is productive : but when one industry is developed in fair competition with another, no such ill-effects are to be apprehended — the presumption is strongly that more are included in it, and that though some may suffer, more must gain.

14. The true problem is twofold: how to qualify men for labour, and how to find suitable objects on which to employ it.   In no other way can the total value of products be increased and duly distributed.   The mere spending of money does nothing whatever to overcome this difficulty. Promiscuous almsgiving tends only to organise pauperism; while restrictions and monopolies go far to make the solution of the problem impossible.

Here is a feather: a mere trifle which would cost let us say 5*l.* to obtain, but it is the fashion of the day, and 10*l.* will be readily given for it. What are the indications of money regarding it? First as to price.   Fashion is urgent and wants it to-day, though it might be had for half the cost a little time hence.   Moreover we may perhaps find that the dealer fears that next year no one will buy such feathers on any terms, and remote considerations of cheaper cost have little weight with him.

Next as to the buyer.   He has no more urgent wants left to satisfy: nothing that he can get for 10*l.* at the moment gives him more gratification than this feather.

As to the seller, or the several sellers, who may have contributed to the supply; the price to them is meat and drink and clothes: a little bonus, perhaps also, to set against bad times past or to come. The next freak of fashion may be quite out of their way.   They have "a right" to the price they can obtain; but if their feathers be not sold they may have to eat the bitter bread of " charity."

N

Take any other article of not quite so capricious a value :—the replies will still be similar, only the sellers will be somewhat more securely within the circle of independence.

Such are the indications of money regarding value in exchange—these or such as these, and nothing more : and what further, as to the necessaries of life. In a wealthy country which avails itself of the best resources the world has to offer, they tend naturally to be relatively cheap. Dealers have no fear that these will go out of fashion : they get them with confidence from the best sources of supply and can sell them for the barest margin of remuneration. "Growing more potatoes" is evidently not the remedy for these discrepancies. A nation not absolutely poverty-stricken has rarely any difficulty in obtaining a supply of the common necessaries of life, and our own country has far passed the stage when such considerations occasion any anxiety. The great problem which has to be solved is how to embrace all members of the community in the circle of reciprocal service and industry best adapted to satisfy not only the physical wants but the higher requirements of a well-reasoned civilization.

Capital :—
the requisites necessary to support life.
15. Capital, as I think, may be most conveniently regarded primarily as the accumulated stock of the necessaries requisite for the support of life during the time when the work of reproduction is being carried on to completion. We have thus as the essential elements of production :

natural agents or the materials upon which labour
can be employed; labour to be employed upon
them ; and capital required to support it until the
products are completed and fitted in their turn for
consumption. Mr. Mill, however, puts forward a
somewhat different view (*Prin. of Polit. Econ.*,
Book i. c. 4. § i.), and writes : "The distinction
between capital and non-capital does not lie in
the kind of commodities, but in the mind of the
capitalist — in his will to employ them for one
purpose rather than another : and all property,
however ill-adapted in itself for the use of labourers,
is a part of capital, so soon as it, or the value to be
received from it, is set apart for productive re-
investment." A definition which seems open to
the grave objection that at the least it assumes,
as a general truth, conditions which obtain only
casually even in countries which are not only
wealthy but prospering. In writing a history of
the development of production it might no doubt
have been assumed that those who carried out the
design of applying their wealth to productive purposes, had, in fact, been able to make the exchanges
required to enable them to do so. Naturally also,
when speaking of the current work of production,
only that portion of capital is referred to which is
actually employed, or is seeking for employment in
it. But when dealing more specifically with the
problems connected with the developement of industry it is asking too much to grant any such
assumption. It may indeed be said in dull times

in the London money-market, "There is no capital anywhere;" but we all understand that there is abundance to be had if the owners can only see their way to employ it to advantage. The will of the owner no doubt determines whether he will attempt to apply it productively, and I am quite ready to admit that the *will* for the purposes of the argument may generally be assumed to imply the skill requisite to give due effect to its decision. But this is a very different thing from assuming that a picture, or a vase of crackled china, or a bale of velvet is capital in virtue of the intention of the owner — especially in the abstract sense which Mr. Mill's definition implies. Before any A can receive value for his picture in the form of capital which can support labour, he must find some B ready to do just the reverse. B goes out and A comes in to the sphere of productive industry when this is accomplished, but not before. Two minds, not one only, are concerned, in what is after all merely a change of ownership. And it is hard to see why an intention to employ the value of property unsuitable to support labour should be held to make capital, any more than an intention to work, or an intention to discover new mines or lands, should be held to constitute "labour" or "natural agents." Capital, labour, and natural agents are equally the material requisites for production, and it is surely far more closely in accordance with the facts with which we are concerned to consider them alike as the resources with which mind and intention have to deal, and by means of which the intentions of the mind are carried into substantive effect.

Moreover, in treating of material substances, it is apt to lead to confusion if a distinction is drawn where materially speaking no difference exists. We have already seen the very unstable kind of equilibrium which arises from the production of mere superfluities : are the workers to be considered as consumers of capital or of non-capital according as they succeed or fail in their efforts to make their labour productive ? And what is to be said of the consumption of paupers and those out of work, which in a civilised country is as necessary as that of any other members of the community. It is in economic terms a drain upon our capital. There is in this case no material requisite of production wanting. No doubt effectual intention only is required, but I submit that, if that can be brought to bear, it is better to say that " unproductive " capital has been made " productive," than that non-capital has been made capital, or that capital has been " created," when the material substance implied has not in any way been changed by the intention. The definition has led, and I think is calculated to lead, to the prevalence of very pernicious fallacies. There is a cry for capital when it is under our hands if only we could make good any intention to utilise it, but neglecting and ignoring that which we have, there is still a cry for more and other capital to be got by the sale of superfluities which by no possibility can be other than superfluities in any one's hand. The making of them was an irretrievable action of the past. Whoever has them can only hold them for the uses for which they have been fitted. They may perhaps be a useful and permanent form of wealth, but can only be exchanged for capital when capital is already in abundance. I refer here to the definition only without reference to Mr. Mill's views as elsewhere more fully expressed, and cannot but think that an apparent simplicity has been gained in it at the cost of real obscurity.

Practically speaking in so wealthy a country as England there is always a superabundance of capital at command without taking thought for a moment of things ill-adapted for labourers' use, provided that the intelligence which directs labour can find labour suitably qualified for the work it desires to undertake ; but in countries which are really poor, an actual want of accumulated capital may be the first great difficulty in the way of improving the conditions under which labour may be made more productive.

Fixed and circulating capital;—objections to these terms. 16. Capital is further spoken of commonly as circulating or fixed : neither of which terms has ever been regarded with any satisfaction. The so-called "fixed" capital sunk in a factory or in workmen's tools is employed to assist and economise labour, which is a very different conception from supporting it. Further, the factory or the tools are worn out and consumed just the same as a workman's clothes, and have in like manner to be replaced, so "fixed" capital does circulate only in rather different cycles. Nor does the term "circulating" itself aptly represent the continuous process of consumption and reproduction which takes place as regards capital properly so called. Money does circulate and it would be well if the epithet could be specially appropriated to money. But a continuity of entirely new and ever fresh production, maintained moreover only by the equally continuous efforts of well-applied industry, is a conception so radically different from that of mere "circulation" that it is to be regretted that the term was ever adopted in its usual connection.

I have already ventured to use the words "productive property" instead of "fixed capital" in a way which I trust will not have appeared either strange or unintelligible. The factory or machinery or other appliances in which capital is said to be fixed have not, it is true, the recuperative power which is inherent in land—neither have mines—nor even in the case of land does this unique quality constitute in itself an element of exchange value. Economic rent thus stands alone as a possession of a peculiarly specialised description ; but for the rest, why should not stock or property, as well as capital, be distinguished as " productive " or "unproductive" ? and if the latter be no longer misdescribed as "fixed," it need no longer be misrepresented as "circulating."

CHAP. III.

There is, however, another side to the question. We speak of labour unskilled, or skilled in greater or less degree; this usually implies that it must be furnished with the appliances and tools necessary to make good the distinction; and a reasonable accumulation of the results of past labour in this form also must be held applicable for its special requirements. It would be a violent figure of speech to call capital skilled or unskilled, but not the less the supply of it must correspond and be adapted to the quality, as well as to the quantity, of labour to be employed, and this very essential distinction must not be lost sight of in the general use of the term.

Labour and capital are factors constantly variable.

17. Nothing can be more absolutely true than the fact upon which Mr. Mill insists, that there cannot be more productive labourers employed than the portion of the products of past labour allotted to them can feed and supply with the materials and instruments of production; and, as he most justly urges, this fact (self-evident as it may appear to be) has constantly been forgotten, and governments have acted, and been urged to act, as though the mere dictum of authority could create value without providing for the use of the means necessary to carry out the work required.

But while keeping this truth fully in mind, it must not be supposed that either capital or labour are fixed quantities which cannot be increased or decreased according to the amount of intelligent energy brought to bear upon them.

The analogy of the balance-sheet of the accounts

of any industrial concern may fairly be cited in illustration of the principles involved. On the one side there is the category of all the assets, and on the other of all the liabilities, at one particular point of time :—strictly speaking it is a *point:* not a day's latitude can be allowed. Everything to be paid must be set against everything to be received, as at one period. If any one, either from folly or fraudulent intention, desires to mystify an account, he will very likely represent that these items have been paid, or those received, since the account was made up, and so make it appear that the balance is something quite different from that which is represented. The specific facts alleged may be true enough, and, if the changes involved were of sufficient importance, might afford a very valid reason for restating the account up to a later date. And when *all* assets and *all* liabilities were again duly set forth in the same way, as they existed in correspondence at some other moment of time, it would be proved that no mere change or juggle of figures could change the true position of the affairs involved. If one side of the account is increased or decreased, so also must be the other, and every investigation which does not include every item on both sides is a delusion.

Not the less is the condition of the concern supposed, changing day by day and month by month for better or worse according to the success or failure of the work actually done within it. So, while we must totally disallow the possibility of a nation, or an individual, increasing its investments in labour or materials without also increasing the capital employed, we must as clearly bear in mind that these factors are constantly varying, and can be influenced—but can only be influenced—by bringing appropriate means to bear directly upon the progressive work of production. Every year's account will show some change for better or worse. Nor is it merely apparently increased accumulation that is to be regarded, but the soundness and due proportion of all the related parts of the whole. This argument is not opposed to the fundamental doctrines which Mr. Mill has expounded; but the desponding views which he has repeatedly expressed that improvement in the condition of the wage-earning class could only be secured by extreme measures for restricting their numbers— and consequently the power of the nation—have tended, as I think, to throw this side of the question unduly into the shade.

Only well directed labour productive.

18. Danger is now rather to be apprehended from quite another quarter, and is to be discerned in the disposition to regard mere capital as though it were in some way a self-generating power. There are many who seem to think that if they intend to employ their funds productively they have a right to look for a profitable result either in the shape of high interest or of profits, almost as a matter of course, without the exercise of any skill, care, trouble, or even discrimination, on their own part. The stolid Transvaal farmer who declared the

banker must be a rogue who offered to give him something, in the way of interest, for keeping his money was consistent at all events. He wanted his cash to be safely put away in a strong box, and was ready to pay for the service. But the fact which cannot be too forcibly impressed upon popular apprehension is, that if interest is to be paid at all, their capital must be made productive, and for this object must first be altogether consumed and destroyed for the aid and support of labour, and in place of it some entirely new "utility" must be produced. Whether any other capital may stand between the investor and the first risks of the undertaking in which he may be thus, perhaps unconsciously, concerned, is a matter of comparative detail and of personal arrangement, but of this nature is the process upon which the success of all must ultimately depend. These conditions however are popularly ignored or forgotten. If the enterprise fail, the money lost is presumed to have been abstracted in some way, and from a confusion of mind between the money of currency, which cannot be consumed, nor can itself be productive, and money as representing capital which must be consumed in order to have a chance of being productive, it is assumed that the "money" must be somewhere, and that some one ought to be forced to refund it. Out of some such delusion as this have grown all the scandals which are from time to time disclosed after every period of speculative inflation. There is, in short, an effectual demand

for investments on impossible terms, which is sure
to be met by that mixture of folly, fraud and recklessness which is always ready to pander to and
profit by irrational selfishness. A great deal of
intelligent hard work, as well as passive integrity,
are required so to apply capital, that the results
may satisfy some presently felt want, and thus
make good its claim to be regarded as productive.
At all times it is quite as true to say that the productive application of capital is limited by the
quantity of suitably qualified labour, as the converse ; and both sides of the truth must be kept in
mind together.

The rela-
tive effi-
ciency of
labour the
chief
source of
wealth.
19. The creation of a new industry does not in
any material sense necessarily call for an equivalent
creation of new capital, for to take the antecedent
conditions at the worst :—if surplus labour exist
at all, there must also exist the means of supporting
it. The aggregate stock of commodities is always
largely in excess of immediate wants. Prospective
requirements are readily met by increased future
production, and only a comparatively slight readjustment of the future application of labour will
suffice for the primary support of a greatly extended
industry. The tools and appliances suited for
highly skilled labour are not thus held in reserve,
and indeed for the most part have to be specially
fitted to the varying nature of the work required.
A double operation may thus be required, and the
second employment of labour and capital must wait
the completion of the first. But it is these appli-

ances, which in a well organised industrial community are the outcome of capital joined to high
technical skill and science, that render ample production possible. They increase the positive efficiency of labour, *i.e.* the actual difference between
production and necessary consumption. It is this
difference represented by the quantity of labour,
which, being supported by the labour of others
can be applied to other purposes,—not the aggregate value of capital employed, which determines
the growth of those forms of wealth, whether permanent or transitory, which are the more remote
objects of desire and ambition. Nay, more ; it is
this surplus of energy which is indeed the great
source of power in a community. There is no physical law of necessity which controls either the production or the distribution of things non-essential ;
but much wealth there must be—at least potentially—within the limits of a community living
under such conditions, and also a wide range of
choice as to the employment of a large number
of workers. In such cases the wise direction of
this labour, and the just and politic distribution
of its results, are problems of far more pressing
interest than any question as to the further accumulation of capital, or as to the greater or less
aggregate of material " utilities," bearing exchange
value which may be produced.

20. In the case of a country actually poor, the
difficulty is generally not so much the transmission
of capital as its adjustment and adaptation to the

other requisites of production. This is indeed a work requiring much patience and judgment and, as has been already shown (I. 25), the mere acquisition of metallic wealth does not do much to solve the problem. If natural agents abound capable of yielding any desired utility, no doubt Capital can transplant Labour, and all that is required to support it, bodily to the place where they can beneficially be employed ; but labour, duly qualified for such enterprises, is generally hard to find and can ill be spared, and a transfer of this kind has little in common with the development of the natural resources of a country, by the labour which, in the main, it can itself supply, in a way which shall afford a margin out of which the new capital employed can be fairly remunerated. The first and most essential object is to increase the efficiency of that labour, and so secure the difference just explained which can be applied to extended production either for export in kind, or for the support of labour locally applied to new purposes. It may be a very great advantage to have capital, in other words to have the use of all the appliances which can at once be turned to good account, without going through the tedious process of accumulating the equivalent of them by gradual savings, but the instruction and technical training which must be imparted before a new people are able to make good use of such appliances are just as helpful and necessary to production as any material aid which can be afforded. The introduction of both must be a work of time, and the kind of appliances required in one state of society is often ludicrously unsuited to another. What can be more out of place than steam ploughs or artificial manures in a district where land is so much in excess of population that the custom of letting a large portion lie fallow is, under existing circumstances, no waste of available resources, but simply the most economical use of them. So with the introduction of railways, works of mining or irrigation, or any other improvements in a foreign country. The quantity and quality of labour which it can afford, how far that has previously been used to, or organised for, any similar work; the wealth and means of circulating it which may already exist; the effect which any artificial aggregation of labour in any one district may have on the price of provisions, and many other such considerations have all to be taken fully into account with reference to any scheme of construction. While as to the ultimate success of the undertaking; the quantity of traffic which any district can afford to use, the population which may be able to take new land into cultivation, the extent to which custom or apathy may operate against changes however apparently beneficial, will all have their effect on the returns to be anticipated from the completed work. Experience in most settled countries where there is no violent interruption to the efforts of industry, warrants strong confidence in their general capacity for progressive development, but quite the reverse as regards any advantage to be derived merely from profuse expenditure. The high rate of interest in many new countries does not represent the insecurity of property so much as the risk of failure arising from the difficulty of adapting the new capital to the existing agencies which have to be modified to carry out the work designed.

It is needless to enlarge further upon such difficulties which must be the subject of careful and special investigation wherever capital has to be applied. Enough I trust has been said to indicate something of the nature and the limits of the uses which it subserves.

Commercial use of the term "capital." 21. The word capital is used in a somewhat different sense in commerce, rather with reference to the very general conception of "money" which will now come under consideration. The balance of the estimated value of a trader's assets after full discharge of his liabilities is, for instance, said to be his capital. It thus indicates in very general terms that which is his own, as distinguished from that for which he is accountable to others. Or it may be opposed to *interest* or *income*, as the capital value of the funds or of an estate : the right to such income being exchangeable for the amount of capital expressed. The term may often be somewhat loosely used, yet will still be found to signify ultimately a purchasing power, which, though expressed in the terms of current money, does not imply the substantive use of either bullion,

coin, or notes, but represents rather means which
actually are, or potentially might be, employed,
either in supporting labour, or purchasing the
products of labour for completion or for final
distribution and resale.

22. Before advancing further in the question, it
may be well to summarize the conclusions just
arrived at, without however following closely the
order in which the several points have been raised.

Summary of the foregoing propositions.

(1). A certain stock of necessaries must be continuously maintained in every country to support
life while the work of reproduction is being carried
on. It may either have been produced directly
within its own borders, or procured by traffic with
other countries. Thus, cattle may be exchanged
for corn, though it does not follow, merely from
this fact, that more of either is raised by the whole
labour of the producers than will be required for
consumption within this period. Population is of
course limited by the extent of this supply, which
supports alike those who do and can, and those
who do not or cannot, contribute to it. This stock
is capital in its primary sense, and that portion of
it which maintains those engaged in the work of
production is distinguished as " productive."

(2). Under favourable conditions, natural or
acquired, the production of all the stock thus
required will be largely in excess of the consumption of those engaged in this special work. Other
labourers, therefore, supported by this surplus, can

only be usefully engaged in supplying other commodities (or rendering other services) than those which are required to satisfy such primary wants. Equal "quantities" of labour must therefore be held to give equal value to all products for purposes of exchange the one against the other ; for the "natural agents" upon which all alike are employed are not the exclusive property of any, and all are engaged in supplying in the aggregate those things or services which are best fitted adequately to satisfy existing demand. As no physical law of necessity governs the application of the labour thus supported, it may be diverted to any objects according to the state of opinion which governs the effectual choice of society.

(3). It may be further observed that no precise general definition can be given in this context of the term " necessaries ;" but physiology and practical experience clearly show that the minimum required merely to support the continuity of life is not the minimum cost of production, for, within certain limits, the "quantity" of labour which can be yielded increases in a far greater ratio than the quantity of products consumed. As a question of current exchange value, the amount of necessaries required to remunerate labourers is just that proportion of the aggregate production for which their demand can be made effectual ; but a well-nurtured labourer can more fully earn his wages than one who is ill-nurtured.

(4). The efficiency of labour is greatly increased

by its specialization, which implies in an extended degree the co-operation and interdependence of all who are directly or indirectly engaged in the work of production. Labour is also aided by various appliances, and skilled labour, *qua* skilled, must be supported by capital, including such adjuncts as are necessary to give effect to its special dexterity ; these being in fact the products of previously applied capital and labour. Capital also may be invested in factories, machinery, and other productive property by means of which labour, both skilled and unskilled, may be more efficiently employed, and the ultimate effect of these redoubled applications of capital and labour is largely to augment production as compared with necessary consumption ; and, consequently, the surplus of capital and labour which can be optionally applied.

(5). This surplus, if applied to the construction of objects of durable value *in use,* increases the wealth of a country. It may equally be applied in the production of perishable superfluities of no real value in use, or to services which do not yield any results in material form,—but in all cases value in exchange depends equally upon the cost which may be required, directly or indirectly, to maintain those who are thus admitted for the time being within the circle of recognised industry.

(6). Fresh capital must inevitably be made productive in order to include other and new labourers within this circle of independent co-operation, but as, materially speaking, this capital is for the most part already in existence (or men could not have been supported at all) the work required, especially in any wealthy country, is rather that of voluntary redistribution, by means of improved industrial organisation, than of any new production of capital in its primary sense.

(7). The cost of all existing property may be resolved ultimately into the value of the commodities produced and consumed in times past. The exchange value of that portion which may be distinguished as productive is based; (*a*) on an estimate of the revenue which can be afforded by it, *i.e.*, by the difference between future income and future necessary expenditure, and (*b*) upon the amount of accumulations of capital at the present time of interchange which the owners possess and are willing to give for the prospective advantages to be derived from such property.

As regards the first (*a*) there will be deducted from the prime cost, the outlay for all labour originally wasted or misapplied, or applied to objects the utility of which has been superseded and passed away :—and added, any increase in the estimated cost of production in the future as compared with the past. The current value of all property and commodities is estimated subject to both these considerations.

(8). As far as the consumption for the support of labour is less than the remuneration (whether earned as wages, working profit, or under any other name) accorded to it, there will have been an accumulation of capital within the limits of the cost of any specific product. This most essential feature of social economy must constantly be kept in mind, though for exposition as well as for practical purposes, it will probably be more easy to most minds to conceive of these as separate accounts to be set the one against the other in estimating the accretions of national capital, rather than to attempt to grasp the innumerable expedients of industrial activity in one common account. The same general principles apply throughout.

(9). The exchange value of possessions not yielding any periodical increase to the owner, rests entirely upon the estimate formed of the advantages of all kinds, whether mental, moral, or physical, which the possessor may derive from keeping them, rather than any other advantages he could get by parting with them. But properties of this description generally can reasonably be regarded only for the uses they are fitted to subserve. Thus, a man who has diamonds or pictures or unique porcelain is, *so far*, altogether outside the pale of social industry, either as a consumer or a producer. It may perhaps be said that an economic advantage of such things is that those who buy them do withdraw completely from all interest in or control over capital or labour in favour of those who may be better able to utilise them : a step which few would be willing to take were it wholly

CHAP. III. irreversible, which it is not as long as such things maintain an exchange value from the demand of others who are willing to accept them under the same conditions.

(10). The current exchange value, and more especially the price, of all property and commodities is in all cases essentially relative, and is worked out by the equations of demand and supply as severally adjusted at any one time. This demand and supply depends not only on the conditions referred to, but also on changes of opinion which may lead to exchanges on unequal terms between one kind of possession and another.

(11). The current exchange value of all these various objects of desire :—property, productive and unproductive, and securities based upon them ; commodities fitted for use or in various stages of completion : merchandize in store or in transit, services of all kinds, are all expressed in the common terms of money, and although the use of it in any specific form is very rarely required, all the multifarious and diversely-related transactions in them are made on the faith reposed in the integrity of our golden unit of exchange value. The fact that the great operations of industry can be thus generally described without direct reference to it, serves to show how little it can be affected by local transfers, however great may be the amount of their value, which are within the ordinary range of social and industrial intercourse. Gold serves as a common measure of value for all,

while its own value depends on a far wider average
of independently working causes.   It escapes and
is exempt from the one-sided and interested
influences to which the objects which are calculated to gratify the ordinary desires of mankind are exposed.   Its own use may be best
understood by the analogy of any other system
of weights and measures.   It is in itself eminently
trustworthy, but just as any conceivable absurdity
in estimates of length or capacity may be precisely
expressed in the most exact terms, or rashly and
falsely expressed in terms which are themselves
accurate, so it may be with the £ sterling or any
other monetary unit.

In proceeding to treat of the means by which
the current work of industrial production is carried
on, we shall have specially to deal not with money
itself, but with estimates expressed in the terms of
money.

CHAPTER IV.

(Value.)

CONDITIONAL OWNERSHIP : CREDIT AND BANKING.

1. THE consideration of fixed and realised property of all kinds may now for a time be laid aside, while attention is directed to those processes by which the work of current production is continuously carried on, and the means by which the necessary transfers are effected from one hand to another of all that is required by those who are engaged together in work, which has not only to be subdivided in an infinite variety of ways, but the results also have to be brought together to suit an infinite variety of wants under circumstances which in a greater or less degree are constantly changing. Not only must every one's section of work be expressed in terms common to all, but meantime, while engaged upon it, each one requires the uncontrolled possession of the materials which he has to use. But it is not at all necessary that he should have the unqualified ownership of them : on the contrary, a very little reflection will show that such a condition would work very unequally indeed. Thus : take for example the first

process required on iron which has cost little or
nothing, and compare it with the latter work done
on fine steel on which a great deal has been already
expended. The labour applied in either case
might well be worth equal remuneration, but necessarily the inherent cost of the material is widely
different. If therefore each kind of work had to be
done only by those who could afford to own the
material, the latter section could only be undertaken by those who were comparatively rich.
There is, in fact, no natural relation between the
present capacity of any particular workman and
past accumulations of capital invested in the
materials on which he works. Thus capital, which
includes in a very general term all that is required
to support industry in every form, must itself be
again generalised and distributed, so that it may
be brought into appropriate connection with labour.
This further generalisation is termed *credit*, and
materially speaking there is no difference whatever
between the one and the other.

To use *credit* is to use capital in a way which
will satisfy the needs of a highly-organised system
of industry and requires a largely extended use of
"money," not in the form of actual coin or notes
representing coin, but simply as a purchasing power
on a definitely fixed scale, in a sense even more
abstract than any which has yet been explained.
And for this reason. Loans can no doubt be made
of commodities : there is no reason whatever why
they should not be so made when it suits the

convenience of those concerned, but loans in money
are generally preferred, as affording the borrower
the wider range of choice in selecting that which
he may require. He can hire or buy just as much
as he wants of labour or of rough material, or
materials upon which much work has been already
bestowed : but the product is something completed,
or in a more or less forward state towards completion, and is not by any means the same as
those things which have been required for its
production. That which has been directly or indirectly borrowed is either consumed altogether,
or so completely altered in form that a return in
kind is out of the question. Very little use could
be made of credit without a basis of sound money
in which to express its conditions in general
terms.

Even to take corn as the article of all others in
most general consumption ;—many things else are
required by the cultivator, especially if he would
make the best use of the land upon which he is
working, and though a rent in kind might be paid
ultimately to a landlord, quantities of corn bear
no assignable proportion to the specific wants of
those who have to be recompensed for the various
commodities supplied to a skilful farmer. Further,
even in this case, though there may be no difference
in the material form of one year's corn and that
of the year which has preceded it, the production
must still be regarded as constantly progressive :
each succeeding month must bring it nearer to the

time when it must fulfil the final purpose for which
it is raised.

So also as regards merchandise in the hands of
an importer or dealer. Its form may not be
changed, but the object is, not to return it back
to the owner or lender, but to pass it on for further
use, or for consumption. The nearer we get to
the consumer, the more advanced is the stage of the
work which has been completed, and the greater
the labour and cost which has been expended.

2. Industrial "money" represents alike all that
is required to sustain labour in full beneficial
activity, and all the products which result from it
to supply the ever recurring wants of mankind :
and though it has been shown that there can be no
usufruct in gold or silver or the representatives of
either as money in mere material form, it by no
means follows that there cannot be such usufruct
of that which conveys the power of purchasing,
ready to hand, all that is required to aid and
support the continuous operations of production.
And this will be more clearly seen as we consider
further not only the form but the nature of the
various obligations expressed in the terms of money.
We have in fact to treat of loans, and the money
market in this context is the market for loans.

Nature of relative rights arising through credit.

There are two juridical terms which so well
express the conditions under which credit is
accorded, that I will venture to introduce them
here. Strictly speaking, they refer rather to the
compass than to the *subject* of rights—and the

Jus in rem.
Jus in per-sonam.

obligations corresponding with them ;—but I trust I shall not be deemed too lax in interpreting *jus in rem* as a right in something, as against all the world; and *jus in personam* as a right to something, as against some peculiar person or persons. These answer to the most essential distinction between the rights of the borrower and lender respectively. Specific commodities must of course be definitely owned by some person or persons. The ownership of them may even be conveyed by any suitable document. Thus the " Bill of Lading " signed by the captain of a vessel passes by endorsement from hand to hand, and conveys the right of ownership to the specific goods mentioned in it. The Receipt or " Warrant " of a warehouse keeper[1] represents goods deposited with him for safe custody and conveys the same right. But these same goods may be, and very generally are, directly or indirectly, also the basis of a Bill of exchange or a Promissory Note.

The right to goods in a man's own possession, or represented by such documents as a bill of lading

[1] This, though only established in law by a very recent decision (Merchants' Banking Company *v.* Bessemer Steel Company), is entirely according to the reasonable exigencies required by the division of labour in commerce. The mere safe custody of goods can be more efficiently provided for by those who lay themselves out for this kind of business than by owners generally. The duty of warehousemen as such, is simply to deliver such goods to the holder of the warrant, and questions of ownership can most conveniently and safely be dealt with by those who hold that document. Further, to illustrate the position, it may be added that should the holder become bankrupt, the warrant vests in whomsoever represents his general estate, and is held as an asset for the benefit of all, as against any special creditor.

or dock warrant, is *in rem*. The right given by a bill of exchange or by a promissory note is *in personam*, and avails only against the acceptor or other persons who are parties to the instrument: any direct right to the goods against which it may have been drawn is not conveyed by any such documents. It is very much the same with an advance in cash made by a banker for any fixed time. The lender may know generally what the borrower wants to buy for the purposes of his trade, but his only claim is against his debtor personally for a specified sum of money to be paid hereafter. Rights of both kinds may be concurrently held in respect of the same property, but they are, nevertheless, essentially distinct.

What is the meaning and object of this duplication of instruments, or rather of terms of concurrent rights affecting the same commodities? Simply this. The person who has work to do with them has the uncontrolled use of them, either for the purpose of turning them into other utilities, or for supporting productive labour. He holds them, or the results derived from them, against all the world, to use according to his own discretion, without let or hindrance or interference. But this *credit* is only accorded on the faith that the commodities, the use of which has been obtained directly from the lender or by the use of the lender's money, are being brought on to a stage of advanced value, so that when the acceptance or loan becomes due in course of time, the promised

" purchasing power " will have been earned and obtained. A bill or note, therefore, does not during its currency imply any purchasing power as at present existing : it is only the promise of those who are parties to it that such a power will be conveyed at some fixed future time : the presumption being that they have not at the time any such power to convey.

So far a man with only moderate means of his own, but in good reputation as not only passively honest, but capable in the work he undertakes to do, is fairly placed on a level as a producer with his richer competitors. And it may be said of this generalisation of capital, as credit, as has been already remarked of the fundamental laws which govern value, that it is essential to any state of society which would rise much above the range of a barbaric isolation of individual labour. It is neither the cause nor the effect of the division of classes into rich and poor, though no doubt those who have only enough for their own immediate wants cannot lend the surplus which they have *not* to others. But small savings are equally available with great accumulations to make up the aggregate of productive capital required. There is, for example, no reason whatever why the 70,000,000*l.* now in the savings banks should not be directly employed in supporting productive undertakings, except—what is probably the fact—that these reserves are better and more safely placed elsewhere, and other resources are more conveniently available for the uses of industrial enterprise.

3. The nature of *credit* may, as has just been
remarked, be most readily apprehended by considering money in the present context as simply an
abstract term, implying a purchasing power.   It is
this power which is transferred, and which has to
be returned.   Uses, rather than the accidental
materials used, have to be considered in the relations between those who give or take *credit*, and it
is on this ground that any question between them
must be discussed.   Now use implies risk which
cannot by any contrivance be entirely eliminated
from mundane affairs, but which differs very greatly
in degree in various undertakings, and the sound
morality of credit depends upon the way in which
these risks are understood and fairly avowed as
between man and man.   The analogies of stealing,
where the thief takes away that which he had
never any right to touch at all, do not apply to
cases where money is given in order that it may be
spent, *i.e.*, employed.   To obtain credit under false
pretences, or to abuse it after it has been obtained,
may involve graver and baser criminality, but it is
no more to be described as theft than as arson.

There may, indeed, be cases where a loan has
been obtained so palpably under false pretences
that an obvious remedy is to get back the money,
or that which has been bought with it, as far as it
can be identified or "ear-marked."   But this is
rarely possible, or, where possible, may only give
an unfair preference to one lender at the expense
of others, who, under quite similar circumstances,

CHAP. IV.   have trusted to the borrower's personal obligation.
The rights of all alike are *in personam,* not *in rem,*
and only further complications of wrong can arise
from neglecting this obvious distinction. Again,
the old traditions of our common law righteously
forbid that any man charged with a crime should
be required to give evidence which may criminate
himself; but no such maxim can be so strained as
to excuse any one who has failed to meet his personal obligations from the duty of rendering, to a
competent tribunal, full and explicit accounts as
to the uses to which he has applied the *power* of
money intrusted to him. The higher form of trust
should imply a higher order of responsibility.

Risk.   If a man be reckless or negligent in the use of
such borrowed money, he is guilty of a very grave
offence ; far more so if he misrepresent the purposes
for which such money is required. For the lender
is thus made to participate in risks of a different
kind from those which he was willing to incur, and
upon an estimate of which the terms of his remuneration were agreed upon. The wrong done is
of the same kind as though a policy of insurance
were obtained upon a ship by false accounts as to
its destination or seaworthiness. The culpability is
none the less because it might escape from all
dangers and realise the great profits which are often
associated with great risks, without actual injury
to any one. But to incur risks is not in itself
culpable. On the contrary, some degree of uncertainty waits on all enterprise which depends on

future conditions which never can be perfectly anticipated. The very meaning of the word experiment implies that danger which arises from a want of knowledge of the results which will follow any particular course of action, and such trials or ventures in commerce are not only useful, but may even be meritorious. If merchants and manufacturers waited for absolute certainty, they would ignore their function in the general economy of life. If dealers in grain waited for an assured scarcity, the risk of famine would be shifted from them to the society which they exist to serve. Hence it is that the graver questions of right and wrong, as regards credit, turn not upon the risks openly incurred, but upon the candour with which the nature of these risks has been disclosed. Nor can it be assumed, as a matter of course, that rashness, want of forethought or discrimination, are the faults of the borrower and not of the lender. Thus, the creditors (or still less the shareholders) of any company formed to extract moonbeams from cucumbers have no ground, *primâ facie*, to charge those with wrong-doing who have failed in the attempt to carry out the avowed object of the association, though no doubt if they have not themselves shared in the risks, a common sense of the fitness of things will draw its own inferences from a prudence so free from all taint of folly.

Moreover the object of credit is to obtain a division of function with which the division of remuneration may suitably be made to correspond.

P

The reasonable desire of those who accept loans is to secure to themselves in a larger degree all the more or less of gain which may be derived from their own skill and experience in the management of some special kind of industrial work. Those who grant loans forego this advantage, but are assured of a more certain income. The "material guarantee" for this assurance is the capital actually owned by the borrower himself, and any wilful misrepresentation on this point, however indirectly made, is essentially fraudulent. But no wrong is done if any one choose to lend his money to another, trusting solely to the guarantee of his competence and discretion, or the interest he may have in the good will of any productive undertaking, though no one is within the limits of reason in urging that support ought to be accorded to him on any such terms.

Reckless adventures are not encouraged by such arrangements, if made with any reasonable discretion. On the contrary, waste and ruin result rather from a blind confidence in the alleged guarantee of capital without any regard to the uses to which it may be applied. Hence it is that we see periodically great commercial failures. The books often exhibit at the first a superabundance of the wealth to which every one had trusted ; further investigation shows that on the most lenient assumption, none of those connected with the undertaking had any conception whatever of the real nature and extent of their obligations ; and the final result proves that the capital which should have been productive, has on all sides, and long ago, been utterly misapplied and wasted.

Capital and credit are, materially speaking, the same. The purchasing power implied by the use of either term is the same. The division is one only of ownership, implying a corresponding division of function, and while nothing can be gained by unduly confounding the individual rights and responsibilities of the lender and the user, all their broader and more permanent interests must be regarded as identical. The result under a fairly conducted system of free competition is the better adjustment of the work to be done to the various capacities of those engaged in it, and a consequent positive economy of labour for the benefit of the community served, especially when the casually adverse claims of those concerned are not suffered to obscure the true sentiment of co-operation.

4. The uncertain sense in which the term *profit* is used is at the bottom of much of the confusion of thought which prevails on many social problems. At one time it was commonly held that wages were paid out of profits, a notion which no doubt arose from such a case as that of a dealer who bought goods wholesale, and sold them by retail at advanced prices : this difference he might call profit, or, more strictly, gross profit, and out of it wages and other charges would have to be paid, the balance only being the actual *net* profit which the

CHAP. IV.

The profits of productive industry.

dealer could afford to spend upon himself. Mr.
Mill also, having divided the sum of products into
wages and (gross) profits, shows that one portion
cannot be increased without a corresponding reduction in the other. He may have had very good
reason to insist upon so self-evident a fact, for that
3 and 2 could be made into more than 5 by some
skilful juggle of legislation, was one of the profound
fallacies of bygone "financial" theories which it
was very hard to kill. But it is to be regretted that
the general drift of his writings tended so much to
encourage the view that it was pre-eminently desirable that the special profits of enterprise should be
generally shared by those earning wages—leaving
out of view entirely the consideration that there
should be a certain correlation between the nature
of the work done and the mode in which it is recompensed. There is no difference of opinion as
to the principle that all workers should be able
by a reasonable exercise of industry and self-control
to save, and thus accumulate capital ; in this most
important sense all should share in the profits of
production. But wages—and in this generic term
must be included "pay," salaries, and all other
forms of fixed remuneration—may be disproportion-
ately too high or too low. Profits represent alike
the very scanty earnings of the struggling shop-
keeper and manufacturer, and the exceptional gains,
usually associated with inordinate risks, of the
fortunate speculator.

Nor, *cæteris paribus*, does any one form of re-

muneration imply more independence than the
other.   The bargain driven for wages or for profits
may be unduly in favour of either.   Nor should too
much weight be given to the argument that better
work is done for profits than for wages.   The same
lax morality which gives too little work for fixed
pay, will soon find out means of getting too much
pay for an undefined amount or quality of work.
What is required is rather that a just and discriminating criticism should supersede the mere blind
blundering instinct of hard bargain-driving, which
is the popular substitute for economic management.
But we are not concerned in following out this
side of the question.   It is enough to say that the
mode of remuneration governs neither its relative
amount nor the quantity or quality of service
rendered for it.

5. The connection between the nature of the
work done and the recompense earned for it, may
be most directly shown by glancing back at the
necessary order in which production is accomplished.   Wages, whether high or low, are advanced out of past accumulations, and, speaking
generally, though the wage-earner may be uncertain
whether he gets work or not, he does not, having
once obtained it, run any further risk as to the
ultimate success of the undertaking upon which he
is engaged ; and fittingly so.   For specific mechanical work, or even that of subordinate superintendence, may ultimately lead to gain or loss quite
independent of the skill and fidelity with which

CHAP. IV.

Profits
specially
associated
with risks
of final
adjust-
ment.

this special work or service is performed. It has nothing directly to do with the risk of loss from mis-adaptation of supply to demand, which may arise either from error in judgment on the part of the employer, or even from causes impossible for him to foresee and provide against. Work of this descrip-tion is a separate study altogether, requiring capacity of a different kind, and constant attention to changing conditions in a very different range of observation. Whether a further payment may be made to wage-earners, dependent on results, as a reward for and an inducement to good work is a point which does not affect the present argument. But wages as a rule are and must be paid imme-diately. The final results are completed, and their exchange value can only be tested, at some com-paratively remote period. Equally if a dealer buys merchandise at home or abroad, he arranges for the payment on definite conditions at once, and the seller may be assumed to have no further risk in the matter. He has supplied something presumably fitted for use, but how far it will ultimately be wanted for use does not directly concern him. That individual or associated labourers should undertake such ventures if they desire and are in a position to do so is most desirable. As far as such "co-operative" associations tend to make wage-earners better acquainted with some of the higher questions connected with the work on which they are engaged, they are worthy of all possible support, consistent with their maintaining an independent position.

But the special work, the recompense, and the responsibility, must go together. Of course the
expectation is that average profits will more than
cover all risks, but this gain has to be earned by
successful adaptation, in fact by saving the waste
from misapplied labour which no perfection of individual mechanical skill could avoid. From a
point of view which may fairly be referred to as
clearly showing one side of a truth, profits are
rather saved out of, than added to, the cost of production. No one, for example, would pay a master
builder if the various artificers could, without undue
waste, put together the parts of a house—every bit
of which is the work of their own hands—without
his aid in adapting their several work to make up
the concrete whole, the value of which depends on
its fitness for present use and convenience. He
has indeed to deal with values and uses, or what
his customers may be pleased to consider uses,
rather than with any special materials.

There is inevitably an uncertain balance of excess
or deficiency at the end of every work of reproduction, and it is this resulting risk which is inevitably
associated with profit. In banking, which has been
reduced almost to a science, the highly skilled head
work required is often paid for by salaries (*i.e.*
wages), but even in this case the small proportion
more or less of profits, falls to those who undertake
this ultimate risk, and would indeed be responsible
in case of disaster. Profit and risk are so in-
separably connected, that " profit and loss " is the

CHAP. IV. appropriate heading of every trader's account which records the success or failure of his several transactions. Indeed, when interest and the wages of superintendence and indemnity against loss are provided for, the final profit may well be termed the remuneration for risk; the risk being of such a kind as, to a greater or less degree, but not altogether, can be provided against by due care, skill, forethought, and good management.

If the "adventurer" accepts a loan, he guarantees the lender against loss to the utmost of his resources. On both sides therefore he bears the first brunt of risk, and it stands to reason that his directions as to the ordering of the labour employed must be supreme within the limits of the undertaking for which he is thus finally responsible. It does not follow that his remuneration should be higher than that of others working with him, but his special function is to direct and adjust, and, in the interest of all concerned, he should have fair scope for the exercise of it.

Interest considered as a charge on industry. 6. Interest—apart from such risks—has well been termed the remuneration of abstinence. Capitalists, large and small, instead of spending money on present enjoyment have accumulated, and apply it to the support of productive labourers. Regarding it further as a charge which may accrue separately to individuals who merely lend to others, not only past abstinence is implied, but also that the lenders further abstain from exercising their undoubted right to expend their funds in purchasing productive property, or supporting productive labourers directly for their own benefit. This lenders could certainly do, were they so minded, and that without raising prices against themselves. For the value of commodities and the rate of wages also is determined by the total capital made available to pay for them : this aggregate can in no way be altered by any mere change in the way the division is to be made of the surplus production hereafter to be derived from the outlay of that capital. Whether A spend his own capital and also that of B, or whether A and B each spend their respective capitals separately, makes no difference whatever in the aggregate demand or in the aggregate supply. The same as to profits— there would be, *cæteris paribus*, precisely the same amount earned, only instead of a division into gross profits with a sub-division for interest, there would be a single appropriation of profits accruing in stricter proportion to the amounts of capital severally owned. So even if *interest* were altogether abolished it does not necessarily follow that the cost of production would be either increased or diminished. The chief difference would be that those who with small means are now in the independent position of employers of capital would have to take a subordinate one as employed by those who own it. Any further difference could only arise from the greater or less practical efficiency of the one mode of organisation rather than the other.

The element of risk, however, cannot be wholly eliminated in practice, and is therefore a fair basis for a compensating charge. The *gross* rate of interest will thus vary according to the nature of the employment and the sufficiency of the "adventurer's" guarantee ; but whereas the difference which forms the estimated indemnity required to provide against the *first* risks will be comparatively large, a far smaller proportion only may be required to recompense the lender for the remoter risks which he incurs.[1]

---

[1] I enter more specially into the merits of this question as the charge has been attacked as a wrong and an injury to industry, and though it is one which will certainly be maintained in virtue of its actual utility and fairness, still the unhappy notion—which is not so uncommon as might be supposed—that though practically necessary, it is not strictly justifiable, is one which, as far as it goes, cannot but have a deteriorating effect.

The most specious objection to the charge of interest is that the receiver takes no share of risk, but this point is entirely within the range of equitable arrangement. It is in simple fact commuted with mutual advantage. If a lender were to share the more or less of profit, it stands to reason that he would also have to retain some right of detailed supervision over the use made of his funds. If any one is concerned in details he must be deferred to in details, and would be apt to insist upon it. It works far better to draw a definite line which excludes all such irritating and troublesome matters. Moreover, if a man is fit for his position at all, he gets on far better when he has the weight of his own work fairly in his own hands. Men's minds are cramped and dwarfed by constant supervision in detail. Even an artificer doing comparatively exact work will not stand being overlooked in such a way. His word is, " I will abide by my results, but I will do my own work my own way, or I will not and *cannot* be responsible for it." A love of gain is no doubt a powerful stimulus to exertion, but too much has been made of this motive, and it is moreover one of those which, unbridled, are so apt to o'erleap their own intention. The sense of freedom combined with a sense of a definite sense of responsibility for the use of it, are the most favourable conditions

One casual advantage of this division of function
and remuneration which *interest* subserves is the
individual security which can be attained by means

for drawing out the best energies, especially of an enterprising race
like our own.

In the commercial association of borrower and lender there is no
place for the idea of favour, the accommodation is mutual; but the
system is certainly to the advantage of the less wealthy trader, who, if
he is at the pains to manage his affairs with discretion, and does not
seek to incur more risks than he is able to meet, has little difficulty in
obtaining at once as much money as he can employ on terms which, in
the very nature of things, must be within the limits of the average
profits of the business on which indeed it depends. The reason for a
want of success must either be in himself, or in the fact that there are
more already engaged in the particular branch of industry into which he
seeks to enter than the wants of society can support. In any case if
he cannot satisfy existing terms, still less could he satisfy those which
would result from such a change as that above referred to. The alternative of confining the direct uses of capital strictly to those who own
it is incompatible with the manifold wants of enterprise in these, or
indeed in any other, times.

In the days when slavery was a recognised institution the wealthy
might no doubt employ their means through the agency· of those
who, by reason of their inferior status, could not openly put forward
any claim for recompense other than their master's favour chose to
accord to them. There is little reason to assume that this servile
service was more honestly performed than the obligations arising under
the more independent forms of co-operation; but the abolition of
slavery, and of the ideas connected with it, were assuredly favourable
to the development of a system under which reasonable interest is paid
for loans made in support of independent enterprise.

On the ground of equal dealing, it is hard to see how any one could
suppose that a return of the principal lent was a fair adjustment between the lender and the borrower of money to be applied to productive uses. The advantages of having the command of products
ready to hand for immediate use, instead of going through the tedious
process of saving the equivalent of them are so palpable : the borrower evidently would have so much the best of the bargain, that
some share in this advantage seems due in common honesty, though
no doubt the interest on loans, just like the exchange value of everything else, depends upon the actual use that can be found for them.
A farmer, manufacturer, or shopkeeper reasonably expects to live on

of it. A worker in any one branch of industry—especially if engaged in some arduous enterprise on which his best energies may be concentrated,—need not depend solely upon it, but may devote his savings to support other selected undertakings without incurring the first brunt of the risks and responsibilities attached to them. For the reason thus suggested, money at interest in the Savings Banks is probably better placed there than employed in directly carrying out productive work. A reserve to fall back upon in case of sickness or old age is thus safely preserved.

Holders of "money" do incur one definite risk ; no one is obliged to take or to pay them for their money. They have no direct hold on productive undertakings, but low rates of interest induce men to invest in real property or to promote new industrial enterprizes ; high interest to aid those already in existence. It will generally be most closely in accordance with the actual conditions of industry in such a country as this, if the questions of risk, interest, and ultimate " net " profit are considered together.

Popular instincts are fully alive to the one valid objection to interest, viz., that a fixed interminable charge of the kind may outlast all benefit derived

the profits of his stock, and at least to keep it up also to its original value. The service of money is not the less real because it is rendered in more abstract form. The owners of it in this sense hold commodities generally—not for their own enjoyment, but for the use of workers whose labours are thus rendered more easy and more efficient.

from the original outlay.　Hence it is felt that the
burden of the National Debt should not be sent
down to posterity in its entirety.　In form, termin-
able annuities would more suitably represent the
limits within which the weight of expenditure to
meet special emergencies should be distributed, but
this does not suit the varied exigencies of borrowers and lenders so well as the expedient of a
" sinking fund " by which the stock of those whom
it may suit to be in the market to sell, can be
bought up and extinguished.　Practically, moreover, new difficulties arise which would warrant new
loans, and it would be useless actually to buy stock
with one hand to reduce the debt, while selling it
with the other to meet present emergencies ;—
though this farce was at one time gone through
with much solemnity—and expense.　Money is in
fact so general an expression of value that no such
proceeding is requisite, but in order to keep the
aggregate of debt within a compass representing a
burden which may fairly be sent down to posterity,
every timely opportunity must be taken to keep
down its proportions.　The benefits which may be
derived from such expenditure are essentially general.　So also is the consequent charge on the
national resources, and it is needless to point out
the immense advantage of unimpeached credit
which enables a State to distribute its burdens in a
way which even in times of the greatest emergency
makes the strain upon its income comparatively
easy to bear.

In commerce no such question as this can arise. The transactions are short and consecutive, though this fact may not be apparent to one who employs his money through the agency of a banker ; nevertheless the continuous interest received is in fact the result of many successive operations.

Into the question of loans *not* made in support of productive industry I do not intend to enter. Loans without interest are sometimes the most effectual mode of rendering aid to those who are striving to win their way back into full independence—but no general law of value can or, in the nature of things, ought to apply to such personal cases.

The distinctive functions of bankers. 7. The commodities required for the aid and support of labour have been generalised as *capital.* Capital has again been generalised as *credit,* which implies that the owners of capital and those most competent to use it are brought into industrial association. It still remains to trace further how this is brought about by means of banking agency. The subject has been much obscured by a collateral question, viz., the issue of notes by bankers to take the place of money in the more exact sense of the word, as a general circulating medium. Those who have been very conversant with the subject in all its details have not always been careful enough to distinguish between such circulation, and the uses of capital made available by means of loans for productive purposes.   Thus Mr. J. R. McCulloch in his well-known treatise on Metallic and Paper Money and Banks does not bring out at all clearly the essential difference between notes and other obligations payable at some future date (§ 2).   He writes when treating of the issue of paper substituted for coin, " Suppose for example that a capitalist issues a promissory note for 1,000*l*.— This he does by advancing it to an individual in whose solvency he has confidence, and who has given him security for its repayment with interest.   In point of fact therefore the issuer has exchanged his promissory note to pay 1,000*l*. for an obligation of equal amount bearing the current rate of interest ; and so long as the note, the intrinsic worth of which cannot well exceed a sixpence, remains in circulation, he will, supposing interest to be at 5 per cent., receive from it a revenue of 50*l*. a year.   The business of bankers who issue notes is conducted on this principle. They could make no profit were they obliged to keep dead stock or bullion in their coffers equal to the amount of their notes in circulation.   But if they be in good credit a fourth or a fifth part of this sum will be sufficient," &c.   When it is said that a banker could make *no* profit if he were obliged to keep stock equal in amount to the notes issued, it must mean no *more* profit than that amount would bring in if well employed and invested, and there is no reason whatever why a banker's stock should be worth more than that of any one else. The issue of notes to the extent of four or five times the amount of his own stock will, no doubt, afford a profit as far as they can certainly be maintained in circulation. But any one with a reputation for wealth might so issue notes, and *if* they were wanted and *if* his credit remained undoubted they would continue in circulation just in the same way ; this throws no light on the special work and service done by the banker. The analogy suggested of a note bearing interest tends to confound together two distinctly different processes. Every one knows that a banknote does not bear interest, and is payable *on demand.* It takes the place of metallic money as a tally or substitute (II. 7). It passes from hand to hand as a *reserve* only of purchasing power, and only so far as the community to whom it is issued will retain such a reserve. But the natural desire of every one is to invest or use, that is, to part with and spend his "money," and all the undoubted credit of the Bank of England will not enable it to keep out in circulation a single note more than is wanted to be held for this special purpose. It is not therefore only the credit of the banker, but the very special and limited needs of the community with whom he deals, which determine the amount of his issues, in this form. An over-issue would no doubt lead to depreciation, but if notes are convertible into gold on demand, the tendency to such an excess is under all ordinary circumstances effectually checked.

As far as notes are kept in circulation the issuer, whether he be a banker or not, does certainly borrow from constantly changing members of the public who hold his notes, but it may be said of each and all of them successively that, as holders of notes, they are not using purchasing power but holding it in reserve, and however useful an adequate amount of circulating medium may be, it is not directly correlated with any work of production which can afford increase or profit to the owner. But any one who can so continuously borrow *value* may continuously employ it. If three-fourths or four-fifths of the total notes issued are kept in circulation that portion of value can be used, but the man represented as borrowing 1,000*l*. at 5 per cent. interest is not the one who will keep them. *He* has to deal directly or indirectly with the consumption of labourers engaged in making new value. More or less of such money will pass through his hands according to the nature of the work he has to do, but most assuredly it will not remain idle in them.

This distribution of capital—this selection of agents who will make good use of loans—is the special work of banking. The issue of notes is not by any means essential to it. Whether a banker issue his own notes, or those of others, the borrower is sure to part with them as soon as may be, and these or some other money or notes will find their way into the hands of those who have no immediate use for this purchasing power. The function of the banker is to take this surplus and find suitable employment for it. Money is like water : one pound is just like another pound, and no matter how diverse the employments of those who severally own that which has exchange value, any surplus is applicable to any deficiency, and the same notes will measure and convey these values over and over again. There is no hard and fast line to circumscribe the compass within which a banker may make such adjustments. This is a point to be decided by his own experience. If he find he has in his connection more borrowers than lenders at one time, and the reverse at another, he will try to extend, not necessarily the aggregate, but the range of his operations, so as to attain a more equable average. His own capital—that purchasing power of which he is the unqualified owner—must make good the aberrations on both sides. He is of course directly liable for all money lent to him. But though his obligations as a debtor are the more stringent, still, on the other hand, if his customers find that he cannot give them the support which they may reasonably expect, he would lose his business and connection altogether. For the end and object of all this industrial borrowing and lending is to give purchasing power to those who can immediately employ it, and to take it from those who have no present use for it. They know nothing of each

other, and have their own cares and risks to attend
to. They severally do their section of work, and
the banker does his, each on his own personal
responsibility. But what the latter deals with is
deposits, *i.e.* with the average balances of "money,"
i.e. purchasing power, which his customers leave
in his hands: the issue of notes is in no way
essential to his position.

8. It is needless to go back upon the question
of the over-issue of substitutes for money, or of
the possible redundance of the currency itself, but
within the considerations already discussed, and
admitting the necessity of insisting upon the convertibility of all notes issued, a further point may
here be conveniently raised, viz., whether the issue
of such notes should be the exclusive function of
one central authority, or, whether it may be left to
any individuals who may succeed in getting their
notes into circulation.

Nature of the security conveyed in a bank note.

A real economy is no doubt effected by the use
of notes, especially in certain early stages of monetary organisation. Instead of counting out amounts
of coin over and over again, which is useless when
money is required merely as a measure of value,
notes transfer ownership without going through
this comparatively laborious and tedious process.
Coin bears a small proportion to the actual transactions in commodities of all kinds. Notes passing
still more quickly and easily from hand to hand do
far more work; or, conversely, a smaller value of
notes will do the same amount of work as a larger

value of coin. Judicious and enterprising bankers who promote the activity of well-devised industry may aid very greatly in making more work for money to do, and at the same time supplying the circulating medium required. Thus the Scotch Scotch Banks, in early days, made admirable use of credit Banks. obtained in this way, and their success in very meagre fields of enterprise is a standing proof how completely well-directed labour, barely supported by what are regarded as the necessaries of life, is the efficient cause of the creation of substantial wealth. Whether the operation is described as making capital where none before existed, or as making existing capital productive, its true nature is the same. All those who successively *held* banker's notes had parted with value for them, and this value was used by those who had obtained loans in notes and passed them on in exchange for such things as they required. The amount of circulation which the community could retain was by no means an inapt measure of the commodities which could be made applicable to supply the continually recurring wants of consumers, and fairly indicated the limit to which current expenditure might safely be extended. With equal discretion fresh capital was also introduced into these new fields of industry by means of cash credits, the extent of which was not limited by the amount of their note circulation, but by a wider apprehension of the more permanently productive uses which capital might be made to subserve. Notes were

an important adjunct : a means of economy which
enabled these banks to work more cheaply in fields
often very poor in the resources afforded by nature.
But their success is due to the rare prudence and
vigour with which difficulties were met and new
adaptations of capital and labour effectually worked
out. Much also is due to the character of the
people themselves who could be so aided, and there
could hardly be a more efficient sumptuary police
in a small community than a shrewd bank agent,
with the purse-strings in his hands, and a keen
interest in the well-doing of his customers.

Still, especially when we come to a more advanced stage of organisation, a more complete
division of function is to be desired. ˙ Banks are
necessarily closely connected with the risks of
industrial enterprise, but are not always managed
with such skill and prudence. And although an
issue of notes in excess of the immediate and
special requirements of the public is impossible,
it does not follow either that the public requirement may not itself be exaggerated in times of
speculative excitement, or that any bank or banks
giving way to a strong tide of popular delusion
might not increase their note circulation, both to
supply an unduly inflated demand, and further, at
the expense of other banks who might be temporarily
cast into the shade by judiciously abstaining from
business which they believed to be conducted on
fallacious bases. There can be no doubt that banks
may do a very great deal to promote bad, as well

as good, business, and that excessive issues might well grow with bad business though neither the leading cause nor the measure of it. If in this way the aggregate currency became redundant and thus deteriorated in value, the evil would be a doubled one, and must be distinctly so recognised. There are not only false and exaggerated estimates expressed in the terms of money to be considered, but the value of the measure of value itself has become depreciated.

Notes the final reserve.

The note-holder may reasonably expect that the reserve which he must needs keep in hand should depend as directly as possible on the large generalisation and wide average of bullion, and not in any way upon the smaller generalisation and limited average of any particular business or locality. The association of those who deal with a bank in the ordinary sense of the word, whether as lenders or borrowers, is voluntary. That of the holder of its current notes practically is not so. Other bills and promissory notes no doubt can be passed freely from hand to hand, but circulate only among those who, as dealing with capital, are conversant with the uses to which it is applied, and can therefore form their own judgment as to the ability of the borrowers to fulfil their obligation to pay "money" within a given period. But a bank-note, if it is to be kept out as currency at all, must circulate indiscriminately and pass freely from one to another without any question whatever as to the uses to which it may be applied. And as only a certain limited aggregate value of currency can be used in this form, if so much unsafe " money " is held in circulation, just so much safe money is kept out: and practically no man in the ordinary course of business can afford to refuse a note which according to existing local custom is considered good payment. Moreover, a note which takes the place of money is not merely a personal reserve, for the very nature of money requires that use inevitably puts this reserve into circulation to the benefit of the community at large. It should serve even in the case of the utmost disaster as a starting-point for fresh endeavours. But if the note-owner's claim is only a personal one against the banker whose general assets may have been largely wasted in abortive efforts of nominally productive enterprise, they have nothing to fall back upon which can serve them or any one else in such an emergency. Nor is their position materially altered by Sir Robert Peel's Acts of 1844 and 1845 which provide that bankers issuing notes above a certain limit then fixed should hold a corresponding increase of coin.[1] This precaution may be effective against the temptation to obtain undue credit by an over-issue of notes, but it affords no special security to the holders of any of them. One note cannot be distinguished from another, nor has one creditor a right to any preference over another: the coin must be shared by all alike as a general asset of the estate in case of insolvency. Such notes are not in fact a reserve at all. In 1824-5, when a

---

[1] 7 & 8 Vic. c. 32 ; 8 & 9 Vic. c. 37 and 38.

large number of country banks failed, the Bank of England had at once to send out about ten million pounds' worth of currency. The daily work of the communities affected had to be carried on, and the reconstruction of credit in any form without the aid of money which can be trusted, is impracticable. The distinction which must be clearly drawn, is between the economy in the use of money which banking affords, and the ultimate integrity of money itself or whatever specifically takes the place of it. The old story of the frightened creditor who violently insisted on taking out immediately his balance at his bankers, and went out exulting with a bundle of their own notes in his hand, very aptly illustrates the difference which is instinctively felt. His first distrust may have been just as foolish as his subsequent confidence, but for all that, money and bank credit are two very different things which ought not to stand upon the same footing. Nor would the case be better if notes were made to constitute a first claim in preference to other debts : the remedy is not complete, nor is there any justice in subjecting the assets on which general trade creditors rely, to such a diminution. To make good the independent value of this ultimate reserve it must have a separate and well-defined basis of its own.

The law of restriction, with the exceptions of long standing continued under the Acts just cited, obtains generally throughout the kingdom ; nor need these exceptions cause any practical disquietude, though the issue of bank notes which virtually cannot be refused, though not actually "legal tender," remains as an anomaly in our system.

It is true that the personal trust reposed in a banker to pay the cheques of a depositor in any way which may best suit the holder of them involves, generally speaking, far less risk than any one would be likely to incur in keeping his own specific money, which might be lost or stolen; and it is equally true that the note of a solvent bank is quite as good as a cheque. Still these allegations do not meet all sides of the question. It is well that the difference between the *jus in personam* which is all that any man has, as against his banker, and the *jus in rem* which he has, as owning money possessing an independent value of its own, should be clearly apprehended. It should be borne in mind also how very limited is the restriction required. Any form whatever promising to pay money, or to transfer it, is open to every one, and may be circulated by any lawful means. Only the use of the one special form which virtually simulates metallic money itself is forbidden.

Some further detailed remarks on local and general currency will be found in the Appendix; also some reference to the manifest abuses of credit when its forms are simulated without due regard to the laws which govern the production of value. Meantime the argument on more general principles is continued without interruption.

9. Though bank notes are of much use in carrying on the ordinary details of interchange, they form but a very subsidiary part of the great machinery for the wider adjustment of credit which has now to be considered. Values of the most diverse nature, as expressed in the common terms of current money, have to be set the one against the other. Even if this money be not so well based or so exact as it should be it must needs be accepted, for the time being, for this purpose. Its instability injuriously affects the work of production, because it may alter and confuse the true value of these terms, but, as a matter of practical necessity, the existing common measure of value must be accepted. All means or instruments by which values are expressed are indiscriminately brought together, and it was for this reason that I deemed it well specially to refer to underlying differences, which, though lost sight of for a while, must not permanently be disregarded.

The great development of banking in recent years has been by means of "deposit accounts." By very long established usage bankers have received "money" both from traders and others, to be repaid when required, but, subject to this obligation, the use of it was left to their own discretion, though, speaking generally, the unwritten code of right has restricted them to those dealings which did not involve the first risks (or contingent profits) of enterprise. They have always deal with comparatively large aggregate values, and their function is to distribute these means of supporting productive work to an extent which they could not possibly supervise in detail. More recently joint-stock banks have adopted the plan of paying interest on the amounts left with them, and have thus attracted for their own uses much "money" which otherwise would either have remained unemployed or have been invested for short periods in other securities.

These cash deposits, as they are called, are repayable either on demand or on short notice. That is: some hundreds of millions of pounds sterling of so-called "money" are in bankers' hands throughout the kingdom, every penny of which may be said to be at the immediate disposal of the depositors. Yet so strictly are the operations of interchange controlled by natural conditions that, for the most part, this "money" can and is used for other purposes of which the depositors neither have, nor wish to have, any specific knowledge at all.

The account of each individual depositor is constantly changing, but that which goes out from one hand comes in from another. For the most part it must needs do so, for the purchasing power put in force by any buyer *must* be transferred to some seller. A somewhat similar remark has already been made as regards tallies or substitutes for metallic money (II. § 5); but now, in a much more advanced stage of the subject, we are treating rather of the *uses* of money than of the symbol itself. To a very large extent the transfers thus required are effected by mere book entries in bankers' accounts. They might be made by a mere word or nod, and are done in practice by means of mere memoranda of the simplest kind that will serve for a record. The familiar form of a cheque is most commonly used, and this is sometimes very loosely classed as an instrument of credit. But it is not so. The true intention of it is merely to cause a transfer to be made from the account of the drawer to the holder of the cheque, who may, if he chooses, at once draw out the sum specified in gold or notes. A may thus transfer "money" on credit to B by means of a cheque on his (A's) bankers. But the reverse of this transaction must be taken before coming to the conclusion that credit is expressed by the cheque itself. It is B who takes the cheque, and may be fairly assumed to have given consideration for it in some form; and he certainly does not give credit to A in any proper sense of the term, though he no doubt does give credence to the fully implied assurance that the "money" is in the bankers' hands for him to deal with immediately at his absolute discretion. A promissory note payable at some future time does imply credit given and the use of money, subject to the risks involved in such use. The two documents represent obligations of a totally different kind. There is no intention of giving credit or incurring such risks expressed by a cheque. A man may sell jewels, and, through mere inadvertence, deliver an empty casket; so may he receive value and deliver a cheque without having provided funds in his bankers' hands to meet it: the one case is very much on a par with the other.[1]   If B choose to hold A's cheque, no doubt in some sense he trusts A, in whose account a certain sum remains, unused, but at B's disposal.   The case supposed serves to illustrate how the compass rather than the subject of rights may come into question.   A's right was a personal claim against his bankers: more than that he had not himself and could not transfer to any one.   If B had claimed and taken possession of that to which he had a right, viz., either actual money or a transfer in the bankers' accounts, he could have held the one as much as the other against all the world.   But if at any future time the bankers have no funds of A's in hand, or should he have failed, they are under no obligation whatever to give effect to his order.   B may thus lose by trusting A, but it is misleading to call this credit.   Cheques kept in any way in circulation have a closer analogy to notes, but they are not intended to answer any such purpose, and need not be taken into consideration as being incidentally used for it.

[1] The exigencies of trade sometimes require very large transfers of securities to be made simultaneously, corresponding cheques being passed against them.   Cases of considerable intricacy may thus arise in the event of unexpected failure to carry out complicated arrangements.   Still the rule certainly is that a cheque means *Cash*, not Credit, and an unpaid cheque implies an incomplete transaction which should be of no effect on either side.

A cheque is, strictly, merely an order for the immediate transfer of value, either in actual money paid on account of the drawer to the holder, or simply deducted from one account and added to the other ; and these together with bills of exchange and promissory notes actually due, and the book accounts in which "cash" received and paid is entered, are the chief means by which the daily transactions of a large aggregate of individuals are adjusted in a way which will seem very artificial as long as the mind is suffered to dwell on the ostensible use of substantive money, but which will be found on looking a little further into the matter to be very simply and closely in accordance with the actual work which is ever going on around us.

General principles affecting all loans.

One general principle affects all loan transactions, in whatever form, which are based on industrial operations whether of manufacture or distribution. The work, as has been already noticed, is not stationary but steadily progressive. Hence all that constitutes its value is, normally, progressive and cumulative. Production may either be completed in one process or in many distinct and separate stages. In the latter case each of these will involve a cash settlement between those who have been successively engaged in carrying on the work, and each will, normally, represent a larger value than the former until the last final transfer to the consumer ; and this gradual increment will include the recompense of those on whose responsibility the several undertakings are carried on.

Another point may most conveniently be noticed in this context.

The multiplication of bills and promissory notes has been regarded as directly raising prices in the same way as an over-issue of paper-money.   But if due regard is had to the relation which all instruments of credit must bear to *cash*, it will be seen that this analogy does not hold good.   For obligations of the kind are of no avail until they are exchanged for cash.   General prices are an equation of all supply, to all demand made effective by existing purchasing power, and the mere transfer of this power from one to another cannot increase its amount.   The effect of any redistribution of credit can only be to employ actually existing capital.   B may discount a bill for A, and subsequently rediscount it with C, and C with D, and so on, but B and C simply get back the value they paid ; the capital they took is actually restored to the general market ; and D stands in their place as regards A.   All these indicate transfers and nothing more.   They may be symptoms of excitement and of obligations rashly assumed by those who are not able to carry them out ; but they cannot be the efficient cause of any change in prices.   The value expressed in the terms of money on all documents implying the use of commodities is not the measure of the value of those commodities, but of the definite personal obligation of those who have the use of them. The amount of a bill accepted by a trader in no way governs the more or less price he obtains from the consumer of his merchandise. It exactly expresses only the extent of his obligation to those who have aided his work with their capital. If the aggregate of such bills in circulation is excessive, it tends to raise the cost of loans, and is, no doubt, a warning sign to bankers. But the appropriate remedy is a more careful selection of bills. There is no reason for an indiscriminate pressure as though mere transfers from lenders to borrowers could make money actually scarce. The same may be said of all loans on stocks or shares or any other securities. So further, if a bill is passed from hand to hand in payment of accounts, it no more enhances prices than would a bank note so used, and such notes only enhance prices nominally by becoming themselves depreciated; but a bill due payable in sterling money cannot be depreciated as long as the parties to it are solvent.

The distribution of credit.   10. In accordance with the general condition set forth, "cash," that is, purchasing power immediately available, is distributed. Gold and notes are in this sense no more cash than an entry in a banker's book against which cheques may be passed. The current *rate* of interest depends on the equation of the supply of cash to the demand for loans, but the amount paid is calculated on the number of days for which the *use* of "the money" (that is, more strictly speaking, of the money's worth) is required, and during which time value will be normally in process of augmentation. Thus A may have sold goods to B and taken his

promissory note payable three months after date in
payment for them. B has immediate use of the
commodities received, and A has nothing directly
to do with the use which B may make of them;
but the recompense for the advantage thus given
by A to B is included in the price charged for the
goods. Cash prices and credit prices are determined
subject to the estimated difference in value just
referred to. This bill however is a "negotiable"
instrument, and by the simple form of "endorsement," A can transfer all the rights he has in it
to any one else; and further, by the universal custom
of commerce, personally guarantees by this act to
all subsequent holders the due fulfilment of the
obligation expressed. The bill may pass by the
same means and under the same conditions to
several successive owners, but whoever holds it can
get payment of the amount at once from a banker,
less the "discount" for so many days, if he or any
one of those who have thus signed their names on
the bill, are in good credit. Or B might equally
well arrange to get a loan from a banker and pay
interest to him, and cash prices to A. All the
very small differences involved are a mere matter
of calculation and arrangement. Or again, X, who
may be engaged in some trade not generally known,
may find it to his advantage to send his merchandise to Y, whose credit is well established, and who
is, as it were, a connecting link between X and the
general distributors of *Cash;* as the bills drawn by
X upon Y and "accepted" by him command the

R

confidence of bankers. Some such arrangements as these suit many of the exigencies of foreign commerce.

It is needless to expatiate on the many and various expedients of the kind which may be adopted : the object of all being to give " cash " to those who are engaged in the processes of reproductive industry, subject to their obligation to return " cash " as the work of production, or the portion of it on which they may be engaged, is completed. The same principle applies to all, whether manufacturers, merchants, or " distributors." Directly or indirectly the full use, though not in an unrestricted sense, the ownership of money's worth is at the disposal of those who can be trusted to reproduce the value advanced. Their possession is subject to the fulfilment of their obligations. Failing this, their creditors—but not any one creditor more than another—can take possession of whatever the debtor may own for the satisfaction of the right which they have in common against him.

There is no rule, as of right, which can determine the exact forms which credit may assume. The more sound and healthy the conditions of industrial co-operation, the more freely will its terms be adapted to their manifold requirements. These are essentially matters of expediency. All forms may be right if mutually understood and rightly used. Divisions, sub-divisions, and associations of all kinds may be made, tested by experience and maintained or abandoned as it may dictate, but the

general tendency of all highly organised life is CHAP. IV.
towards division and specialisation of function, and
that of industry forms no exception to the rule.
Some joint-stock and private firms carry on banking
operations in London or throughout the country ;
some confine themselves specially to dealings in
bills of exchange.   Some do business, modified in
form but essentially banking, with foreign countries,
and for all parts of the world.   All alike deal with
values implying the *productive use* of commodities
with which they are not brought into direct contact.

Speaking broadly, the rate of remuneration, cal-   And its re-
compense.
culated always with reference to time, is in inverse
proportion to the extent to which values, however
represented, can be generalised and appropriately
dealt with in larger or smaller aggregates.   Early
in the century the operations of commerce and
industry were on a comparatively limited scale, the
work was restricted to few hands and little subdivided, while the rate of profit bore a very large
proportion to the values interchanged.   Now, an
average gain of 2 or 3 per cent. on the transactions
effected will represent a large amount of mercantile
or manufacturing service of this kind : bankers work
on differences between interest given and interest
received, giving a far narrower margin.   Very substantial service is rendered for the equivalent of
less than a penny in the pound.   One class of
brokers dealing in large aggregates of bills of exchange, usually receive at the rate of $\frac{1}{16}$ per cent.
per annum, or five farthings per £100 per month.

Some of the leading Joint-Stock Banks pay 15 to 20 per cent. to their shareholders, but this large gain is earned partly on capital, which, though not specifically appropriated to them, has accumulated in addition to the nominal amount of their shares, but chiefly on ten or twelve times the amount of deposits belonging to others on which interest is paid, which is made to circulate by their agency, at a somewhat higher rate, and which is so distributed as credit accorded to productive industry that the average of waste on the very large aggregate employed is extremely small, though every now and then the public are startled by hearing of losses and frauds to a vast extent. Such exceptions with such average results only prove the rule of general stability. It is not implied that these low rates of remuneration are inadequate. The ultimate profits in some cases indicate very much the reverse, but all that need here be remarked is that these adjustments which give so much force and elasticity to that part of the available wealth of the country which constitutes its capital stock are efficiently made without weighting either industry or the consumer with any heavy burden.[1]

[1] Taking figures which roughly represent the position of some of the leading banks, let us suppose a share capital of £1,500,000—a reserve of undivided capital of £1,000,000, making £2,500,000 in all : and deposits amounting to £25,000,000. 3 per cent. on *all* their own capital would give £75,000—or 5 per cent. on the total of the *share* capital only. An average gain at the rate of 1 per cent. *per annum* on £25,000,000, of course implying very many shorter transactions to very many times that large amount, would give £250,000 more or 16⅔ per cent. on the share capital, in all 21⅔ per cent. Banks

Moreover all these divisions of functions are merely empirically made, and have no claim whatever to be maintained further than they serve to promote better economy or higher efficiency.

Dealers having funds of their own will naturally avail themselves more sparingly of credit, *i.e.* of the capital of others. Yet the complaint is sometimes made by the wealthy that they suffer unduly from the competition of those who avail themselves freely of its advantages. This suggests two replies. It cannot be urged that a banker should not lend cash to enterprising men, merely because they choose to work better or harder, or for a smaller profit than those who have no charge for interest to meet. The banker and his customer may surely be allowed to judge what is best for their own interests, and further, cheap production means normally service done on the best terms, for the general interests of consumers. If borrowers risk other people's money more recklessly than any prudent man would risk his own, it is the lenders who lose, and the remedy is not the general restriction of credit, but a due insistance upon the obligations attending it. The other reply more nearly affects the general question of the use of credit. Bankers of course are liable to have cash deposited with them when they do not know how to employ it at once, and have not always cash to spare when good occasions for using it are

gain or lose like any other capitalists by a high or low rate of interest, but, as *employers* of capital, work for a *difference* in charge which does not depend upon the general rate. The service they render is substantially the same whatever it may be.

presented to them. This, *mutatis mutandis*, is the case with every one who has to effect adjustments of any kind, and the utmost skill and forethought cannot quite overcome this disadvantage. Those who use credit enjoy the corresponding advantage, they need only take and pay for loans as they may actually require them. Subject to this necessary correction, sound theory would require that the average rate of interest on loans should not trench unduly upon the share of those more directly engaged in the active work of production. There is no reason why more than interest, and a fair indemnity for risks incurred, should accrue to capital in whosever hands it may be, and the complaint alleged merely goes to prove that the system of credit is in the main well and efficiently organised, and as far as such cases are concerned is on an equitable basis.

General demand governs production, though not the cause of it.

11. I have made no reference to the abuses which may be made of credit, for it is the system, and not the way in which it may be misapplied, which is now under review. One point however may be noticed. The distributors of credit no doubt undertake grave responsibilities ; they can do much to encourage sound enterprise, and to check ill-directed or ill-devised projects, for within certain limits they have the disposal without any direct control of the money of the general public (§ 9). But not the less does the selection of the completed products offered, rest absolutely with those who ultimately exercise the rights of unqualified owner-ship over this money, that is, with the consumers

who spend it according to their own discretion, over which neither banker nor producer, as such, have any control whatever. Those who dispense the funds of the public can only do so on the condition of promoting the production of those things which this public, the value of whose money has been expended, will accept as value on completion of the work. Generalise demand and supply as we will it is impossible to escape this conclusion : though mere demand does nothing whatever towards aiding the work of production, it effectually determines the direction in which labour must be employed in order to be recognised as productive or serviceable.

12. The extent to which these means, the nature and form of which I have endeavoured to describe, are used to adjust all commodities, in the widest sense of the word, to all the various changing wants of the community, may best be exemplified by a reference to the results shown by the bankers' "clearing house" in London. Nothing can be more simple than the principle upon which it is conducted. Its object is to effect an interchange of all cash obligations. Bills of exchange and promissory notes *due*, implying completed uses, are taken as *cash*, so are all cheques implying book transfers. A bill or note discounted before it becomes due and thus implying continued obligation, remains in the discounter's hand, but the cheque given for it is *cash*. On the other hand, all

The bankers' "clearing-house."

CHAP. IV.   the accumulation of purchasing power expressed by the aggregate of bankers' accounts due to their customers is *cash*. All these form, as it were, the contents of one vast reservoir, which supplies and is supplied by innumerable streams. All values, like water, form one undistinguishable mass, but not the less surely does the preservation of its equilibrium depend upon the due inflow and outflow of every tiny rill and conduit connected with it.

Each bank of course makes for itself the transfers required, as between its own customers. If A, B, C, &c., all deal with one bank, all their transactions can be arranged by transfers in that bank's books, made upon bills due, cheques, &c., drawn upon, and paid into their several accounts as *cash*, and this alone will represent a very large aggregate of adjustment. The clearing-house shows the interchange between bank and bank of all the cash obligations which each severally may hold on all the others, the final adjustments being made by transfer orders on the Bank of England, which, to a certain extent, is the bank of all other bankers, and the use of "money" in any specific form is dispensed with altogether. The transfers adjusted by London bankers alone amounted in the year ending 30th April, 1875, to a total of over £6,000 millions. In 1876–7 to 4,873 millions, of which about 500 to 600 millions [1] were in connection with transactions on the Stock Exchange.

Large amounts passed through it.

[1] The published returns show about 950 millions for the Stock Exchange " settling days," but from this total an allowance must be

It is difficult to form any idea of such quantities without reference to some standard of comparison. The total amount of the National Debt funded and unfunded is under £777 millions. Our whole import and export trade for the latter period was together about £660 millions. The total value assessed for income-tax was £543 millions, of which land and houses in Schedule A form 160 millions, and railways, mines, &c., trades and professions in Schedule D 250 millions. The entire farming stock of the country is roughly estimated at about £300 millions, and this for the most part will require two or three years for its consumption and reproduction. Mr. Dudley R, Baxter in 1867 estimated the aggregate income of the United Kingdom at £814 millions, and was probably rather under than over the mark (III. § 12), and £1,000 millions a year, or say roughly three millions daily, may be taken as an approximate estimate of the expenditure of the United Kingdom, the population of which is thirty-three millions.

Certainly a total of about £5,000 millions of transfers, even for so great a centre as London, appears somewhat astounding, but let us try to see generally what is indicated by them.

As regards Home and Foreign State and Muni- cipal loans, railway, mining, bank, and other shares, made for the ordinary transactions of business which are in no way intermitted at these times. There is, however, a Stock Exchange "clearing" in anticipation of the "settlement," so the increase in the bankers' clearing gives no positive indication whatever of the actual amount of Stock Exchange transactions.

Nature of the adjust- ments effected.

and securities based on them, the values transferred represent the estimate of many years future production (III. § 6), and necessarily are out of all proportion to the income of any single year. Hence we may more readily infer that these transactions are in reality to a great extent mere exchanges of one property for another, although the buyers and sellers may not directly meet in the market. It is impossible to distinguish in these returns what portion of the value may be made up of newly-acquired accumulations. Stocks and shares especially can be dealt with in large or small amounts, and small individual savings, gains, or losses lead to innumerable transfers of them.

The great gambling transactions in "time bargains" on the Stock Exchange do not contribute much to swell the total; for in these cases the differences only between the prices quoted at the time the contract was made and on the "settling day" are ultimately paid. Even in the case of purchases *bond fide* for actual delivery, one transaction may quite rightly be set against another in any broker's account, so that the total given is no measure of the actual dealings effected, as only the cheques given for the final balances go through the general clearing-house. It is most desirable that property of this kind should freely pass from one to the other; but the more clearly the general public understand that all this buying and selling of stocks and shares is quite outside of the work of production, the better. It may be of vital consequence that a government or a public company should be in good credit, but their corporate energy is by no means directly affected by any such dealings ; and apart from considerations of this kind, all the national debts, and all the railway stock, and debenture stock in the world, might be sold and bought ten times over without altering the amount of taxation, or the pay of any one official, to the extent of a single penny.

Setting aside Stock Exchange transactions, which for the most part indicate transfers of this nature, we have still fourteen to fifteen millions of value dealt with in some way or other for every working day of the year. In this, however, will be included dealings in land, houses, factories, ships, and other income-yielding properties, which will also indicate many mere exchanges made indirectly and be bought and sold at a greater or less multiple of their estimated annual return. These transactions are far less frequent than those in shares, and the changes of ownership often affect the productive uses which such properties may subserve.

Many of the entries in this category may, however, represent mere transfers of ownership in no way conducing to productive agency. Thus merchandize may be, and in times of speculative excitement often is, sold over and over again, without affecting its ultimate use one way or the other. The difference between last year's total and that of 1874-5 is no doubt largely owing to the reduced amount of mere transfers of this kind.

But making full allowance for all such dealings, there will still remain a total which would indicate that the aggregate of daily transfers of value by means of cheques passed is a large multiple of the aggregate of daily consumption. For it must be remembered that the same kind of work which is done in the London clearing-house, is also carried on wherever there is a bank throughout the kingdom, only with somewhat less perfect machinery; and all this moreover is in excess of the innumerable small transactions daily carried out by means of the currency. The most perfect system shows the results most clearly, but exactly the same principles of interchange obtain throughout.

Whatever the ultimate estimate may be, it must indicate a very large amount practically associated with industrial work, and which represents the extreme activity and adaptability of credit to the various requirements of society. There is no reason whatever to wish to limit the number of times the value of any commodity may enter into successive cheques passed through bank accounts. The inception and completion of every separate stage of production will, as a rule, be represented by cheques, each of which is a settlement, so far, for a definite share of work completed: so also the collection of various items required for further production: and again the aggregation of completed articles in the warehouses of wholesale dealers, their appropriation to retail distributors, and to a large extent their final dispersion among

consumers and the re-collection from them of the
value delivered :—all this work may be completely
effected by mere book transfers of value.   The
same means are applicable for all the transfers
required in this country to carry out our import
and export trade with all parts of the world.
Further as regards the more special adaptations
of credit.   A man, let us suppose, enters upon a
transaction which will require six months for
completion.   At the time he has *cash* in his own
hands, and of course uses it.   After a while he has
other cash obligations to meet, and borrows on
valid securities, perhaps for a month or more or
less, when again funds of his own become available
to him for a while :—and so on.   It is impossible
to follow all the details of adjustments of cash
and credit loans of this nature, but every one
engaged in business, except on the very smallest
and simplest scale, will have to spend some time
and thought every week or every day in planning
such arrangements.   And with the strictest regard
to probity in exposing no one to risks—beyond
those inseparable from the nature of the obligations
which he may have severally with those with whom
he deals—will find means of avoiding a needless
use of borrowed funds, which as regards himself
personally involves loss of interest, and as regards
the public a waste of "purchasing power" which
had better be actively employed.   Even if new
products are brought into the country, they will
be for the most part absorbed into the great stream

of traffic entirely by these means. Thus if we suppose the sale of a cargo of wheat from Australia, no one here having any prior claim upon it, payment in the ordinary course of trade will be by a cheque, *i.e.* banker's *cash* will be transferred from the buyer to the importer, who may draw out the whole amount in gold, but in all probability it would not serve his interest to do so. He might buy land or shares or consols, all of which could, as a rule, be paid for most conveniently by cheques simply transferring value within the same banking circle. It would be just the same if he bought merchandise for export. It can equally be obtained by mere book entries in the common terms of money. In his turn the buyer becomes a seller, also getting cheques to replace his cash at the bank. But following this wheat a little further we come to a change. It must be fitted for use. Suppose it to be bought by a miller. If he have not accumulated cash of his own, he will readily be able to discount his promissory note, drawing thus upon the general fund of capital in banking circles ; probably taking out little or nothing in notes or gold. Indeed, to keep more closely to a simple illustration, it may be supposed that the miller's cheque transfers the value of the cargo to the importer. By the time the obligation of the former becomes due, the wheat has been ground and turned into bread, and it is quite within the limits of possibility to say that every loaf of it may have been paid for by cheques ; but these cheques represent, normally, other and different work which has already been accomplished.   If consumed by non-producers it must still be paid for by the value of other products to which they have in some way acquired a right.   Continuous consumption is balanced by continuous production without the necessity for using actual money at all.   Circulation of this kind works automatically.   All that producers have to care for is that their several products are fitted to meet an effective demand. Whose money it may be that supports them meanwhile is no concern of theirs.

Such extremely useful and simple operations swell the total of the clearing-house returns, proving, as regards any special undertaking, neither success nor the reverse in the work actually attempted, but indicating the great flexibility of the system by which supply and demand are constantly in course of adjustment, with the minimum of waste and confusion.   Many cheques moreover are passed as a record, and (as bearing the stamp required by law) a legal voucher of payments made, where, if notes and gold had to be counted out, a balance only would actually be paid over.   Every one knows the practical service which banks freely render in this way.   The vast total of the clearing-house transfer is thus very fairly accounted for, though any great increase or decrease in this total naturally suggests inquiry. Very much as if the streets were unusually full, or deserted, we should ask the reason for such a

CHAP. IV.

change in the ordinary signs of traffic. No effects can be produced without some adequate cause for them, but the fact itself may admit of many different interpretations.

Inferences deduced.

13. Two points must be clearly realised in this context. One is that every single transfer in this vast aggregate represents value in pounds sterling, just as fully as if sovereigns were handed over in every case. Any change in this unit of value would substantially alter the terms of every document passed, and every entry made, whether representing the inception, the completion, or any intermediate stage of the work to be done; and also the relative position of every borrower and of every lender, in a way infinitely complicated according to the different periods over which the different obligations dealt with might have extended, or be designed to extend.

The other, which I propose to examine more at length, as illustrating the present argument, is, that by no possibility can the aggregate balance of "money," held among the banking community who contribute to these returns, be changed by any transaction passing through the clearing-house. Every entry has its reverse; there is a "debit" for every "credit," an addition for every subtraction. Thus, if any man is unable to meet his engagements, his bills due are unpaid, and, with his cheques, are returned "dishonoured." At the time nothing is done. His bankers do not pay and those of the holders of his obligations do not receive. Simply no transfers are made on either side. One failure may, and generally does, lead to others with the same immediate negative results. If this were to continue to a sufficient extent general bankruptcy must inevitably ensue, and a readjustment of the working conditions of industry on a new basis altogether would be forced upon us. But though we have in this country repeatedly seen that the system of credit has been momentarily paralysed, because in times of panic men did not know whom to trust ; still, the remedy has substantially been found by a readjustment of the internal resources held within the limits of the banking community.

When great failures occur the popular impression *Adequacy of existing capital.* naturally is that great losses are then incurred. But this, as I have already shown, is far from the truth. The losses have probably been made long ago, and it is *past* accumulations that have been dissipated. Creditors who were living in a false security then find out that their capital has been spent or wasted, or at best "sunk," in some form of production the value of which is not recognised, and does not call forth any effective demand. Now although this fact may afford but little consolation to those who are suffering from heavy losses, it is of great importance to the general issues concerned. For no loss is implied of a nature which should lead to the interruption of any of the productive work required to supply all the acknowledged wants of society. If the cause of failure has been loss owing to misdirected production, that of course must cease [iii. 6], but, unless unreasoning credulity is followed by equally unreasoning suspicion and timidity, all well-directed industry can and ought to receive the support of capital currently accumulating to support current wants.

Those who have the misfortune to hold unpaid obligations have to become borrowers, either upon securities they hold, or perhaps upon the general balance of assets which they may be able to show as adequate to warrant further advances. The tendency of this borrowing is to make "money," *i.e.* loans, dearer, or in other words to raise the rate of interest. The exact nature of the change of position is this: Certain items of (nominal) capital, now for the first time known to have been lost, are struck out of the estimate of those whose money has been dissipated; the existing "cash"—which might, but for this exposure, have gone the same road—is available for those who *have* valid securities, but *not* the cash which they expected to receive. The corrected estimate shows a larger proportion of borrowers to lenders, but that is all. The fact that loans can be so raised and paid by a cheque, simply transferring cash from one account to another, proves conclusively that banking resources are adequate to meet the strain put upon them. If a trader or banker to meet deficiencies arising in this way sell securities, land or consols for instance, he is set financially at ease, and so are all concerned in his solvency as far as he is concerned; but the cheque which brings about this desired result indicates merely a book transfer from a rich account to a poor one. The mind can hardly follow all the changes involved ; the impression of abundance in place of scarcity is so palpable, that it is·hard to realise that this benefit is effected without some addition to the actual supply of money. Still we know very well that in such cases the buyers have not to rummage the country for notes or gold or any other means of making the required payment ; what is done is, that a pur-chasing power not only actually existing but im-mediately at hand is in some way made available for active uses, and the buyer of such property, who owned that reserve, retires so far with his property from the field altogether. It is not more capital, but more efficient or more suitable distribution, that is required.

14. It must not be supposed, however, that the operations of the clearing-house comprise the whole system of credit in the country, or even all that part of it which is carried on through the agency of bankers. Their chief *raison d'être* is no doubt the division of function implied by credit ; but those who carry on their undertakings in the main with their own means, have an equal and a com-paratively independent share in the great work of productive industry, though their cash transactions may still be carried out in detail by the convenient machinery afforded by bankers. The value of a commodity may even pass through the clearing-house repeatedly, while the commodity itself

The incre-ment of capital.

remains without the limits of banking agency.
Thus, if a bar of gold sent from abroad be taken
to the Bank of England, it would be included in
the total shown in its weekly returns. But, if it
were sold to a bullion dealer who paid for it by a
cheque, the result would only be a deduction from
his account, and a corresponding addition to that of
the vendor in the books of their respective bankers.
The bullion itself remains, a third item, as a commodity specially available for foreign traffic or for
use in the arts or manufacture at home, but outside
the circle either of bankers' cash or of the currency,
though it may at any moment be brought within it
at the option of the owner. So also with all property and products—except in so far as they may
be the subject of credit—until they are brought
into the general market. Then the price of every
item has to be determined according to the current
equation of demand and supply. The money existing, even in the most general sense of the term,
cannot be commensurable at any one time with all
the property of the country, but the interchanges
made as occasion may require are carried out by a
machinery wonderfully subtle and effective. The
innumerable specific utilities of all kinds offered for
sale successively, represent the special interests of
every producer or owner who affords supply, while
the "purchasing power" by which demand is made
effectual is generalised in the highest degree. Any
demand, or any prospective demand, can at once
be made available to him who sells, and who

would in his turn have the use of this purchasing power.

Nevertheless there is a constant ebb and flow of value into banks by means of the currency. Thus, if a contractor requires notes and coin for any unusually large payment of wages, he draws directly from his banker's stock, though, if not required for circulation, this currency quickly reappears in bankers' accounts. So further, currency may be paid in, but the cheques drawn for the equivalent value may merely be passed through to other accounts. In this way the aggregate of "cash" balances may be increased or lessened, though the currency which represented the value is not in any way changed. A shopkeeper, for instance, doing an active business, receives daily a large amount of notes and coin which he pays into his bank account; but his payments to wholesale dealers or manufacturers are usually made by cheques, which the receivers pay into their accounts, and which thus go through the clearing-house. Notes and coin go out rather for cheques paid over the bank's counter to the general public who have small purchases to make. Bankers acting in this way as "cashiers," greatly facilitate the general circulation of value however represented; but the circulation for productive uses, and that for consumption, though equally expressed in the common terms of money, touch only. They can be seen to be distinct as soon as we follow the course of the transactions effected.

If by dealings of this kind a banker's accounts

are increased, such portion of them can be used as he expects to retain for any certain length of time ; or if, on the other hand, values are drawn out, the supply of cash applicable to loans would be so far lessened. It is only by accretions and diminutions arising in this way that the aggregate of capital in bankers' hands can be affected. It is not by any recondite theory that we conclude that it is not changed by cheques passed through the clearing-house. Simple arithmetic compels the belief that if A pays B's cheque into his bank account, and the sole consequence is that just so much as is deducted from B's balance is added to that of A ; the aggregate cannot be changed. And as, further, we do know by ample experience that vast payments for state and other loans, for the purchase of large properties, for the settlement of such unexpected difficulties as have just been referred to, and so forth, are arranged by means of cheques so passed, the inference is irresistible that a readjustment of the resources actually within the limits of banking capital is found adequate for all these purposes. But we know also that capital is constantly being consumed, and must as constantly be replaced. It is not to be supposed that this vast consumption and reproduction maintains an absolutely perfect equilibrium, leaving an unchanging balance held in anticipation of future wants. We must look outside the great adjustments of the clearing-house to find how this aggregate may be affected.

If payments are made by or to a bank in

notes or coin, although they do not for the
purposes of this agreement signify "cash" any
more than a cheque, its balance is so much the
greater or less without a corresponding change in
the total held by any other bank, and thus, and
thus only, can the aggregate of balances be changed.
The well-known fact that transactions of this kind Made only by gradual savings.
are generally much subdivided and comparatively
small, serves as an incidental proof that true gain
and loss is, and can be, made only by gradual
savings, and by the gradual increment of production over consumption.   Very little reflection is
indeed required to show that it is in this way only
that the ultimate success or failure of our various
enterprises is tested and proved.   Special industries
may be stimulated by means of borrowed money:
say, for instance, the iron trade for railways.   The
casual advantage will at once be shown by an
increase in a much subdivided outlay as far as that
stage of the work is concerned.   But if the railway
is not wanted, a reaction surely follows, and many
who have indirectly spent their money in paying
for useless rails must not only curtail their daily
expenses, but also afford diminished support to
productive industry by withdrawing their "money"
from it.   There is a very generic difference between
the way that money's worth may be thus lost or
made, and the way that individuals may gain what
others lose by the mere fluctuation of prices.

15.   In referring to the calls made upon our finan- "Creation" of capital.
cial resources for such undertakings as railways,

manufacturing companies, or even foreign loans, financial statisticians commonly use the phrase "capital created." The words may convey a meaning which is sufficiently well understood; but that we may more clearly see what is actually done, let us take the case of a foreign loan, and trace in general terms what has to be effected in order to carry out such an operation. No government can be supposed in reason to want to borrow and pay interest for " purchasing power," unless it is able to make some speedy use of it. It requires and obtains the immediate use of capital already made, or at least to be forthcoming as the instalments in which the loan is payable may become due. So, that which is said to be " created " must be understood as being already made, and the fact of its creation only implies that a ready mode has been found for its expenditure forthwith; presumably, however, in some connection with labour which is to be made productive. It may perhaps also be regarded as " fixed capital " yielding periodical interest. In some way or other, substantive value has to be delivered either in the foreign country itself or in such places as the borrowers may determine. Whether materials of war or materials for the productive enterprises of peace are required, they are alike obtained under the condition that lenders are to be found who can afford the means to pay for such things at once in consideration of receiving an annuity or dividend hereafter. As far as regards the security for the ultimate fulfilment of the stipulated conditions, it may very nearly concern the lenders to know what kind of uses their capital is to subserve. A new country, rich in natural resources, may benefit greatly by the immediate use of capital judiciously applied, even though the advantages of the works made by its aid are of a very general nature. The increased wealth of the country, and its consequent ability easily to bear the additional taxation required out of that general increase, may be as good a security as a lender need desire.

But in any case that which has to be done in the first instance is the same : a comparatively large amount of value has to be immediately transferred, which comes back only by slow degrees. We can no more tell in detail how this work is done than we can describe how this great city of London is daily supplied, without its being the special business of any one in particular to look after its requirements. But that it is done we know full well.

Nevertheless it would be an entire mistake to suppose that such financial operations as result in thus placing value in substantive form at the disposal of others, and especially of a foreign country, could be carried out if the high organisation of banking agency did not facilitate an infinite variety of adjustments by means of which the labour and burden of the work is distributed. Actual value can only be transmitted from one country to another in substantive commodities having in some way a value in exchange. Traders' bills are based upon

Foreign banking agencies.

the value of such products as they become vendible at the place of payment. Bankers moreover are to be found throughout all Europe, and indeed in every country where commerce is active, who again generalise these values. They deal habitually in bills of exchange, using their own capital, and credit obtained partly by the sale of their own bills in different quarters, to mitigate the fluctuations which may arise in the ordinary course of trade ; and extending their operations into every place where industry can take root and flourish. It is impossible to trace all the adjustments that can be made by these means in support of any operation conducted by those whose names command financial confidence. It is easy to see that if a man who had lent money, say to a Baltic merchant, were suddenly to withdraw his support, on the ground that he could do better for himself by lending it to the French government, a most injurious dislocation of credit would be the result. Indeed a probable reply to such a demand would be, "You cannot possibly have your money until I can sell my commodities." But, generalised as values are, any one who desires to subscribe to a loan draws, as it were, the bucket of water to which he has a right, not from any one particular stream, but out of the general reservoir, and no violent disturbance of its level can ensue. But large loans imply the withdrawal of many bucketsful, and if the aggregate withdrawal exceeds the available surplus, the deficiency is shown on all sides. If the capital seeking employment is thus absorbed, the terms of credit at once indicate that instead of owners of cash seeking investments for it, borrowers have to offer better terms to those on whose support they depend (§ 6). This may be shown in two ways. The price of current loans, *i.e.* the rate of interest, rises, and the price of the special loan tends to fall, especially if unpaid instalments due upon it throw upon the holder the obligation of finding further capital. Under these conditions further adjustments may take place. The conduct of a large loan will only be undertaken in some large monetary centre; but if the amount subscribed is so great as to make money scarce and raise the interest on current loans, every banker in connection with it has a new inducement to send "money" for temporary investments, which might very probably be used in the discount of ordinary trade bills. So that a money market in this condition gets just what any solvent trader may obtain, who is engaged in an undertaking rather in excess of his immediate resources, that is, time, during which readjustments may be made and the surplus of production be again accumulated. No system of interchange can do more than this. Not all the money in the world can make a bad undertaking into a good one by any jugglery of finance; but hardly any limit can be assigned to the resources which may in this way be made available from all sides on any reasonable occasion.

16. From very early times such work as this has been done by means of bills of exchange. The

wonderful increase in the security and facility of transit have only given scope to the development of a system which began with the earliest ages of commerce, and here also it is only the ultimate differences which have to be adjusted by that common medium of exchange which possesses an independent value of its own. A reserve of purchasing power in the form of bullion must be held in every country; and the mode in which it regulates the course of international exchange may very briefly be shown. Just as every individual account must in some way or other be balanced, so it is with every country. After all possible sets-off have been made, some surplus or deficiency will usually remain. One of the chief fallacies of the old "mercantile systems" arose from the amazingly profound ignorance and narrowness with which this truism,—for such it really is—was interpreted. The economists of the day looked only to the direct transactions which they could trace as between one country and another, never recognising the plain fact that if A owes B a debt it is as effectually discharged by payments on B's order to C, D, and E as in any other way, which, provided always that A can send value to C, D, or E, more easily than B can do himself, will be the course naturally adopted. As far as the conditions of any trade can be broadly defined, nothing can be more obvious than the process. The inter-relations of very numerous industries are more complex, and the possible adjustments are so numerous and so delicate, that this branch of banking naturally be- comes a special study, but the essential simplicity of the principle remains the same. The state of politics, of the harvests, of the prosperity or decay of industries in all countries, especially concern the international banker. Local difficulties are usually met by local resources, but any unusual strain upon them may call for a transmission of substantive value from one country to another which must affect more or less the rates of international exchange.

It is only after all expedients have failed for the adjustment of the values to be interchanged that trade falls back upon its reserve. The way in which it comes into use is this. In every centre of trade, bills of exchange are offered for sale, drawn, let us say, on London, promising value to be paid there, generally some months after the time of sale. For the sake of clearness of analysis and illustration let us, in the first instance, suppose these to represent commodities sent to London to be sold there in order to realise the value indicated on the bills; and further, that the buyers of these bills are those who, having received and sold commodities from London, do not themselves desire to send back the equivalent in other commodities, but merely to return value in the general terms of money, *i.e.* in pounds sterling. These are very ordinary conditions of trade. Now if the value of bills offered—which of course indicate conversely substantive value sent in the opposite direction—

CHAP. IV. may be represented as 100 and the value required as 102, the only possible adjustment is that the bills must be bought at 2 premium. As French money is expressed in francs, German in marks, the United States in dollars, &c., the fact cannot always be stated in so simple a form; but the "par" of exchange given as francs 25·22½, marks 20·43 per £ sterling; or 4s. 1¼d. per dollar, indicates nothing more than equal weights of gold of any common standard of purity. The sole difficulty arising from such differences in terms can be overcome by any practised clerk in a very few moments, and it is idle to talk of them as any obstruction to trade of this description. But the proportional difference is based on a fact which cannot be got rid of, and appears equally in the quotation of exchange from our Australian Colonies, though their sovereign is not only taken as identical with ours, but is actually a legal tender in this kingdom. Where the legal currency of a country is in inconvertible paper the price of gold in such paper is in reality, if not in form, taken as the basis of the calculation. So also if exchange has to be arbitrated between one country with a gold and another with a silver standard, the estimate of the price of one metal in the terms of the other forms a shifting item in every transaction. The work is of the same kind, though somewhat less cheaply and accurately done in such cases.

The assumed difference of two per cent. being primarily apparent, we may now suppose bankers to come in;—they are, in fact, rather the first than the last in the field, but their special function may best be thus separately considered. At so high a premium, they will naturally desire to sell bills, provided either that they expect to buy trade bills on the spot on better terms hereafter, or that with the cash they receive for their own bills sold on London, they can buy other bills on some other place, and with the money *there* received, buy bills on favourable terms to be sent to London to be set against their first drawings. Bills for this purpose will be bought and sold, not only in one, but in several places successively, provided that an ultimate advantage is shown, and some slight margin in favour of the banker secured on the amount thus indirectly remitted over the amount directly drawn in the first instance upon London.

But if we suppose that gold can be sent to London at a cost, including all indirect and incidental charges, of one per cent., the banker would never expect to sell at so high a premium as two per cent., for the bullion market is practically open to all, and some at least of the traders would take gold, which could be transmitted at a cost of one per cent., sooner than pay double that charge for a banker's bill. If only one hundredth part of the demand for bills is superseded in this way, the natural arbitration of exchange brings down the rate to the equivalent of that to be secured by the transmission of gold. So likewise, *mutatis mutandis*, no one would sell a bill for 100 on

London at so low a rate as 98, but in preference would direct his London agent to send him gold which, after paying the one per cent. for charges, would give him 99.

Practically, therefore, in dealing with bills of exchange the banker's range is limited to two per cent., i.e. from one per cent. premium to one per cent. discount, and only when no further adjustments of value can be effected, directly or indirectly, will these extreme points be touched, and gold be actually transmitted from place to place ; and then only to an extent sufficient to reduce the divergence in the rate of exchange within these limits ; for as has been repeatedly shown, there can be no direct profit made by dealing in bullion.

Extended inter-changes of capital thus made.
The resources of banking are very inadequately exemplified by the case supposed. International dealings in stocks, for instance, afford scope for operations which are very large as compared with the value of the income derived from them ; or, to put the point with more regard to the exigencies of the arbitration of exchange, dealings in such stock may often be made with less adverse effect against the operator than dealings in the current values of bills representing the transmission of merchandise. Thus, if London, having funds in Paris, buys an amount of French Rentes, just so much value is left there, less only the periodical income payable upon it. It remains merely as a debt till other needs arise. London may thus get interest for its capital instead of dead bullion,

which it does not require.   Such Rentes, or, "the
funds," are, however, somewhat uncertain as a
banking security : for the market price of them is
liable to fluctuate ; and the value of securities
payable in current money within some limited
period can be more precisely estimated.   Hence
good commercial bills are pre-eminently the security
most in favour with bankers, and it may further be
noted that the cause for this preference, which is
so well justified by experience, lies partly in the
fact that behind them, as a rule, there are the
commodities which are required for current use
and consumption.   Even if prices are depreciated
by excess, time thus is ever tending to restore
the due proportion of supply to demand.   No
such process of necessary consumption aids the
price of shares or stocks, which depends therefore more exclusively on mere opinion, or on
the surplus left for the purchase of such property after the satisfaction of more pressing
requirements.

International bills of exchange are also largely
used as a means of obtaining credit.   Thus a banker
in London may draw on Paris, and, when his bill
is due there, may draw on Berlin, and so on.   Such
bills form a special commercial currency, their
amount is limited to the sum which the general
body of traders can afford to hold in circulation,
and the gain of course depends in the long run on
the uses to which the "money" so obtained is
applied : *i.e.*, as a rule it is lent in support of

commercial enterprises, earning a profit which can be shared with the lender.

International trade is naturally concerned rather with the transmission of products fitted to the use of other countries than with the preparation of such products themselves. These ultimate results, therefore, come to be represented by documents in forms easily transmitted, and in currently vendible forms. The service done is specially the adaptation of supply to the time and place where demand requires satisfaction. Regarding this adaptation as an essential condition of utility, the *rationale* of all this machinery of international bills of exchange is evident. Bullion here also, as a common measure of value, keeps the terms of every transaction upon a certain and intelligible basis. But, as the intimacy of commercial relations extends, so will the capital of the world become more completely generalised, and the great law of average be more effectually applied to equalise the fluctuating surplus or deficiency which arises in each one of all the centres of industry which can thus be associated together.

17. In the early part of this Treatise it was shown that the primary use of metallic money was to serve as a *reserve* of purchasing power, to be used only in compensation for the natural inequalities of production. And further, that, as far as trade consisted—as for the most part it does

and must always continue to consist—of the interchange of property and commodities of various descriptions, the secondary or inferential use of such money as a common measure of value might, to a considerable degree, be superseded by means of tallies or substitutes of different kinds, though it is of very great importance that they should be maintained at the same value as, and be interchangeable at will for, the standard weight of the precious metal which they purport to represent.

The review of the most highly-developed system of commercial interchange shows that the uses of metallic money are essentially the same as those first indicated, theoretically. But over and above any system of tallies which can be used to represent metallic money, or even money in any way vested with an intrinsic general purchasing power, we have had before us a system for facilitating to the utmost extent the interchange of values of all kinds.

It will have been observed that, not only are the values of all commodities which can be made available for current use set the one against the other, but, further, in the more stable and civilised countries, "capitalised" property, representing the present value of products to be yielded in the future—perhaps in many future years—is also brought into the circle of international adjustment. The tendency of the peaceful development of civilisation and mutual confidence is to make these means yet more fully available for this purpose, except of course in the case of bullion-producing countries; but with the increase of general wealth a comparatively large value of the precious metals may be retained for their customary use as money, and any lasting change in their purchasing power can only be effected by influencing the vast aggregate of demand and supply for them throughout the whole world.

General Conclusions.

I will submit only very briefly in conclusion some further remarks of a more general nature. I have endeavoured to show the conditions upon which value in exchange is based—how on the one side the *quantity* of labour necessarily employed governs all value of this kind which can be continuously maintained, and with this quantity of labour is connoted the consumption required for the support of the labourer; there is on the other side the *value in use* to the consumer—or, to express the relation more adequately, to all men as consumers—which value must depend upon the demand which they can, and actually do choose to, make effectual. Hence, from the calculation of value in exchange will be eliminated (a) the cost of labour needlessly employed on any act of production, and (b) on the excess generally of any production, however necessary may be the thing produced, beyond the requirements of consumers (III. § 22). And similar reasoning applies also to services rendered. This process of reciprocal adjustment and adaptation is constantly going on, and is most effectually accomplished where free competition is neither restricted artificially nor thwarted by dishonest artifices. Into the defence of the principle of competition I need not enter at length. The practical tests which are the result of it are as needful in material matters as is free discussion in the world of thought and of politics. Both are liable to similar abuses. False work, misapplied, wasteful, and slovenly work, perverted statements of fact, bad logic, confused and reckless argument, are equally sins against truth, the best interests of which are not the less bound up with the full knowledge and varied experiences which only such freedom of action and of thought can adequately afford. Work and the capacity for work must be proved, and the right of each man to offer the best he can afford on the one side, and to select that which most fully satisfies his own wants on the other, must be fully accorded as the basis of justice on which an organisation of free men can be developed, subject to no other restrictions than those which are, in fact, required to insure the impartial application of these principles to all alike.[1]

The means by which the aggregate resources of the country are mobilised, so as to be adapted in an innumerable variety of ways to the ultimate production of such things as society effectually demands, have also been referred to. The mechanism of interchange is admirable; the very attempts to simulate its processes serve only by their speedy failure to prove the stability of the basis of credit on which the industrial fabric rests. It is not within this mechanism—regarded as a means to give effect to the choice practically made by those who avail themselves of it—that remedies are to be found for the evils which afflict the body politic, but by action of a far wider and deeper kind brought to bear upon the wills, desires, and capacities of its several members. Nevertheless while no good work can ever be done by the mere manipulation of money, infinite waste, mischief, and confusion may arise from any falsification of it. Hence the importance attached to the preservation

---

[1] No better practical rule can be cited to prevent freedom from degenerating into license than the time-honoured maxim—

" *Sic utere tuo ut alienæ lædas;* "

and this sole restriction on our own rights must be applied not only to what we do, but also to what we abstain from doing, by which the interests of others may be affected. To this may be added one more pregnant dictum from the same source—

" *Non omne quod licet, honestum est.*"

The great masters of jurisprudence did not hold him "honest" who acknowledged only the sanctions of the law as indicating the extent of his social duties.

of the integrity of the currency and of all symbols
of value represented in the terms of money. Any
attempts to overlay and obscure, by any juggle or
mystification of finance, the indications which it
affords, tend to the advantage only of those who,
however refined may be the methods of their
operation, can only be included among the predatory classes of society. Still, an ignorant credulity
is ever ready to believe in the magical production
of wealth, and the alchemy of past ages is suc-
ceded by currency nostrums of various kinds in
the present. All delusions of this nature lead to
incalculable loss, not to be measured only by the
expectations which are stultified, but also by the
consequent diversion of energy from objects of
rational utility. It is not the mere mechanism,
but what is done with it, and especially what are
the limits of its powers, and to what extent its
utility can be made available, that we have ultimately to consider. The very perfection of the
system within its legitimate range is apt to hide
from us some of the considerations which are most
important for our social well-being, rigorously conditioned as it is on the one side, yet possessing such
abundant latitude of resource on the other.

I venture to invite consideration to the results " Neces-
sary " and
of industry distinguished as " necessary " or "optional"
produc-
" optional," rather than as " productive " or " un- tion.
productive" in any material sense. No one denies
that there are many services, which, though not
" productive" of wealth in any form, are yet

peremptorily needed to satisfy the primary wants of mankind, so that the consumption required to support those who render them must be regarded as indispensable ; while many material products which, as having exchange value, are practically accepted as utilities, satisfy desires only of a most capricious and transitory character. It is true the distinction suggested cannot be accurately defined, but though indicated only in general terms, the very discussion of these terms is pregnant with issues of the greatest practical consequence.

The conditions with which we have to deal, especially in a highly organised system of industry, are that the labour of a part of the community is fully adequate to satisfy the primary wants of the whole (III. §§ 11 and 14). In other words, the consumption of those so engaged is reproduced with a greater or less increase, which, being in excess of their own wants of this kind, can only be utilised by supporting others, who can only come into the circle of industrial cooperation by rendering services of some other kind. Much labour must in the nature of things be devoted to the production of commodities which perish in the using. What proportion of the energies of a country must be used subject to necessities thus imperatively ordained, depends upon the resources, both natural and acquired, which are at its disposal. Hence the inherited and trained skill of workmen, the habit and power of conjoint labour, the growth of laws calculated to give freedom and security to industry become the most important factors of productive power, and speaking even on purely economic grounds, the first essential of prosperity is rather to secure this ample power of reproduction than to restrict consumption, or even to embody the results of labour in material objects of permanent utility.

Beyond this it was truly taught ages ago that the " object of labour is to secure leisure "—not for slothfulness, but to devote to such progress and such enjoyments as life can yield; and whether, and how far, in this sphere, the results achieved may be clothed in material form is altogether a subordinate and casual consideration. Leisure also has its economic alternative. It must be duly correlated with labour, but in it reside potentially all that makes man thrive, and enables him to rise above the level of the savage. According to the use made of the option thus afforded, nations which have once emerged from the first struggles for existence stand or fall, and assume the characteristics which distinguish one race from another. Social science if restricted by the usual definitions of political economy may indeed be the philosophy of the sciences in relation to the material prosperity of the State, but is debarred from dealing fully with the higher problems both of labour and of all its ultimate results. For the reasonable test of that prosperity is the ease with which necessary production is provided for, and the highest gain may be conceived of as the greatest balance of energy

CHAP. IV.

Economic
conditions
of this
country.

remaining to be used at the option of the community. Here other sciences take up the question.

Let me briefly refer to the general conditions which obtain in our own country. Dealing as we have to do with highly generalised conditions, we must perforce look to concrete results with a knowledge and recognition of the principles which underlie appearances, rather than attempt to follow out in detail the processes by which these results are obtained. The rapid increase of population in a limited area has already forced upon us, in some respects, rather the conditions of life in one vast city, than those which obtain in a country which can draw all its most needful supplies from its own soil.[1] The import of provisions of all kinds is large and continuous, and includes wheat enough for the use of about half the population of Great Britain. This has to be paid for by exports of native produce (iron, coal, &c.), or of manufactures, by the services rendered by our shipping, by the interest earned on our capital employed in every

[1] This factor is one of very great importance and is too frequently overlooked. The last census returns give the population of England and Wales for the decennial periods :—

1801	... ...	8,892,000	1841	... ...	15,914,000
1811	... ...	10,164,000	1851	... ...	17,927,000
1821	... ...	12,000,000	1861	... ...	20,066,000
1831	... ...	13,896,000	1871	... ...	22,712,000

The same authority gives the population in A.D. 1600 as 4,863,000 and in A.D. 1700 as 6,045,000.

The density of population per square mile is also given, viz. :—

A.D. 1600 ...	83	A.D. 1800	153
„ 1700 ...	104	„ 1871	390

part of the world, and in innumerable other ways. So completely and perfectly is the aggregate of our resources generalised for all the purposes of industry that it is impossible to analyse the value of these exports, or to identify the links of interchange by means of which products consumed are specifically replaced. The material production of such links, and the uses which they are made to subserve as exchangeable commodities, form indeed the subject of work of very different orders (IV. § 4). Commerce effects the interchange of current values of all kinds indiscriminately, and no labour-saving expedient is likely to be neglected in its subtly adjusted operations. We must take the results, and it matters nothing to the argument whether a larger or smaller proportion of the value, say of silk or cotton manufactures exported, has been paid for previously as an import. Value created here is equally sent abroad, and our imports are received in like manner, though the cost of British exports may have entered into the total cost of their production. It is not the less true that we have the choice of every market in the world from whence to draw the supplies we require of those primary necessaries, the cost of which must be the chief factor in the exchange value of all products, and that we pay for these in the way which best suits our own interests. We are fed by the products of our furnaces, our looms and our workshops as effectually as by our own soil. Whether this great "natural agent" is, or is not, used to the best advantage, is a very important question ; but nevertheless it is far less fundamental than that which is now under consideration. We must, and safely may, so far take for granted that the production connoted with necessary consumption is well adapted to the ends desired ; and the process which primarily concerns us is that from necessary consumption to the replacement of that consumed : the difference between the two being that which is available for the support of other labour, the application of which is largely at the discretion of the nation considered generally. We may take it for granted, I say, for the purposes of this argument, that all the interchanges involved are fairly and reasonably made as far as they are made at all ; but it does not follow that they are adequate to all the conditions that we should desire to see fulfilled in the body politic—in other words, that all are brought within the circle of independent and self-supporting industry, who might and ought to be included within its limits ; or that the large portion of our resources, the disposal of which depends upon the exercise of a voluntary discretion, is most wisely and beneficially employed.

It were a waste of time to enter upon proofs of the wealth of this country, or the extent to which surplus labour is devoted to production which can in a very large degree be modified at will to suit the changing demand of those who can make their demand effectual. The returns of our foreign trade give ample indication of this, and, being published in clear and exact form, naturally attract special attention, but the strongest proofs probably lie at home, and there can be no doubt that domestic enterprise has benefited still more largely by the margin for optional labour secured directly and indirectly by free trade.[1] Indeed there seems to be some reason to think that the relaxed rate of progress which has lately been shown in our foreign trade is in some measure owing to conditions of our home industries by no means unfavourable to the interests of the community at large. And be it remembered that though the due supply of primary necessaries is an essential condition for the production of wealth, it does not in itself constitute wealth ; although all that can be fairly so termed— or the leisure which may be the equivalent of it—is materially based on the excess continuously produced. The fact of wealth accumulated in permanent forms proves that this condition has been fulfilled. That it still subsists is proved by the capacity of the nation to employ continuously a large portion of its resources upon objects which, as far as any immediate pressure of want is concerned, might very well be dispensed with altogether ; and, further, by the existence of a large amount of capital which is constantly seeking for employment. That is to say there is a large

---

[1] Mr. Brassey, in his *Work and Wages*, states that what are termed the building trades support as many labourers as those maintained in the three great industries of cotton, wool, and flax manufactures. It is difficult to trace this result exactly in the census returns, but the large numbers engaged in domestic industries are very strikingly shown in them.

power immediately available for purchasing that which will support labour calculated to yield results of more or less permanent advantage, or to await for compensating returns hereafter—perhaps in a comparatively far distant future.

Concurrent wealth and destitution. Now if our commerce secures us an abundance of natural agents, and makes good the deficiency of the necessaries of life which our own soil cannot yield, on terms which admit of the rapid accumulation of wealth and of capital ready to be applied to the support of labour which can in any way be made serviceable, how is it that there are many who want to work, and yet remain on the verge of destitution ? The want felt in the midst of plenty clearly does not arise from any scarcity of necessary products, but from the inability to earn wages to give in exchange for a share of them.

Here is the sharp contrast between superabundance and destitution which must be looked in the face. What is the remedy for the evil ? The reply at once suggested is, " A more adequate distribution." True. But let us see what a more adequate or more perfect distribution implies and requires. I have already explained (III. § 12—14) how the wealth of the rich must inevitably go to the support of labour, and that, to put the case in an extreme form, the mere substitution of almsgiving for expenditure on products or services in themselves superfluous, would only perpetuate a race of paupers to the detriment of comparatively independent workers, and further, that however capricious may be the choice by the wealthy of the objects for which they will pay, the ultimate equation of wages received to the total value expended in this way, is a matter quite beyond any individual control. However much there may be to deprecate in the manner in which our optional production is governed, production implies distribution on some terms. Money must be spent in order to enjoy its fruits, and no mere volition on the part of the wealthy can increase or diminish the total amount which they have to spend. If this amount be inadequate when divided among the numbers wanting wages, are we therefore driven to the conclusion that the population has already exceeded the limits which can be supported in the country? The question is a grave one : for large numbers, fitly maintained, mean the power and strength which only will enable this kingdom to maintain its position at the head of a mighty empire.

If the increasing cost and scarcity of the primary necessaries of life were the cause of the distress experienced, it would be useless to deny that this insuperable difficulty must be met by a reduction of the numbers which had to be supported, but it is clearly shown that this ·is by no means the state of the case. The classes who minister to the wants and pleasures of the wealthy are, speaking generally, among the most thriving in the community. Naturally those are preferred who can do the most acceptable work. Behind them lie many others

CHAP. IV. far less favourably circumstanced, and behind these
again those whose work or services no one seems to
require. So we have a residuum, who, though but
poorly provided for, are still supported at a minimum of direct cost, yet are a burden on society
because they contribute still less to the general
Distribu- stock or to the general convenience. With many
tion.
wants to be supplied, there is yet the cry of "no
work." Why should not those thus supported, but
thrown out from the circle of industry, work for
one another ? The suggestion sounds almost like
cruel irony, yet the germ of the only remedy
adequate to the extent of the evil lies in it,—even
if we only get back the hopeless reply that no work
remains to be done which they are capable of
doing. The demand for unskilled labour is necessarily limited in any community where industry
is highly organised (III. § 9), and the society which
suffers-its members to grow up merely as unskilled
labourers must pay the penalty of its shortcomings.
Yet even here there is some mitigation, for there
are many swamped in this class who might yet with
some rightly-applied help be able to struggle out
of it, to the benefit both of themselves and even
of those whom they left behind.

Radical   The popular remedy, especially among the com-
fallacy of
"mono-   paratively favoured classes, for any distress arising
poly."
from a depression of prices is "protection," disguised perhaps as merely "a restriction of undue
competition ;" which on examination will be found
to resolve itself into this absurd anomaly : Because

there is a want of commodities against which commodities can be exchanged—all trade being ultimately an interchange of commodities—therefore reduce the supply of commodities. Unless all the wants of all the community are fully satisfied, over-supply means in fact a supply which has no exchange value because it can find no counterpart. If the aggregate supply of any product loses its value because, as far as it is in excess of a decreasing demand, it wants utility, the obvious remedy is to diminish the supply, and apply the labour set free to other production : the capital for its support is certainly already in existence ; so also is the power of purchasing the finished product without any new augmentation of either. But if a fall in prices consequent on a reduced cost of production is met by a corresponding increase of demand, there is an absolute gain in the increased supply of utilities, for although those immediately engaged only receive as much as before, the actual value of wages to all consumers is increased, inasmuch as they can get more of what they require. Those who advocate restriction read falsely and imperfectly the indications afforded by money, for it is useful only as a purchasing power, and high prices, thus artificially maintained, mean simply low purchasing power. Money measures only relative cost : relative utility can only be estimated by a well-reasoned comparison of results. No one doubts that a monopoly may secure to a class or to an individual a relative advantage, but that requires not only the monopoly of one kind of production, but that all, or at least most, other kinds of production shall *not* be subject to any such restriction. There must be a monopoly of monopoly itself to make it of any effect, for a system under which all strive to get as much and give as little as they can, obviously must end in the impoverishment of all alike. Legalised monopoly is legalised robbery and extortion as against all consumers, and a combination of any one class to secure to itself special and exclusive advantages is a declaration of civil war against the community at large. That men engaged in the uncertain issues of trade should prefer high prices and large profits to low prices and perhaps heavy losses is perfectly natural, but not the less are " cheapness and plenty " the essential conditions of permanent and general prosperity.

There moreover is a far greater advantage in the freedom of industry than any which can be expressed in the terms of capital conceived of as a fixed quantity. The facility of applying labour to new forms of production is the great incentive for saving capital and applying it to new adaptations of reciprocally beneficial industry. It is not so much by elaborately devised schemes, as by innumerable small experiments, by expedients known only to those intimately acquainted with varying minor local considerations, that the circle of independent and self-supporting industry is enlarged. The reduced cost of living puts the power of saving

capital within the reach of many who can best feel,
or have felt, their way to using it to advantage.
This no doubt implies changes, and it is impossible
to say that some may not casually suffer from them.
Dangers and difficulties of this kind were urged as
against free trade with foreign nations by those
whose sole notion of supply was limited to that
passing through their own hands. They are now
urged again, with even less reason, against the free
circulation of labour in domestic industries. But
if we are well assured that the common reservoir
is increasingly filled, it is needless caution to insist
beforehand on knowing the precise means by which
the necessarily consequent overflow is to be drawn
out. There seems to me no room to doubt that the
benefits which have arisen from the freedom of commerce are small and insignificant as compared to
those which would accrue from the unreserved
adoption of the same principles by trades unions
and all who have any influence in the direction of
labour. The want acknowledged on all sides is of
a wider distribution, which can only be attained by
giving the fullest scope to that work of adaptation
by which mutual work and mutual wants can be
extended and co-ordinated.

It may perhaps be urged that free competition
will lead to low wages and to the increase only
of profits. Were capital a fixed quantity and
employers the sole owners of it, there might indeed
be some casual danger of this result; but generalised
as it is, its distribution cannot be restrained from

any uses which will satisfy the terms on which credit is usually granted, in other words, from any uses which any of the dispensers of it are assured will be reproductive. With a flowing tide of accumulating capital no difficulty can reasonably be apprehended on this score. Even if it were so, the accumulated profits must at the least afford new employment for new labour, which will readjust the balance of demand for it, and that with the less difficulty if labour be not in any way restricted from adapting itself to the change of production required. So also as regards the argument that cheap prices benefit the rich : they must needs do so for they benefit all alike, but only on like conditions. But whenever industry can acquire vigour and freedom of action, both profits and interest, regarded as modes of remuneration, tend surely to a minimum, and do not under any circumstances necessarily imply a superior or still less an exclusive power of accumulation (IV. § 4–6.) We may go further, and say that all forms of remuneration tend to an equality under the influence of free competition, remembering always, however, that this competition to be valid must imply a capacity effectually to do the work competed for. Nothing can be more inane and futile than to cry out for special remuneration of any kind without acquiring the skill or undertaking the cares and responsibilities of the work associated with it. In short the natural laws which favour such a equalisation are so irresistible that they are

only to be thwarted by that diminution of production which the mistaken policy of restriction
would enforce.

So, on the other hand, little weight need be
given to the threat that capital will be sent out
of the country if not duly protected. The experience of late years has shown that its employment abroad is not so easy a task (III. § 20). It
depends upon labour for its reproduction—upon
competent and well-organised labour—and must
come to terms with it wherever it can be found.
It is perfectly just and right that trades unions
should look after the interests of labour in all
questions which may arise as to the apportionment
of wages and profits, and that co-operative associations should fairly compete for the latter if they
deem it for their welfare to do so. But, above all,
the general interests of the public which all trade
subserves must be clearly recognised. Any one
who will be at the pains to realise how great and
varied are his own interests as a consumer, as
compared with the value of the product with
which he is individually concerned, can hardly fail
to recognise the soundness of the policy which
aims at the diffusion of industry and the general
efficiency of production, rather than grasping at
an undue share—of what?—a relative "purchasing
power" as expressed in money, which the dearness
of things to be purchased renders nugatory.

The fact that the nation is so much dependent
on other countries for its supplies of food adds

further weight to the argument. Cheap production will always give us a command of foreign markets, but it by no means follows that the low rate of living which may obtain in them will depress wages here. The cost of production in any country is governed by those causes which have relative effect within its own boundaries (II. § 19). We *must* come to terms with the foreigner, no doubt, for our supplies of necessary food; but cheap production generally within our own borders renders a cost of production, low as compared with that of other countries, quite compatible with high wages as measured in what can be bought with them. It is only by relative cheapness of this genuine kind that our position can be made secure. The spurious prosperity shown by high prices is open to the direct competition of any nation whose necessities may induce them to resort to those markets of supply on which we are ourselves dependent, and which, it may be added, though reciprocally dependent, are not indissolubly dependent *upon us*, for the supply of those things which they take in exchange.

The efficient adaptation of labour.

Still the adaptation of labour to the various occupations required is a task presenting many difficulties, which cannot be removed without some toil and sacrifice on all sides. That new labour cannot be supported without some fresh application of capital is fully to be admitted, and this lesson, taught by former economists, tells as strongly against the merely declamatory resolutions and superficial legislation which are the foibles of the present day, as against the attempted official regulation of all industry by the mere *dicta* of authority, which was the delusion of the past generation. All that I urge is that the capital needed is at hand, ready and waiting to be applied. It is "mind," not "matter," that is wanting. It is a problem of life, not of mechanism. To say that things must be left to take their course, and that we cannot alter the law of demand and supply, is either to assert that the quotient cannot be altered if the figures remain the same, which is a truism hardly worth reiterating; or to imply that the factors themselves cannot be modified, which is mere abject fatalism. If no change can be shown in the effects the inference is irresistible that the causes have not really been modified, whatever amount of *dilettante* enthusiasm may have been brought to bear upon them.

As far as the condition of the masses of our population has been ameliorated, the results shown are valid tests of the efficiency of the means used, but their imperfection is not a proof that the ends desired are unattainable. No branch of enterprise ever yet was opened up which did not involve some loss and disaster to the early adventurers, and some persistence, in spite of difficulties, may well be urged in favour of attempts to introduce new industries, or a better organisation of industries, which may help to develop a wage-earning power, especially among the poorer classes.

As far as such industries can acquire the support of this class the fresh wages earned and expenses lessened by improved production are indeed a doubled gain.

I have insisted much on the abundance of capital in this country. Probably no nation has or ever had so great a command of this necessary element of production. But it is well to keep in mind the relative force of words, and, when we speak of supporting labour by capital, to show how necessary it is that that labour itself should speedily be made self-supporting. The estimate of our total annual expenditure has been given (IV. § 12) as at least about £1,000 millions. The whole capital that could be raised, even in this superlatively rich country, is small as compared with such a total, and would not represent more than the outlay of a few months ; or, to put the point in another light, this minor sum represents all our purchasing-power which is not already appropriated to definite objects of conventionally recognised utility. These estimates are vague enough, it is true, but the proportion roughly indicated does serve to show in a striking manner how palpably impossible it is to raise the condition of the poorer classes generally without raising also their power of labour. Nevertheless, I repeat that our available capital is most ample for all the purposes which it can possibly subserve, for true work can only be accomplished by those gradual processes which nature requires in every field of development.

But there is no room for waste. The resources which can be applied optionally are far less than those the application of which is restricted by the imperious necessity of satisfying the primary needs of the community. Endowments wasted or public funds misapplied cannot be regarded as a matter of little consequence even to a wealthy country. They may apparently form a small part of its total expenditure but bear a far larger proportion to the means which can be devoted to higher aims of public utility.

Very homely truths have to be urged in treating of the condition of those dependent on precarious wages, eked out perhaps by alms, for their meagre sustenance. The attempt to bring them into connection with luxurious expenditure is hardly to be commended, though the ostensible show of wealth seems to point out this way as the most easy solution of the problem. But that demand is already made fully effectual, and the extension of it can only follow a further increase in the aggregate profit accruing to the richer classes. The interchange of commodities of ordinary use, and which satisfy commonly felt wants, rests on a far more secure basis than any which can exist where the demand on one side is governed by mere favour or caprice.

The first beginnings must be made by the aid of Thrift. thrift. I use this word in preference to "parsimony," for it is a fuller term, and implies that, and more also which is much to the purpose. It is not so much associated with the bare and somewhat indadequate idea of saving, as with making the best use of all available resources by dint of good management. Parsimony is indeed quite consistent with an ignorant and obstinate persistence in cheap, but in reality inefficient and wasteful, methods of working. From the want of it there arises that vast amount of needless waste which so much increases the expenditure required to satisfy primary wants. A knowledge of the properties of food ; of the laws of health ; of the art of cooking and of clothing and other such true household economies, may not result in any immediate saving of money, but in the far better gain of increased energy and capacity both for work and for enjoyment. Indeed the notion of getting on in life by saving a little money " to start a shop " has been a somewhat mischievous delusion, tending to a superabundance of "distributors" who would have been far better, and quite as independently, employed in earning wages in any productive undertaking. On the advantages and independence which result from reasonable saving it is needless to dilate, but it does not quite follow that it is necessarily the first step towards amelioration.

But closely connected with this question is one in which the owners of larger capital may be more directly concerned. Who can venture to estimate the waste of energy expended in fighting against foul air, bad water supply, damp, insufficient space, fever engendered and spread by these causes : intemperance often induced by conditions which in turn are fearfully aggravated by its effects; and countless remediable evils of the kind, both in urban and rural districts? To remedy crying evils of this kind we must boldly anticipate the action of the law of supply and demand. To provide suitable houses, and, in town, the space for them, requires the outlay of an amount of capital which it would take a long time for those who need them to accumulate., Indeed there is too much reason to fear such a saving could never be accomplished, crippled as they now are with the heavy disadvantages of most insalubrious dwellings. To create a demand by affording a suitable supply is no new thing in commercial enterprise. Those who undertake such ventures often do so on the very imperfectly secured hope that future profits may recompense their first losses. Moreover we have all to buy our experiences and grow wise only by repeated failures. Now it is just this chance of being ultimately recouped for their first ill-adapted efforts and experiments which the pioneers in this great work may, from philanthropic motives, wisely forego with unmixed advantage to the community. They take the first risks, try the first experiments, undergo all the incidental crosses and losses to which all pioneers are subjected, and create the demand by affording the most suitable supply. When this can once be accomplished the field may be left open to those engaged in the ordinary conduct of the trade, and further operations thus become thoroughly self supporting. It is the first steps which are the most difficult and the most costly. A higher order once established will be more easily maintained, for better work can be done under it with less exhaustion of energy, and experience will make its true economy apparent. A more adequate standard not only of comfort, but also for work, will thus be promoted.

Nor should it be a cause of offence that those who have attained a position of some independence should largely receive the first benefits of such a movement. Why should this class be grudged an advantage which they could not indeed obtain for themselves without some aid, but for which after all they pay just as much as any one who gives a fair rent for the house in which he lives, but which he could not afford to buy? By these steps progress towards the end desired is most speedily made. To be ready to help those who are most ready to aid in helping themselves is surely the best way of inculcating the useful lesson of self-help. Some indirect benefit is open to all by the increased supply of house room afforded, and even those worst off may be advanced a step though not forcibly carried over the heads of others. Help is not less help because it is given on terms compatible with the independence of both giver and receiver.

But it chiefly concerns my argument to point out the certain economic gain which must follow every successful experiment of the kind. The

immense saving of energy which is secured by
these means must inevitably increase the capacity
for production without in any way calling for a
larger consumption to satisfy primary wants on
the previously existing scale : though as a consequence, consumption with manifest advantage
may be largely increased. It may be difficult to trace
the results in detail: they may not be shown directly
by any test in money, and it is not even desired
that the gain should fall in any special degree
to those who have led the way to so beneficial a
change.   But not the less certainly are new and
better conditions secured for life itself, and every
problem of industry will be worked out under
more favourable conditions.

Not inferior in importance to this is the great National
question of National Education, which may also education.
make some direct call upon the capital of the
country. Regarded even from a purely economic
stand-point, it is of the last importance that our
Public Elementary Schools should be vigorously
carried on and conducted on sound principles.
The primary object during the scant time which
is afforded for the formal instruction of the
children of the great mass of the population is to
train the young mind in habits of cheerful moral
discipline and rational self-control: to draw out
the faculties, to cultivate the powers of intelligent
observation and accurate comparison ; to teach not
so much mere "useful facts" as the true art and
method of learning. However rudimentary the

course of instruction may be, it should of all things
be thorough in its degree, and specially directed,
as far as may be, to imparting knowledge, and
especially principles, of widely general application.
If teachers can succeed in maintaining their due .
authority without an assumption of their own
infallibility, they may the better succeed in imparting by their example one of the most useful
lessons that can be taught in the cause of "order
and progress." Duly to connect these schools with
those of a higher range of study is for many reasons
most desirable, but the former must be in many
cases the only, and should be the fitting, preparation, not merely for the field and the workshop on
the one hand, or the university on the other, but
for all that work and that education which for better
or worse must be carried on through life. Technical
training in all its many branches should be associated with, but must not be suffered to supersede
this necessary preparation, which is of such para-
mount importance. For while the exigencies of
civilised life require the early specialisation of individual labourers, the interests of every one are intimately associated with and dependent upon those
of many others. It becomes daily of more and more
importance that every member of society should
acquire some capacity of understanding the true
relation which other, and perhaps apparently conflicting, interests bear to those in which he is
personally concerned. It is not the advance of
education that tends to bring different interests

into collision; that is rather the inevitable consequence of the growth of population and the constantly increasing numbers who have to work
their way into our industrial organisation. It is
the densest ignorance that most blindly follows
those who promise all kinds of impracticable and
self-contradictory advantages. The old fallacies
will crop up over and over again, till a better
power of discernment dissipates these delusions.
Nothing is more rare than any original thought
on these or any other matters : all but a very
small minority necessarily adopt, more or less consciously, some leadership. As the average power
of discrimination can be increased in any appreciable degree, even if exercised only in the choice
of leaders, so will the issues raised as between
" capital and labour " and on all such other social
questions, be brought more fully within the range
of sound reasoning.

Further : the special conditions of industry are
constantly changing. Just as in commerce large
profits arising from scarcity are so frequently followed by the losses (and actual waste) arising from
an over-supply, so is it in other branches of
industry where interests of a more permanent
kind are involved. Even were the general cultivation of the faculties of far less consequence than
it is, a premature specialisation of the training
of the young should be avoided, as entailing in
a needless degree the risk of mal-adaptation to
the work ultimately required. This necessary

specialisation itself is indeed more adequately conceived as the concentration of many active faculties
for one definite purpose, rather than as the merely
mechanical development of one faculty at the expense
of all others. A certain degree of intelligent mobility
may often be of more advantage than exclusively
technical training, however excellent. Take, for example, the case of the Spitalfields silk weavers. A
highly artistic and delicate training led for years to
nothing but the extreme of poverty. A little more
general knowledge, conveying a greater power of
adapting their taste and dexterity to kindred purposes, would have been of the greatest advantage,
both to themselves and art manufacture in general.
It is only by such continuous modifications and
adaptations that labour can secure an adequate
return of value, either " in exchange " or " in use " ;
and all such considerations involve economic results
of the most directly practical consequence.

In all cases, too, where the direction of action,
and especially of conjoint action, is required, the
call is for that rarely well-ordered exercise of all
the faculties which is often termed " common
sense." It is a good thing " to do one thing and
do it well," but another side of the question,
equally important, is concerned not so much with
doing any one thing, as with adjusting many things
together ; and these two sides, representing as they
do interests common to all, should be so far understood by all, that the irrational discontent arising
from mutual misunderstanding which tends to so

much waste of energy, should give place to the acute but discriminating criticism which affords the best stimulus for the general maintenance of a high standard of efficiency.

Above all, the man is more than his work. Though he needs must toil to live, he does not live only for toil. And this truth also, in the harmony of nature, has its economic side. However closely the science of labour may be restricted to the consideration of material production, the reflex effects of leisure upon the powers of the worker exert an influence, which cannot be disregarded, upon the problems which it has to solve. The mere rest and food of a brute will never suffice for the recreation of a reasonable being, or supply that incentive for exertion which will call forth the full exercise of his energies. The brain-worker requires some physical exercise : those engaged in manual labour equally require some healthful exercise for the mind. Nature does not permit one side of our being to be wholly ignored with impunity. This is no far-fetched theory. We have only to look around us to find ample proof that the mere oblivion of sleep and the monotony of some one form of toil will never fill up the true measure of man's wants. The instinctive craving for something more than this will be deadened by dissipation, or find some irregular vent, if it be not met by reasonable means of satisfaction. The leisure which nature imperatively requires must either be a degradation, or a recreation, even of man's " productive " energies.

X

Regarding therefore merely the increase of material wealth, without looking further to the higher uses which it should subserve, the judicious outlay of capital for all purposes of sound education, for sanitary improvements of all kinds, for all which may tend most effectually to promote the well-being of the masses, may be regarded as most truly " productive," though the benefits which result from it may be of so general a character that they cannot be made the subject of that personal relative advantage which constitutes the profit of an investor in any definite work of utility. But this increased power of labour, of skilled labour, of organised labour, of labour capable of adaptation to every exigency of society or of the State, is a far higher and more permanent gain than can be attained by any one effort of production. The expenditure required might be a matter of difficulty to a poor country, but it is assuredly the best investment that can be made by one so rich as our own.

But just the same rigid law which limits the application of capital in any other undertakings restricts it also in these. There is the same urgent necessity for looking to the *uses* to which it can actually be applied, and our advance must be made step by step as the work to be done can effectually be provided for. Some capital, but much more than capital, is required to carry out such works of far-reaching beneficence as are emphatically labours of love. The inexorable laws of cause and effect know nothing of "good intentions." Means must be adapted with equal care and forethought, whatever the ends desired ; waste for an ostensibly good purpose is too often the most pernicious form of prodigality.

But as far as money can aid in promoting the ends desired it is idle to talk of a want of means, or of "withdrawing capital from productive purposes." The whole of our " optional " expenditure, so ample and more than ample for all our wants, is capable of any modification that our true interests may require, either for peace—or, if need be, for war. We get just that for which our demand is made effectual. True it is that "capital" must be content to take the best that labour at the time present is capable of giving; and just as the preparation of fitting appliances must precede the application of skilled labour, so must the preparation of suitable agencies be often the first step to social reforms, and ultimate results may best be secured by means which appear indirect and tedious.

Whether these agencies should be under individual direction, or organized in connection with local or imperial government, or under the control of the State altogether, is a question the reply to which should depend entirely on a reasonable estimate formed of the comparative efficiency of the modes of operation which can be brought to bear by these several means respectively, or by any combination of them. Experience will, I believe, show that for most purposes, the more the functions of the government can be limited to those of a supreme court of administrative supervision and appeal, the fuller scope will be given to local and individual energies, which are as yet so partially developed for the public service throughout the country, and these it is especially desirable to call into activity where the success of the work to be done largely depends on individual zeal, capacity, and local knowledge, exercised under a due sense of public responsibility. Be this as it may, the true issue is still the same. By what means can the work required be best accomplished ? It is absurd to argue as though work ill done by lavish private expenditure were a saving to the country merely because the items do not pass through the public accounts. As wealth becomes more diffused, public spirit more active, and local government purer and more efficient, the work paid for by rates naturally tends to increase, but it by no means follows that any greater weight is placed on the "productive resources" of the country. Arbitrary or ill-adjusted taxation, and still more "irregular" expenditure of public money are indeed evils which sap the foundations of all prosperity, but they are not to be met by an inane wail that the country cannot afford to find money. The plea is neither true nor to the purpose. If public spirit be not wholly overlaid by personal and selfish considerations, a little practical manifestation of it suffices to clear away most of the difficulties which beset such questions.

As far as the influence of public opinion is con-

cerned—and who can doubt the weight of it?—the
wiser direction of *demand* can arise neither from the
operation of the law on the one hand, nor merely
conventional ethics on the other. The influence must
extend to the "positive morality," which is tested
with such unsparing impartiality by the money
which gives effect to actual preferences. Not that
material production, as such, is to be disparaged, nor
anything that adds a charm or a beauty to life to
be sourly rebuked. No economic law invites us to
sympathy with the ascetic materialism which would
rule out the heavens like an account book, and
clothe the lilies of the field in drab by the lowest
contract. But still less should the miseries and
evils and incongruities which society presents, be
accepted as ordinances of a fate over which our
wills and actions can have no control.

Those who study the sadder problems of social
life with an adequate perception of the depth and
magnitude of the evils to be combated, know full
well that money alone is powerless to remedy them.
Alms are to charity much what capital is to enterprise; useless and far worse than useless if not
applied with the vigilant exercise of that discretion
which is required to adapt such means to ends truly
beneficial. We cannot stop short at the relief of
casual distress while the causes of it remain un-
attacked. It is not that economists feel less for the
sufferings of the destitute, but because they perceive more clearly the inadequacy of the remedy,
that they so strongly deprecate that wanton outlay

in indiscriminate almsgiving which is constantly found to drag down the poor into the abysses of pauperism, in great measure by the forced and one-sided competition which it induces against those who are striving to maintain their independence. They realise more fully the fundamental truth that man must live on the fruits of toil, either his own or that of others, and that the only adequate cure is to fit men, not for supposititious work, but for that by means of which they can take a real share in the work of the community. No doubt mono-polists and privileged classes have set the tone of morality which disparages labour and leads the un-successful to seek for a share in unearned wealth rather than to struggle for fair conditions under which industry may thrive. The stricter correla-tion of rights and duties is the only adequate remedy for this perversion of aim by which an opposition of interests which should be casual only, and easy of timely adjustment, is rendered irrecon-cilable. It is the moral state and conditions of pauperism under any disguise that are the most intolerable evil, and least of all can sympathy be given to those who encourage it on the preposterous plea of hiding the "disgrace" of poverty. Cruel indeed are the mercies of those who confound the two. Success and failure are alike generalised under our complex industrial system, and present the extremes of results arising from many different causes. There are many misfits in the world, and many whom a well-organised charity can help to make good their footing in the circle of industry. The simple and easy conditions of primitive life—which indeed are rather a dream than a practical reality—cannot be afforded, but no means should be spared by which all can be qualified to earn and to receive a due share of that which appropriately belongs to the civilisation of which they are members.

The increase of population that will probably fully quadruple our numbers within the present century, is a fact that can neither be ignored nor disregarded. But an exaggerated notion very commonly prevails as to the nature of the difficulty which may thus arise. The increase, and that on the augmenting increase, is cumulative, and shows in startling figures when taken over a range of years. The annual excess, however, of births over deaths, is now only about $1\frac{1}{4}$ per cent., and in the early part of the century was only $1\frac{1}{2}$ per cent. No very violent change can possibly be required; the exercise of a very little more prudence, forethought, and self-control by a better educated community would be an adequate remedy for the worst evils which have ever been apprehended.

How far a growing sense of responsibility may impose a rational and timely check upon this increase remains to be seen. But I cannot agree with those who regard this as the weight which presses most immediately upon the energies of the country. The more so as children born and reared under conditions the most unfavourable for mental and physical health are unquestionably ill-fitted to take their place in the march of life in any quarter, and it seems equally true that numbers do increase in even more than average proportion under these conditions. Herein is the true gravamen of the complaint. In the rapid march of our wealth and civilisation too many stragglers have been suffered to fall behind. It is the helplessness of a large portion of our population, rather than the aggregate numbers of it, that presents the most serious difficulties against which we have to contend. Still, imperfect and misdirected as many of our recent efforts have been, some progress has been effected. We are getting to know by the teaching of experience more and more of the nature of the work to be done, and never can we know rest till the full measure of our duties is accomplished. The British Empire is not confined to the limits of the United Kingdom. Though these islands are closely peopled, our magnificent dependencies are hardly occupied at all. The whole dominion of Canada does not comprise together much more than the population of London alone, and the five Australian colonies about half that number. The Cape of Good Hope and Natal contain not more than about a single million. New Zealand as yet contains fewer inhabitants than Liverpool. There is still much even of our own portion of the earth to replenish and subdue. But though we might well spare money, we cannot yet afford to send to our Colonies the men whom they would willingly receive. To send out, as a class, those who are now outside the pale of productive industry at home, would be a crime as monstrous as it is, happily, impossible.

But there is yet time to train those whom we now regard as a "surplus population," so as to fit them for this alternative, which should be open to all who would carry the traditions of our name and race throughout the limits of our empire. If this country is to be indeed a mother of nations, she must recognise and adopt the high task of fitting her children to embrace, and to be worthy of, their destiny. In them is vested the value which is worthy to be the ultimate object of our aspirations.

APPENDICES.

APPENDIX I.

SOME FURTHER REMARKS ON LOCAL AND GENERAL CURRENCY.

THE foregoing treatise has been confined as far as possible to the consideration of principles of general application, but it may be of interest to explain somewhat more in detail what means are adopted in this country to preserve the amount of coin and bullion required; 1st. Duly to guard the integrity of our internal currency, which consists not only of gold, but also of notes, representing multiples, and silver and other tokens representing aliquot parts, of the standard coin; and, 2nd, To provide for all such exigences as may arise in connection with our foreign commerce. No line of demarcation can or ought to be drawn between the funds available for these several purposes, for the object is to provide that the common measure of value which serves for our domestic trade shall be identical with that which will inevitably serve for that of all foreign trade throughout the world, and that its value should be thus based on the world-wide average which affords the greatest attainable stability. This naturally leads also to some further consideration of the conditions affecting the interchange of the precious metals between different countries.

I do not propose to enter at any length upon the vexed question of the Bank Charter Act of 1844, but without here expressing any opinion as to whether or in what way its provisions might be amended, I shall proceed to offer some further explanations as to the constitution and position of the Bank of England, and as to the work with which it is so closely associated as the centre of our financial system.

1. *The Currency of the United Kingdom.*—Since the resumption of specie payments by the Bank of England in 1816, the coinage of gold by the Mint has amounted to nearly three hundred million pounds sterling, but it is estimated on very competent authority that only about 40 per cent. of this value remains in the kingdom. The actual waste of coins is indeed very small, for, notwithstanding some not very fair usage to which they are subjected, it is found that, on the average, it takes eighteen years' wear to reduce the weight from 123·274 grains troy, at which the sovereign is issued, to 122·5 grains troy, below which it is rejected at the Bank as light. But the British coin is known everywhere, and there has certainly been a steady outflow in innumerable small dribblets to all parts of the world : moreover, as sovereigns are not guarded by any seignorage or charge for mintage, they are frequently melted and perhaps recoined in other countries. It will appear hereafter that it is very desirable that they should in this way flow out as freely as they flow into circulation.

We have, however, chiefly to deal with the more active and visible portion of the currency, and though it is satisfactory to know that there is a large fund held in reserve in the country, no practical question turns upon any exact estimate of its amount. For the most part it lies below those fluctuations which afford any indication of the changes in foreign or domestic commerce. First as to our home circulation : It is well known that the issue of legal tender notes is now confined to a separate issue department of the Bank of England. As far as the Banking Department of the Bank of England is concerned, the notes it holds constitute no claim whatever upon its resources. Their value is independently based, and they are an asset in its possession just the same as they would be if held by any other corporation. They are based to the extent of £15,000,000 (increased by certain provisions under the Act of 1844 from the £14,000,000 then author-

ised) against "securities," including £11,015,100 of debt
due to the Bank by the public for money advanced at
different periods. It has been shown (III. § 5) that
securities of this kind are not to be relied upon in a time
of monetary pressure, but this point is never likely, in
this case, to be brought to the test of experience, for in
truth the value of notes to this extent is far more effectually guarded by the inevitable operation of the law of
demand and supply (II. § 6). Far more than this amount
is required for carrying on our domestic trade. In fact a
further large supply of notes is necessary to prevent their
undue appreciation, and all above this £15,000,000 are
issued only against the deposit of gold coin or bullion in the
Issue Department. According to the quarterly averages
published, the bullion there held ranged during A.D. 1861
to 1866 from £12,000,000 to £15,000,000, the notes issued
to the public ranging from £20,000,000 to £22,000,000, the
difference between this issue and the amount of gold, *plus*
the £15,000,000 of securities, constituting, as it always
must do, a reserve in the Banking Department. From
A.D. 1866 to 1871 the amount of bullion ranged from
£14,000,000 to £23,000,000, the public circulation being
from £23,000,000 to £25,000,000. From A.D 1871 to 1876
the bullion ranged from £21,000,000 to £35,000,000, the
circulation showing a gradual increase from £25,000,000
to £28,000,000; the reserve of notes in the Banking
Department being at one time over £20,000,000. The
last return of the year 1876 shows a total issue of
£43,000,000 against the fixed £15,000,000, and £28,000,000
of bullion; of which total £28,000,000 were in the hands
of the public and £15,000,000 [1] in the Banking Department. This excess of notes representing the available
reserve of gold will be shortly referred to. The increase
in circulation is probably owing in great part not so much
to the mere growth of trade as to its diffusion among
those classes who chiefly use such money for their trans-

---

[1] The coincidence of these totals is purely accidental. At the end o
1877 the total issue was about £39 millions, £27 millions being in circulation and £12 millions held in reserve.

actions. The returns of the savings banks somewhat confirm this view, having increased from £45,000,000 in 1867 to over £70,000,000 in 1877. Not that the sums paid into such banks directly imply the holding of specific money, rather the reverse; but the fact does afford satisfactory evidence of a more general diffusion of wealth, which would put it in the power of some millions of people to keep a few more notes in their pockets for current uses,

Be this as it may, it is evident that the *more or less* of our internal circulation directly rests upon a gold basis. The note also is a legal tender everywhere in England, which ensures its retention in circulation as far as money is required at all in any such form; thus, though all holders of Bank of England notes have not literally rights as *in rem* to the specific amounts of gold expressed upon them, nothing short of disasters which absolutely destroyed our industrial system altogether could endanger the convertibility of any note at the will of those holders who could possibly have any occasion to demand payment in standard coin. The holder of a legal tender note has moreover, as such, a right *in rem* to a document vested with a purchasing·power of altogether a specific and exceptional character.

In addition to the notes of the Bank of England, there are those of private and joint-stock banks which fill a place in the currency, the amount of issue legalised being on an average taken to indicate their existing circulation at the time when the currency was made subject to legal restriction.

In England out of £8½ millions thus authorised in A.D. 1844, the right to issue over two millions has been suffered to lapse, and the actual circulation is now only about £4½ millions. This diminution may account for the increase in the issue of the Bank of England to the extent of one to one and a half million pounds.

In *Ireland* and *Scotland*, however, the circulation shows a considerable increase, though in accordance with the provisions of 8 & 9 Vict. c. 37 & 38, A.D. 1845, coin must be

held (though it is not specially held) for all issue above
the amounts then authorised. Both Irish and Scotch
banks issue £1 notes, which the people are used to, and
prefer to sovereigns. In short, the effective demand is for
that form of money with which they are most familiar.
The *Irish* authorised issue remains at the sum of
£6,354,494, as determined in 1845. The actual issue
is nearly £8 millions; coin being held for £3½ millions;
or two millions more than the Act requires.

Of the *Scotch* issue authorised, £337,938 have lapsed
(owing to the failure of the Western Bank of Scotland in
1857), leaving £2,749,271. Their actual issue has, however, steadily increased, and is now over £6¼ millions,
coin being held to the extent of over £4¾ millions.

So, especially as regards the latter, it will be seen that
setting well-established issue on the one side and the
aggregate of coin held on the other, the Irish Banks
taken together, and the Scotch Banks also taken together,
are in at the least as strong a position as regards the
proportion of bullion held—as the Bank of England,
though as the law now stands the coin is, in the case of
each several bank, only a general asset for the whole sum
of its liabilities : 44 per cent. of the Irish Issue, and 73
per cent. of the Scotch Issue represent Coin, held in the
banks of the two countries respectively.

The note circulation of the *United Kingdom* therefore
at the end of last year (1876) may be taken as :—for the
Bank of England £43 millions, of which £28 millions
only were in the hands of the public, other English
Banks £4½, Irish £8, and Scotch £6½, together £19 millions
more, or in all £47 millions of active circulation. This
showed an increase (somewhat lessened in 1877, but), for
the most part steadily progressive, of about 25 per cent. in
this note circulation since 1861. The issue of the Bank
of England being then about £21 millions, other Banks
about £17 millions, in all £38 millions nearly.

2. *Fluctuations in the Amount of Circulation* may be due
to causes of a merely temporary, as well as of a more
permanent nature. There are certain well-known periods,

Y

such as harvest time, when extra wages are largely paid;
and in Scotland especially, term times when rent, half-
yearly and other hirings, and many such matters are
arranged according to local custom. The notes and coin
sent out on such occasions return with perfect certainty
and regularity. The social conditions which may give rise
to more permanent changes in the amount of notes and
coin held in circulation are very various. Thus a thrift-
less population, always in debt for the necessaries of life,
would have to pay the money received as wages immediately to the shop-keeper or publican. A more
provident community would keep much more money in
hand and hold it in reserve. Again, a population as
thrifty but acting on a more intelligent plan, might so
divide its earnings between the shop and the Bank as to
reduce the use of current money to a lower rate than
ever. A curious side-light is thrown upon the use of
money by reference to the well-known "truck system."
Nothing could appear fairer than the idea of a great
employer buying goods wholesale and retailing them at
saving prices to satisfy the wants of his workmen. The
result, however, was such flagrant abuses and so much
discontent, that the legislature had to step in to require
that wages should be paid fully and solely in the current
money of the realm. The effectual way in which it
secures to the owner the power of free choice (II. § 5)
affords an adequate remedy for the wrongs suffered. But
this requirement of the law no doubt tended to increase
the circulation ; the establishment of co-operative stores
would tend again to diminish it. Such illustrations serve
very fairly to indicate the way in which specific money
may be most largely required in certain intermediate stages
of society, and are applicable both to questions of internal
currency and of international trade with nations whose
industrial system is imperfectly developed.

I have advisedly abstained from laying much stress
upon exact estimates of the quantity of currency either
of gold or silver held for domestic circulation, not only
because they cannot be determined or verified with any

degree of accuracy, but also because the demand for such
money must also be constantly shifting from the most
opposite causes, the working of which it is very difficult to
discern. The fluctuations in the ultimate reserve of the
currency shown by the returns of the Bank of England
are facts definitely, certainly, and promptly known, and,
at present at all events, afford the most trustworthy
indications of the actual changes in the ultimate balance
of supply and demand with which we are practically concerned ; but these indications must be intelligently, and
not blindly, interpreted.

3. *The Cost of a Metallic Currency* has often been the
subject of estimates, but there is a want of reality in the conclusions, which are indeed in excess of the premises that in
ordinary questions may be safely assumed. There is no doubt
an inevitable waste from abrasion, and it would be well if
some means could be devised by which the pre-eminently
public charge of making good this loss should be borne by
the State, and not arbitrarily thrown upon individuals. But
the great item of alleged expense is that of interest. If,
however, in order to carry out any of the economies proposed we were to attempt to sell the bullion "saved" we
should find it difficult if not impossible to carry out the
operation. If by an issue of fifty million one-pound
notes in England we were able to withdraw the same
amount of sovereigns, we could not sell the gold to foreign
markets without causing a perturbation in exchange value
by which we should probably lose far more than we could
gain in account by interest. The precious metals are
fitted for certain uses as money, and this gives rise to the
effective demand which is one of the chief factors in
determining their relative value. If these uses are
generally lessened or superseded this value must be so
far lost. Gold or silver should not for any such reason
be used in preference to other forms of money which are
better or more convenient, but the notion that on the score
of economy it would be well to dispense with the use of
them somewhat overleaps the conditions of the laws of
relative value. The practical question is not whether the

ordinary work of domestic interchange could be carried on with less metallic money, but rather, how far it is desirable for the country to hold a greater or less reserve of value in this special form, which in case of emergency could be passed into international circulation. If the exchange value of gold or of silver were less, they might indeed be more applied to useful purposes in the industrial arts, but it is not on this score that the suggested economy is advocated.

4. *Silver and Bronze token Currency.*—The old traditionary silver standard is now completely superseded. Since A.D. 1816 it has been coined at the nominal rate of 5s. 6d. per oz., standard, or $87\frac{1}{2}$ grns. for the shilling; that is, if any one had melted it down and sold the metal he would not have got more than elevenpence for it. At the present market price of silver (about 4s. 6d. per oz.) he would hardly get tenpence; and during the late scare in the silver market, the bullion contained in the coin could hardly have been sold for ninepence. Silver coins are purely a token currency representing aliquot parts of the sovereign. They are "legal tender" only to the amount of forty shillings. Thus if a shilling a week were paid into a Savings' Bank, it would not be a legal tender to offer to pay back the fifty-two shillings at the end of the year—part at all events of the debt could be demanded, as of right, in gold coin. The right to coin such tokens must necessarily be restricted to the State; for if the Mint were compelled to give silver coin for bullion to individuals, it is evident that there would be no limit to the demand to get coin worth $\frac{12}{240}$ of a sovereign, in exchange for bullion worth in the open market only say $\frac{10}{240}$ of the standard coin. The government provide only as much as is required for actual use, and the value of current silver as representing aliquot parts of a pound cannot be the subject of any rational doubt. It is absurd, however, to refer to the value of the silver coinage as maintained by its scarcity, and to adduce the currency of the shilling as a proof that a seignorage (that is, the charge by the State of the difference between the cost of

the bullion actually in the coin, and the legal value
assigned to it) is sufficient to create an independent value.
The effect of a seignorage is not in this case put to the
test at all. The safeguard is the practical convertibility
of the token into the standard coin which it represents.
The slightest difficulty in getting two sovereigns for forty
shillings, or even a half-sovereign for ten shillings, would
at once impair the currency of the silver. It would not
willingly be received into circulation. If silver be coined
in excess the only result is that it accumulates as a dead
weight in bankers' hands. The burden falls upon them in
the ordinary course of business, inasmuch as they usually
receive broken sums, from their smaller customers
especially, who, if they do not want silver, draw out only
round sums in gold. Bankers put up with a comparatively
small inconvenience sooner than disturb the even course
of the monetary circulation, but the loss would be intolerable if the extent of it could be increased by unrestricted issues, nor can it be supposed that any banker,
for a gain which in the first instance must be extremely
slight, would attempt to force money into circulation against
the wishes of his customers in sums not exceeding forty
shillings. An over-issue of tokens under these conditions
cannot affect the value of those which can be got into
circulation. The redundance is so palpable that the
excessive supply is checked at once.

The silver coins being mere tokens of the aliquot parts
of the gold pound, it follows, as has been already noticed,
that any calculation based upon the intrinsic value of the
metal in them is altogether illusive. But there is a very
adequate reason why our subsidiary currency should be
made of that precious metal which approaches in value to
the equivalent in gold represented by it. If bronze tokens
of no appreciable cost were used, they would indeed normally serve the purpose just as well as silver; but
practically we have to take into consideration the risk
which might arise from fraudulent counterfeits. As long
as the intrinsic values of the metals show a small difference only on which illicit gain could be made, we are

comparatively safe. A shilling made of pewter or any
such base metal, however well executed, can certainly be
detected. But how would it be if there were an adequate
inducement to make any actual facsimile in all respects of
the lawful coin? The detection of such a fraud would
be extremely difficult; but the difference of a penny or
even twopence in the shilling is no adequate gain to set
against the risk, as long as only small amounts can be
passed into circulation without exciting attention. In
this very important respect the security of our subsidiary
currency does depend upon the intrinsic value of the metal
used. *Bronze and Copper* coins are equally tokens representing the smaller aliquot parts of the pound. A
manufacturer could no doubt make them on a large scale
so as to yield a very high profit on their value as tokens,
but could not pass them out to any great amount without
the certainty of speedy detection.

The silver and bronze coinages are of course exclusively
for home use. So are the notes of banks other than those
of the Bank of England; and a portion of these notes
also, and of sovereigns, will be constantly required for our
domestic commerce. But a further portion of notes, representing coin and bullion held as equivalent to them in the
Bank of England, is constantly applicable to the requirements which may arise for foreign trade.

5. *The Bank's Reserve of Gold fittingly held in common
both for Home and Foreign Trade.*—The reserve in the
issue department of the Bank of England is therefore the
fund pre-eminently common both to our foreign and our
domestic trade; and it is needless again to refer to the
way in which these are indissolubly associated together, or
to the incalculable advantages which every member of an
industrial society derives, often unconsciously but not the
less surely, from the vast band of fellow-workers with
whom he is thus associated. I have already shown how
the transmission of bullion from one country to another
is only required when all the ordinary resources of trade
immediate and prospective, offer no better means for the
exchange of international value; and further, how very

finely, and with how little strain, operations for this purpose are ordinarily carried out. But the point deserves some further notice : for it is sometimes speciously urged that home industry ought not under any circumstances to be exposed to perturbations arising from foreign trades. A very direct issue is suggested in this context which may come home to some of those who care little for more general considerations. If gold, which, as has just been said, is only transmitted as a last resort, were not to be had, or equally if it were to be had only at a high premium on the legal (domestic) currency, those who were under the imperative necessity of meeting their obligations abroad would be compelled to make forced purchases in the general market—contrary to the natural course of trade—of anything that at the least cost and sacrifice would convey value to the place where their debts were due. They would have to face a loss, and all who were engaged in the branches of trade thus interfered with would suffer also, the aggregate loss being in a far greater ratio than the excess of supply thus abnormally forced upon the market. It is impossible to say whose or what interests might be injuriously affected by such operations, and equally impossible to prevent any one from buying or selling at forced rates under such emergencies. That reckless and ill-judged trading affects the interests of others besides those who are directly responsible for it is most true, and the hardship cannot be denied ; but even the immediate evil is mitigated by throwing the pressure thus arising rather on the great market for bullion than on individual interests, which might be ruined in detail, one disaster leading to others, in far greater proportion than if the burden were, as it now is, more generally diffused. The reserve of bullion is common to all, and contributes greatly to the safety of all alike. Moreover, it is the business of every one to look to the general indications which the state of the " money market " affords, and which are open to all alike far more readily than the circumstances of special trades, which may adventitiously come into rivalry with their own.

6. *An Excess of Gold an Uncertain Banking Asset.*—
Looking back to the incidents of former commercial
crises with the light of more recent knowledge, dearly
bought by experience, it is clear that the derangement in
the monetary system which preceded them, and of which
they were in some degree the result, arose from a want of
discernment of the true principles by the aid of which the
indications afforded by the bank's returns should have
been interpreted. A surplus of bullion was taken as a
sign of a superabundance of capital seeking productive
investment, whereas it was merely an excess of circulating
medium in want of immediate employment. If the conditions under which bankers hold the deposits with which
they deal are kept in mind, it will be seen that an unusual
amount of gold thus is, and must be, a very uncertain
banking asset. The average value of deposits left with
them for use in the money (loan) market depends upon
conditions which are comparatively stable. The banker
occupies a central position as regards these conditions, and
it is, moreover, his well-recognized business to look out
for and interpret any changes which may affect this
stability. The value of gold no doubt depends upon a far
wider average, and possesses therefore a still higher degree
of stability. But we must carefully bear in mind in this
case the process by which the equilibrium of value is
secured. Neither this country nor any other can be
regarded as a centre. Bullion flows to all parts on the
least possible gradients, and that it should do so is essential
for its full utility as a common measure of value. An
unusual supply in this or any other place is therefore
primâ facie evidence that this equilibrium is somewhat
disturbed, and the return to a normal level is an event
which, though it may be more or less delayed, must ever
be expected.

Superficial appearances were no doubt deceptive. A
superabundance of money in one sense was apparent, and
even though the amount of loans were increased, it did, as
it ever must, come back again and again. For there is
nothing in the fact that a few millions of bullion have

been imported in the fluctuating course of trade, to increase
the amount of it required for, and held in, local circulation.
In a community where banking was little known such a
surplus would necessarily be diffused among its wealthier
members and have a very direct effect upon prices (I. § 22).
But in so well organised a system as our own, a superfluity
of currency is simply rejected from circulation, is returned
in the ordinary course of traffic to bankers, and by them
is paid into the Bank of England. Extended as commerce
now is over the whole civilised globe, an increase in the
quantity of the precious metals is rapidly diffused to
every part of it before there is time for the casual excess
to have any very marked effect. For though the relative
cost of production in any one country as compared with
another is not governed by the value of metallic money
(II. § 19) the relative value of such money as compared
with all commodities generally, can be changed permanently only according to the conditions common to all,
not according to the local and temporary excess or deficiency
in any one country.

It would, moreover, be quite contrary to fact to assume
that because England is a very wealthy country it will
therefore absorb an unlimited amount of bullion. It can,
and does on occasion, afford to hold a very large surplus
for which no appropriate employment can immediately be
found; but that is a very different matter. Thus, as has just
been noticed, the Bank of England held in the beginning of
1876 £21 millions of bullion; in September this had increased to £35 millions. In May, 1877, it had fallen to £24
millions, at which point the banking department of the
Bank of England raised its rate of discount from 2 to 3
per cent. per annum. The practice of the bank during
the year may be cited as entirely in accordance with
sound theory. This accumulation of gold was simply held
as it were for safe custody until it was required for those
purposes of international trade which alone could relieve
us from it. The reserve in notes and coin being £8 millions
in January, 1876, £22 millions in September, and £10
millions in May, 1877: these varying reserves being over

and above the comparatively stable amounts required for internal circulation. Further, the amount of private deposits, including those made by other banks, shows a close correspondence with these fluctuations, increasing with the increase of bullion and decreasing as it was withdrawn. But no attempt was made by the Bank of England to force any part of this exceptional supply into circulation. Had it done so the results under these headings could hardly have shown any material difference, but the futile attempt would have been disclosed by that item of their accounts which shows the amount of " securities " held by it, that which in fact comprises the loans made to the public. If these had been increased to correspond with the increase in deposits, the diminution of that part of the bank's assets, consequent on the withdrawal of surplus gold, would have been a valid cause for apprehension. For having unduly stimulated enterprise or speculation by lending *capital*, because it had an excess of *gold*, this supposititious asset would escape from its control. It would have to come into the money (loan) market for the capital it had lent, for it is not the amount of a bank's deposits, but that proportion only which the depositors on the average leave with it that can safely be employed; and gold is specially liable to be drawn out under the circumstances supposed. This was essentially the error of former times, not that the bank had to undergo the overt humiliation of becoming directly a borrower, but what in the relative position of banking agencies comes to very much the same thing, it was unable to afford its usual quota of support to *credit*. In short, it found itself weak just when it should have been strong, from trusting to a deposit on which it had no sound reason to rely.

7. *The Rate of Interest as affecting the Transit of Bullion.*—As the custodian of the available reserve of bullion, the Bank has to take timely precautions to maintain this reserve at the level which prudence requires; and this it can most effectually do by its action upon the rate of interest. It cannot indeed govern the price of loans negociated through all other channels, *i.e.*, through the

Joint-Stock and private banks throughout the kingdom, but it can and does appreciably influence it. The certainty of the effect of a timely resort to this expedient has somewhat magniloquently been called the great banking discovery of modern times. The mode of its operation is not the less beneficial and well adapted to the end desired. London being the great lending market, interest entering into every transaction involving the *use* of money, and banking profits also being on so fine a scale as, for the most part, to lie within the charges made as interest, it follows that a change in the cost of money here will tell everywhere, and of course most promptly, on neighbouring countries. Foreign bankers who have found use, or may expect to find use, for English "money" at a low rate, draw it from us, selling their bills on London. If these are in excess of the demand which any foreign market will afford, the rate of exchange is turned, as has been already described (IV. § 16), and a portion of the amount goes out in bullion. A rise in the charge for interest here checks any such demand for English floating capital, or may even turn the current the other way. Bullion is, however, the more likely to be sent one way or the other, because these operations are in their nature somewhat in excess of the ordinary demand and supply of the markets affected, that is, every market which deals directly or indirectly with England. A comparatively small amount of bills of exchange bought or sold thus turns the scale in very many places. A favourable rate brings forward buyers or sellers as the case may be, as far as they are in a position to avail themselves of it, but a rise in the rate of interest in London, being a cause of very general operation and everywhere felt, the limits in the rate of exchange beyond which bullion becomes the best means of remittance are sure to be reached first in one place and then in another, sooner or later, according to the strength of the inducement held out for prompt action.

It is in this way and to this extent that the stock of gold is directly affected by the rate of interest in the loan market, and, indirectly may be influenced by the current prices of more permanent investments.

The same reasoning applies of course to every banking centre, but England, as pre-eminently a banker, has the command of the reserves thus generally held, in a special degree, and as long as confidence in her monetary stability remains unimpaired, can always control the supply of bullion without putting an undue strain on any quarter.

If the functions of bullion are clearly seen, the reason for reliance on this expedient will be apparent, and also, which is of quite as much importance, the limits within which it will be justified. Action too tardily taken, or taken under the influence of panic, is likely to be thwarted, for, though England cannot rightly be described as a borrowing nation, she is yet one largely trusted with the funds of other countries, and a shadow of weakness or suspicion tends to induce a withdrawal of such funds, which might reverse, or at least retard, the due course of international exchange, for nothing can be more free and spontaneous than its action.

8. *The Charge of a Seignorage on Coinage.*—Slight as are the fluctuations which serve to turn the flow of bullion, especially as between the chief monetary centres of Europe, the position of this country is such that usually no further action is required than suffices merely to arrest a portion of the supply coming from bullion-producing countries. Roughly speaking our average receipts for the last few years have been about £30 millions, about two-thirds of which are gold and one-third silver. The former only is specially dealt with by the Bank of England, but even the whole of this portion does not go to it. For though the Mint is under obligation to return sovereigns, weight for weight of standard bullion delivered, the operation of coining cannot be performed at once. The practical alternative is to sell bullion to the Banking Department at 77s. 9d. instead of 77s. 10½d. per oz. (III. § 1), the former thus being the selling and the latter the "buying" price for the public. This difference of 1½d. per oz. is less than ⅙ per cent., and may most fairly be considered as a dis-

count for prompt payment, being equal to 20 days' interest at 3 per cent. per annum. Any immediate demand for gold to be sent abroad may therefore be supplied directly from arrivals coming in from Australia, America, or elsewhere. If, however, there is the least check to this immediate demand, the gold is sold to the Bank, which must take it at 77s. 9d. per oz. The result of this is that the Banking Department has to send the bullion to the Issue Department, receiving for it notes, which, as has just been shown, often cannot be turned to any present use; while the seller gets the money of account which *he* of course can spend or employ at his own discretion.

Although the issue department has in this way some latitude as to the amount of bullion it may actually turn into coin, it is under the imperative obligation to pay sovereigns for every note presented. Coin as coin is sometimes required for exceptional reasons, and in many cases sovereigns as being generally recognised even abroad, possess a more effectual purchasing power than bullion could afford (II. § 4). Such temporary use being completed the coin naturally flows back, not being permanently required abroad as currency. If it were guarded by a seignorage, say of one per cent., 100 parts coin would be at first equal to 101 parts bullion. So far there is an apparent gain. But whenever the former became redundant it would lose the special value which depends on use being found for the whole quantity, and the intrinsic value (II. § 31) of the coin being one per cent. less than that of bullion, the whole currency would be liable to depreciation before the surplus could be utilised. It might seem easy enough to levy such a charge upon the supposition that those who applied for coin could readily recoup themselves for the facility afforded by a single operation, but no such charge would be paid as long as coin of the same weight could be drawn from the currency. Practically all coin must be minted on the same terms and it would be impossible so to regulate the issue as to avoid the occasional accumulation of an over supply. With the present large production of gold a large traffic in it is inevitable and this very much changes the conditions upon which, five and twenty years ago, economists argued in favour of such a charge. The highly perfected machinery of modern mints makes coinage a very cheap application of labour to render such a commodity as gold applicable, in the highest degree, to the uses to which it can be applied, and the only way now of maintaining intact the value of the sovereign is by issuing it free of cost, *i.e.* as the exact equivalent of the bullion contained in it. The uses of money are so general that it is for our own interest to facilitate these uses in every way. We trade so largely in "values" that it is sound policy for us to make no charge for any use of the common measure of value. In thus giving the standard gold coinage freely to all, the highest attainable stability is secured for it. The State does all that can be done to avert the evils of temporary or casual fluctuations, and in undertaking this work at the public cost does not lay itself open to the charge of incurring a needless or useless expense, but exercises a judicious liberality befitting the position which this country holds in the commercial world. The argument evidently does not fully apply to all countries, or indeed to British India, and the charge of a seignorage on the rupee there, as far as it is required to cover the cost of coinage, is fully justified.

9. *The Cost of Maintaining Reserves of Bullion.*—It is hard to say in the case of an excessive stock of bullion who it is that bears the loss or expense of holding it. The Bank of Issue has it in its vaults, but that department is charged with very special functions and has nothing to do with the uses of money under any circumstances. The banking department has notes which it may not prudently be able to use; but only under such circumstances would the notes have been issued to it at all. It certainly loses nothing by keeping so much more paper in hand. When other notes come in from circulation for payment in gold, these supply their place; the aggregate circulation, and the amount of deposits which can safely be utilized, not being affected by the change. Those who pay in gold have

the immediate use of money in account without any care as to the use to which the bullion as such can be applied. The loss, if it can so be called, is diffused over trade generally and is of that very supportable kind that a wealthy man endures who has to keep money lying idle till he finds something he thinks worth buying with it.

The banking department of the Bank of England being liable to have deposits forced upon it in the way described, could not afford to pay interest upon them, and indeed does not pay interest on any deposits whatever. And rightly so as a matter of principle. Because as the bank of bankers and holder of the ultimate banking reserve, it should be under no sort of pressure to use money which should be kept sacred for this special purpose. Just as much as activity and enterprise should characterise those who are pressing on to extend the commerce of the country into every field which can be laid open by their energy, so should prudential forethought be the cardinal virtue of those who guard the reserves of the army of industry.

10. *Silver as a Medium of International Exchange.*—The principles involved in dealing with silver bullion are the same as those which regulate the transmission of gold, though it is bought and sold at fluctuating prices as measured in the gold currency, entirely according to the demand and supply in the open market, and in so far as calculations cannot be so exactly made, the work done cannot be carried on with quite so fine margins. Moreover the great markets for silver are in Asia, and the stream runs very steadily in that one direction. The nature of the dealings, therefore, is somewhat modified. Bankers have not so much to do with fluctuating balances of international indebtedness as with regulating a greater or less supply according to the ability of the trade of Asia to afford suitable means of payment for the balance of treasure sent both in gold and silver. A certain process of adjustment goes on between India, China, and other parts, but as England, and indeed Europe generally, owes, under present conditions, almost a constant balance to Asia, this adjustment can only be partial. These conditions of course

cannot be regarded as permanent in any strong sense of the word, though for the present it may be said generally that England supplies manufactures to the bullion producing countries, and with the precious metals so obtained pays the balance due for raw materials drawn from Asia. The "friction" in the way of interest and transit charges is of course much greater. There are differences also in the details of the operations required. Thus the weight of silver required to obtain the rupee current among the millions of India is exactly known, but the price shifts constantly here. The price of gold also as measured in rupees in India is equally variable. In China again, though the weight of the "*tael*" is well known, much of the bullion sent is in Mexican dollars, which bear an uncertain premium, simply as a common measure of value more available, because now better recognised in some of the districts opened to European trade, than the "sycee" silver of local bankers, into which however it is melted down whenever this occasional premium is lost from slackness of demand specially for the coin. The old Spanish imperial dollars are in some parts used as tokens of a tael, though intrinsically worth less than 72 cents of a tael, and have actually been at a premium on the weight of silver which they represented ; only particular coinages being so accepted. Anomalies of the kind are illustrations of the way in which value may be arbitrarily and exceptionally represented under special emergencies ; they are essentially casual and temporary. But weights of metal are the standard to which such tokens are ultimately referable, and notwithstanding such eddies as these, the value of gold and silver respectively, and also their relative values, are worked out according to the world-wide average by banking agency, the extension of which to every considerable centre of traffic throughout the world is as remarkable as any of the industrial developments of recent times.

11. *The Abuses of Credit.*—Throughout the foregoing treatise I have endeavoured to exhibit clearly the essentials of the work of production as well as the machinery by which it is carried on. Where these essential require-

ments are not fulfilled a strain surely falls upon the adjustments by which credit is dispensed, though this strain in the first instance is slight and inappreciable. It is the cumulative effects of a misapplication of capital which result in those crises which periodically occur in the financial world, and no mere change of form can be an adequate remedy for the evil. Nothing is easier than to simulate forms, and nothing tends more than complicated forms to distract the attention from the realities which they should express, but not disguise.

The great financiers who framed the *Bank Act of* 1844 were not altogether free from the traditional delusion which ascribed to the currency a power of regulating and controlling the whole course of commercial and industrial enterprise. It is said that the Act has repeatedly failed. If by this is meant that it has not secured objects of this kind, the charge is no doubt perfectly true. The attempt thus to supersede the necessity for individual forethought and discretion is wholly illusory. But so far as it was reasonably designed to secure the currency, properly so called, from any of the vicissitudes of trade, the principles upon which it was based have been fully justified. The suspension, by the authority of Orders in Council, of the restriction upon its issue have not been required so much for the safety of the Bank itself, as to enable it to render exceptional assistance to trade under circumstances not only wholly abnormal, but, in their very nature, transitory. The relaxation of the letter of the law has been the remedy for a "panic." To expect any law to provide against such a condition as this seems as unreasonable as to call upon a physician to prescribe a regimen adapted both to the requirements of health and the delirium of fever, or the collapse which follows it. The vindication, in fact, of the Bank's exceptional issue on these occasions has been either that the notes were not really required at all, or that they took the place of those which were hoarded under the influence of panic; and it must be remembered that, however unreasonable the cause or the mode of manifestation of a panic may be, the dread of its unreasoned effects is one

z

which those even of the most steadfast judgment are compelled to take into account.

It has, indeed, been contended that Government has no right to suspend the Act, but that its restrictions should under any emergency be rigorously maintained, on the avowed ground that those who have held back their resources ought to reap the advantages of their policy. This argument, however, is in excess of that which the public interests require. There is no administrative Act, not even those relating to the supreme interests of " the liberty of the subject," which may not be suspended on fitting emergency ; though it would be obviously irrational to define beforehand the conditions under which a suspension of the law became necessary.

Dangers of an opposite kind to those which have come under observation might arise if this discretionary power, exercised under the direct responsibility of the Government, could be prohibited. Let us take an extreme case, for every theory ought to stand the test of assumed cases of the utmost stringency, though it may not be able to account for every vagary of individual caprice. A certain class of speculators are ever ready to take advantage of popular excitement when expectations are unduly exaggerated. They are equally ready to make their gain out of exaggerated fears. It is quite within the limits of possibility for a band or " syndicate " of such speculators, at a time when the Bank's reserves were unusually low, and credit had been severely shaken, to operate upon the currency by taking up and hoarding it in amounts which would appear very large in such an emergency, calculating that prices would be so forced down by the panic thus intensified as to enable them to buy securities on their own terms. The Executive Government, acting with due insight into the principles on which the currency is based, could without hesitation counteract such a predatory attack on the general interests of trade, by supplying the deficiency artificially caused. Those who attempted to wreck credit would thus have the tables turned upon them ; not because the issue of notes would directly raise prices, for that it could not do, but the pressure artificially brought to bear would be relieved. Those who had hoarded "money" would have to spend it sooner or later, and come into the market, not on their own terms, but on the best terms they could obtain; and when they did so, the redundant notes would simply be withdrawn, or rather drop out of circulation. No loss to the public need be apprehended in such a case, for the issue would in fact be made merely to supply the natural demand for circulation, not with the view of "regulating the currency" (II. § 14). It is those who attempted thus to disturb it who would find themselves working against the natural laws of supply and demand.

A position not unlike the case supposed is actually brought about during a "panic," though notes may not actually be hoarded. For credit is then in fact locked up. Not only may the timid withdraw their "money" from use altogether, but the usual currency of loans is impeded. Under ordinary circumstances any one with good securities will not take up money upon them until he requires it; but when once a dread of scarcity arises, an exceptional anxiety is felt to secure it beforehand. It may remain in bankers' hands, but unused, for it will be obvious to them that it does not fall within the average balance which, under all ordinary circumstances, they can safely venture to employ. It is "bespoken" specially, though not immediately wanted. Thus, though the amount used is not increased, the loans, being taken for longer periods, will form an unnaturally large aggregate as taken at any one moment.

The Bank of England, as the ultimate resort, is then hardly pressed, not by its own necessities, but to aid those of others; and if the temporary derangement of credit is so great that exceptional relief has to be given, the more distinctly it is then given as exceptional the better, and there is no doubt that its notes do convey in the most absolute form the purchasing power immediately required. If credit were generally degraded, and not merely shaken, a larger amount of coin or substitutes for

it might permanently be required: we should have drifted
back a step towards a semi-barbarous state of mutual
distrust; but there has never yet been any indication of a
calamity of this magnitude. If the knowledge that the
Bank has authority to issue an extraordinary amount of
legal tender notes allays panic, and gives assurance to all
that the system of credit is not to be suffered to break
down, there is no practical use in insisting upon what has
always proved to be the fact, viz., that more notes
are not really required. It is enough to have the assurance that the currency itself really is sound.

Whether the Bank's ultimate reserve is as large as
prudence requires, considering the magnitude of the interests concerned in it, is a question which may fairly be
discussed; so also, whether the Issue and Banking Department might not be altogether separated; the functions of
the former being assumed more directly by the State: or
again, whether any means could be devised by which the
Bank of England, as the central bank for all other bankers,
might command more efficient support from them either
for precautionary or remedial measures. Any such changes
may fairly be urged on their merits, and if better organisation and more perfect co-operation can be brought about,
an unquestionable advantage will be secured. Much may
be done by knowledge and forethought to mitigate the
aberrations of international exchange, and avert an injurious strain upon credit, but only in so far as these
means may tend to bring the inevitable perturbations of
the industrial world more fully within the scope of the
great law of average can they be of any avail.

Many of the fallacies which give rise to exaggerated
expectations at the time of the Bank Act of 1844, as to
its restraining effect upon the course of trade have passed
away in the light of fuller experience; yet still the belief
lingers that the whole monetary condition of the country
may be in some way controlled by regulating the action
of the Bank upon the currency. But no such means can
counteract the effects of a perversion of enterprise or a
waste of capital in adventures which are radically un-

sound : the laws of production will work out their necessary
results. The attempt to provide by anticipation a special
remedy for cases of extreme pressure which may consequently arise, would probably be found to involve far
more serious objections than the relaxations of the law
with the sanction of a Government responsible to the
country.

12. *Panics and Manias.*—It is very well known that
every inflation of prices which has preceded a panic has
been caused by some characteristic delusion. Before 1825
it was joint-stock banks that were to create wealth at will
all over the country. Before 1836 new *El Dorados* had
been found all over the world, only waiting the application of British capital. Ten years later no enthusiasm in
railway enterprise could be injurious, for all the money
was to be spent at home. Before 1857 one very prevailing
delusion had been that, owing to the then recent discoveries
of gold in California and Australia, "money" was always
to be cheap and abundant. Before 1866 one financial
house of very great influence had, for the sake of profits
exceeding the ordinary rate of remuneration, attempted to
prop up numerous undertakings where the capital embarked
had been hopelessly lost (III. § 6), and notably most
flagrantly disregarded the character of the schemes which
they supported. A reckless misapplication of capital
obtained by means which, in mere point of form, were
open to no objection, was the result; and the crises which
followed were little more than an exposure of the true state
of accounts of those who had borrowed largely, accom-
panied by a sharp spasm of dread on the part of lenders
that no one was to be trusted. The revelations of the
Foreign Loans Commission and the recent exposure of the
way in which joint-stock companies, limited, are "promoted," show that we have not been free from such
delusions in more recent times; though this mode of
association is quite well adapted to most forms of enterprise which are fit subjects for joint-stock organisation
at all.

When a superfluous currency was regarded as a proof

of substantial wealth, over-issues of notes no doubt led to
capital being rashly lent, and this again led to reckless
purchases and an undue inflation of prices. It was easier
to blame the banker's note than his want of judgment for
the consequences which ensued. Those who deal only
with the more abstract forms of money are sometimes apt
to lose sight of the essential differences which may be
behind them. They see only the apparently sudden
collapse of credit, and assume that this is the cause of the
disasters which are made manifest. Any question as to
the forms of credit, or any far-fetched reason that ingenuity can invent, is eagerly adopted to avoid facing the
wholesome but unwelcome truth that only that capital
which is faithfully spent in the support of well-directed
labour can yield value in exchange.

A very few words will suffice to show how entirely the
kind of schemes which characterise a speculative mania
lie beyond the true field of commercial credit or industrial
enterprise. Gambling in commodities soon comes to an
end. It is generally founded on some basis of fact that
the value of the thing dealt in is actually enhanced by
scarcity. To buy up and monopolise the whole stock of
any article of consumption is, in these days of rapid communication all over the world, an operation which finds
favour only with the writers of sensational novels.
Traders must follow and not attempt to force the law of
supply and demand, though wildly exaggerated estimates
on the one side or the other may occasionally obtain
credence. But such transactions as these afford little
scope for the spurious financial ingenuity which brings
about a mania. For this it is required that the imagination should be excited with the largest possible expectations,
with the smallest possible necessity for present actual
outlay. From the South Sea scheme and the Mississippi
bubble downwards, this has been the characteristic feature
of all such delusions. The amount required for present
expenditure is comparatively insignificant. The shares
sold at preposterous premiums represent in form the "capi-
talized" value of income to be earned without limit in

future years. (III. § 6.) The usual dispensers of credit
do not support such amazing developments of enterprise,
and are thrown out of the field. Special banks and
" financial " associations are formed to " promote "—what ?
The " floating " of the undertakings, by which is meant
the sale of the shares at a premium. Of course if new
capital can be brought in merely to buy previously existing
shares, prices must . advance. The nominal success is a
mere question of arithmetic, but affords no proof whatever
that any productive work has even been attempted. As
long as the feeling of elation can be kept up there is
literally no limit to the quotations at which shares may be
bought and sold, provided always that the buying and
the selling go on together, so as to be in fact nothing more,
in the aggregate, than mere interchanges, and it is just as
easy to write tens of thousands as hundreds under such
conditions. The whole is in one vicious circle, from which
escape with their unearned gains may be possible for a
few, but anything like a general attempt to sell betrays
the utter baselessness of this fabric of spurious credit.
Indeed the victims are often half conscious of their
position, and the prayer after a while is for only a few
days more of the mania in which each one may hope
to sell out before his neighbour.

All the millions thrown about as premiums on such
occasions may be set down as mere phantasms. It is
a needless exaggeration even to talk of their *loss*. The
industries engaged in supplying the materials for further
"productive" works may be in the first instance so stimulated that prosperity appears to progress by "leaps and
bounds" as long as the period of borrowing lasts. It is
only when the test of ultimate utility comes to be applied
that the chaff is ruthlessly sifted out from the wheat. It
is, materially speaking, very much the same as though the
money had been consciously expended on luxurious superfluities of no permanent value ; but the effect is widely
different, for many of those who are led into extravagance
of the kind are unable to sustain it. Those who have
laid themselves out to supply the wants thus created are

forced at considerable loss to find other means of employment, and the social dislocation which ensues entails many
aggravated evils. Nevertheless, though many individuals
may be hopelessly ruined, it is hardly possible to anticipate the national income of future years for unproductive
schemes. Some may be hampered by long-reaching obligations, such as arise from the "calls" made on shares for
railway construction, or future instalments on loans; but so
far as the general fund of substantive capital is concerned,
this is a transfer only which cannot directly diminish the
amount available for use. An infinity of waste and misery
is often caused, not from any real want of capital, but
partly from an inane attempt to save that which is lost
beyond all hope of redemption, and still more from a want
of discrimination between the fair risks inseparable from
all enterprise, and the ruin which has inevitably followed
the most preposterous imitations of it.

There are different ways and degrees, even during a time
of speculative excitement, in which undertakings may be
unsound. A design may be fairly planned, and adequate
provision made for working it, except that the capital
provided is not sufficient for its completion. The shareholders of a concern in this position have rashly placed
themselves at the mercy of lenders in no way pledged to
adopt their undertaking, and come into the loan market
with only half-finished work at a great disadvantage, especially when over-credulity may have been followed by
undue suspicion and timidity. A scheme so devised is
financially unsound, even though it have in it elements
which might ensure success if fairly worked out. Some
again are utterly rotten. Got up perhaps to buy some
land, or mine, or concession from some promoter, and
with borrowing powers moreover, so that the small value
secured goes as the only asset to some special creditor.
Between these come many schemes not irrational in themselves, but altogether overweighted. Many a design might
perhaps do very well with a moderate capital and a good
working staff. But it is charged with some outrageous
addition to the capital really required for promoters, who

"rig the market" so as to get shares sold at a premium—
not for the benefit of the undertaking, but for the gain of
those who abandon it. Then there will be a Board of
Directors and officials enough to swamp double the profit
that would satisfy a competent executive. This was the
type of a large number of the joint-stock companies,
limited, which were brought out a few years ago, many of
them apparently feasible enough if there had ever been
any honest intention of giving the workers fair play. But
a good scheme in such times is a thing to sell; the work is
a matter of ignoble detail for any one to attend to afterwards.
The collapse of such credit as this is an unmitigated gain,
though it may come in the guise of a newly discovered
loss, and though it may take some little time to readjust
the conditions of working industry which have been thus
disturbed. Aberrations of this kind on a large scale are
a serious calamity, especially when, as has recently been
the case, not only different sections of the community but
different nations have entered into rivalry in a reckless
spirit which has disregarded all the fundamental laws
which govern the creation of value. Still the great stream
of commerce and industry flows on with wonderful little
disturbance from causes which attract so much casual
attention, though there can be no doubt that our progress
not merely in wealth but in the due diffusion of it, which
is of quite as much importance to the well-being of the
body politic, is materially checked by such perversions of
our resources. As far as the limits of the present question
are concerned, we come back to the old very plain and
wholesome truth, that, while the forms and machinery of
credit are an inestimable convenience and economy they
cannot in any way determine the nature of the work
which can be done by their means. Security and prosperity can only be found by looking behind them to the
uses to which capital is effectually applied.

APPENDIX II.

THE DEPRECIATION OF SILVER AND THE INDIAN CURRENCY.

THE recent fall in the relative value of silver is so marked an event in the history of the precious metals, and is of so much importance to our Indian Empire, that the subject seems to call for some further notice in detail. My remarks will be confined chiefly to the application of those principles which have already been discussed, with reference both to some of the extreme opinions held as to the effects of this perturbation, and also to the artificial means proposed, in some quarters, to counteract the natural adjustment of the relative value of gold and silver as measured each by the other.

1. *Changes in the relative value of silver are no new phenomena.*—It will have been observed that such changes are nothing new in the course of events since the discovery of the New World; though, since the early part of the eighteenth century, the proportion maintained both in Europe and America has varied only within comparatively narrow limits. Asia has followed rather more tardily; and, as has been noticed, Adam Smith stated that the ratio of twelve parts silver to one gold, subsisted even in his time in China. Their experience of a fall in the value of the former—or at all events of a change in the relative value of the two metals—must therefore be much more recent than our own. American treasure has certainly for many years past, found its way through Europe to Asia in a continuous

stream both round the Cape of Good Hope, by the way of
the Levant, and over the Siberian frontier. Baron Humboldt
estimated the amount early in the century at fully equal
to £5,000,000 sterling. The precious metals now bear,
practically speaking, the same relative value throughout
the civilised world.

2. *The total stock or present supply of gold and silver
throughout the world cannot be estimated.*—I shall only
enter very cursorily upon the question of the various
estimates of former supply; partly because these, however
carefully made, were necessarily founded on very imperfect
data, and further and chiefly, because the conditions of
commerce throughout the world, and of the industries
more or less directly connected with it, have changed so
rapidly that we are only now beginning to test by experience the quantity that can be utilised, either as coin,
or as bullion held for international traffic. Exact sources
of information are so utterly wanting as regards oriental
stock or production, now or at any former times, that it
seems almost an aberration of statistical ingenuity to
attempt to reduce estimates to exact figures on such a
question, and present a total which shall fairly represent
the aggregate which is in reality affected by the changes
now in progress. Although abating somewhat of the show
of precision, we shall in reality be dealing far more strictly
with facts, by confining ourselves to the experience afforded
by the effect of operations comparatively well known on
this vast but indefinite aggregate ; and shall be better able
to infer its extent from the examination of these effects
than from any elaborate compilation of statistics which
must be extremely imperfect, and cannot possibly be
verified.

It is difficult to determine the order in which the many
causes bearing upon this very complicated question may
best be considered. I shall refer first to the changes
during comparatively recent times in two important
currencies. Next to natural changes affecting the sup-

ply of the two precious metals severally, and to the exceptional requirements of trade which gave occasion for an unusually large export of bullion to Asia within that period. Then, to the reaction which eventually followed a prolonged period of abnormal excitement, especially in Oriental trade, aggravated by further changes affecting the production and marketable supply of silver. And lastly, I shall again refer to the causes which must tend to dissipate and to mitigate the effect of such changes on the exchange value of the precious metals.

3. *Changes in the currencies of the United States and of France.*—In the early days of the Republic a gold dollar was legally current in the United States of America at fifteen times the value of the silver dollar of the same weight and proportion of fineness—viz., 416 grains troy nine-tenths pure, being the same as the old Spanish dollar; but the value of gold in the open markets of the world being somewhat above this proportion, it inevitably flowed out, leaving the silver, which thus became practically the sole currency. In 1837 the weight of the silver dollar was reduced to 412½ grains, and the gold equivalent of it fixed at 25·8 grains of the same standard of purity, being in the proportion of very nearly 16 parts [15·988] silver to 1 gold. The gold coins were struck of multiples of this unit :—5, 10 dollars, &c. as convenience dictated, but these proportions were the bases of the standard currency. The rate thus fixed for silver is expressed in British standard at 4s. 11d. per oz. (nearly) : a price sufficiently below that which ruled in the open market to encourage the export, while yet the difference was not so great as to prevent the more convenient gold coin from being received readily into the home currency as a fair equivalent. Under these conditions the outflow of silver was, under then existing circumstances, so large and continuous that by an Act passed Feb. 21, 1853, the coinage of it could be restricted to the fractional parts of a nominal dollar of 384 grains ; (legal tender to the extent of $5 only), to be used merely as a token currency representing aliquot parts of the gold standard coin ; and, practically, a gold standard was fully

established long before 1861, when the outbreak of war led to the suspension of cash payments altogether.

In France the ratio of 1 part gold·to 15½ silver had been formally established by law since A.D. 1803. This, as expressed in British standard, gives a price of 5/0 ⅞ per oz. nearly; and as long as the price in the general market remained under this rate, the old silver five franc piece of 25 grammes weight $\frac{9}{10}$ pure (or in English terms, 385·808 grains troy 6 W.) was practically the standard coin of the country. And even though some large portion of the £14,000,000 of gold rejected by Holland on their adoption of a silver standard in A.D. 1847-9 was recoined in France, no movement of importance took place in French silver till 1853, when the price in the open market rose to about one per cent. over the equivalent fixed by law. A steady outflow then commenced, stimulated from time to time by a higher rate of difference, but continued also on even a narrower margin, until by A.D. 1856 the great bulk of full weight five franc pieces in circulation had been drawn out and "napoleons" substituted for them, weighing 6·457 grammes $\frac{9}{10}$ pure (99·561 grs. troy 1⅜ W.) being in the same ratio of 1 gold to 15½ parts silver; only, the former being the cheaper metal for the time, was established in the currency. So much so, that by a convention finally published in that year between the different countries of the "Latin Union" (viz. France, Belgium, Italy, and Switzerland) which then formerly adopted the same system of coinage, the issue of silver was restricted to "tokens" of a lower standard (viz. ·835 instead of ·900 parts pure) in limited amounts to be determined by convention. The total value of the French currency thus influenced was estimated at £340 millions. It by no means follows that any such vast amount was moved, but the change from a silver to a gold basis was fully effected. Taking this range of about thirty years, these operations were carried out at ratios varying in the open market from rather less than 16 parts to rather more than 15 parts silver, to 1 of gold; leaving the ratio in 1866 and for a few years afterwards at about 15½ to 1.

The subjoined table gives the price of British bar silver corresponding with the equivalents of gold and silver assumed in various proportions. These figures afford a means of comparison expressed in the most familiar terms, and may be useful for reference. A higher price than that set opposite to the equivalent would indicate that silver is worth more in the general market, and preferable, therefore, whenever there is an export demand for the precious metals. A lower quotation would of course indicate a similar advantage to be gained by exporting gold. The *differences* shown by comparison between these fixed rates and those ruling at any time in the open market, are of the kind referred to previously (II. §31 IV. §16, App. I. 80), and give the measure of the motive power which tends to overcome the friction opposed to any change. I append further the London quotations of silver since 1833:—

NOTE I.

Gold. Silver.	Brt. Std. per oz.	Gold. Silver.	Brt. Std. per oz.	Gold. Silver.	Brt. Std. per oz.
1 to 10 =	7/10·³	1 to 15 =	5/2·⁶⁶	1 to 18 =	4/4·³⁹
1 „ 11 =	7/1·⁷³	1 „ 15½ =	5/0·⁸⁴	1 „ 18½ =	4/2·⁹⁷
1 „ 12 =	6/6·⁵⁸	1 „ 16 =	4/10·⁹⁵	1 „ 19 =	4/1·⁶³
1 „ 13 =	6/0·⁵³	1 „ 16½ =	4/9·¹⁵	1 „ 19½ =	4/0·³⁶
1 „ 14 =	5/7·³⁶	1 „ 17 =	4/7·⁴⁷	1 „ 20 =	3/11·¹⁵
		1 „ 17½ =	4/5·⁸⁹		

Highest price touched in March
and July, 1859 ... ... $5/2\frac{3}{4}$ = 1 gold to 15·028 silver.
Lowest price touched in July,
1876 ... ... $3/10\frac{3}{4}$ = 1 gold to 20·17 silver.

The shillings and pence represent, of course, only fractional parts of the British sovereign : thus 5 shillings = 60 pence = $\frac{60}{240}$ or $\frac{1}{4}$ of a £ sterling. It must be remembered that the British standard for silver is 222 dwts. fine in the pound troy of 240 dwts., while the British standard for gold is 22 carats or $\frac{22}{24}$ths = $\frac{11}{12}$ths fine. As alloy is eliminated, as of no value, in bullion, the result is that though the quotation of both is given per oz. troy of 480 grns., in reality 444 grns. of pure silver are quoted as against 440 grains pure gold. A correction has been made accordingly, giving the price which would have to be paid for the proportionate weight indicated of silver of the same purity as the gold.

4. *Natural changes affecting the supply, and the general uses of gold and silver.*—The first point that strikes attention here is the substitution to a very large extent of gold for silver in the currencies of Europe and America. Whence came the available supply? Baron Humboldt estimated the produce of South America at the beginning of the century at £9½ to £10 millions worth, and that of Europe, including Western Siberia, at one million more; which aggregate was increased by some two or three millions up to A.D. 1809 when the revolt of the Spanish American colonies threw all mining operations there into confusion, but the yield after a while seems to have been maintained in all at about ten to twelve millions of pounds worth: the total value of the silver being at the least three times that of the gold produced. The great extension of gold mining in Russia (Western Siberia) first disturbed this balance,

NOTE II.

London Quotations of Bar Silver per Oz. Standard, taken from the Returns of Messrs Pixley & Abell.

A.D.	Ann. Avrge. Pence per oz.	A.D.	Ann. Avrge. Pence per oz.	A.D.	Ann. avrge. Pence per oz.
1833	59 $\frac{3}{16}$	1848	59 $\frac{1}{2}$	1863	61 $\frac{3}{8}$
1834	59 $\frac{15}{16}$	1849	59 $\frac{3}{4}$	1864	61 $\frac{3}{8}$
1835	59 $\frac{11}{16}$	1850	60 $\frac{1}{16}$	1865	61 $\frac{1}{16}$
1836	60	1851	61	1866	61 $\frac{1}{8}$
1837	59 $\frac{9}{16}$	1852	60 $\frac{1}{2}$	1867	60 $\frac{9}{16}$
1838	59 $\frac{1}{2}$	1853	61 $\frac{1}{4}$	1868	60 $\frac{1}{2}$
1839	60 $\frac{3}{8}$	1854	61 $\frac{1}{4}$	1869	60 $\frac{7}{16}$
1840	60 $\frac{3}{8}$	1855	61 $\frac{5}{16}$	1870	60 $\frac{9}{16}$
1841	60 $\frac{1}{16}$	1856	61 $\frac{5}{16}$	1871	60 $\frac{1}{2}$
1842	59 $\frac{7}{16}$	1857	61 $\frac{3}{4}$	1872	60 $\frac{5}{16}$
1843	59 $\frac{3}{16}$	1858	61 $\frac{1}{16}$	1873	59 $\frac{1}{4}$
1844	59 $\frac{1}{2}$	1859	62 $\frac{1}{16}$	1874	58 $\frac{5}{16}$
1845	59 $\frac{1}{4}$	1860	61 $\frac{11}{16}$	1875	56 $\frac{7}{8}$
1846	59 $\frac{5}{16}$	1861	60 $\frac{13}{16}$	1876	52 $\frac{1}{4}$
1847	5$\frac{11}{16}$	1862	61 $\frac{7}{16}$	1877	54 $\frac{13}{16}$

N.B.—These quotations are given as they are made in the London Bullion Market, for British standard silver 222 dwts. fine.

the value having been increased from a very small amount in A.D. 1820 to over £3,000,000 worth in A.D. 1848. Then came the discoveries in California yielding at first £10 to 12 millions, followed in 1851 by those in Australia giving even larger results, though the outturn from these two latter sources has now declined to within £14,000,000 together. Still the aggregate supply from what may be termed new sources was very largely increased, while the proportion of gold to silver was reversed; the estimated total value of the former being at least twice that of the latter. These figures, however, do not afford any measure of the total production, or still less of the total stock of the precious metals throughout the world open to civilized commerce. There is no reason to suppose that the sources of supply in Asia have failed, Africa also has always exported gold from both its Eastern and Western coasts. The old civilisations in the East have yielded both gold and silver from time immemorial, and, when their numbers and prosperity were comparatively great, must have accumulated vast stores of metallic wealth which, according to changing circumstances, will, to a greater or less degree, be set free for general uses. Asia is evidently able to receive some large portion of our supply, but we cannot tell what proportion this bears to its total requirements, or to its capacity to take up the precious metals; so that this known quantity affords no basis on which to estimate, with any degree of accuracy, the effect of any future excess or falling off of Western supply on the nations of the East. I refer specially only to those sources which from our point of view in Europe are not only best known, but have been made most directly available for effecting the changes referred to.[1]

There is shown, thus far, a larger supply of gold and a more general use for it. Some high authorities have been of opinion that this supply had led to a reduction in value. So far as this were the case a proportionate increase in the

[1] Some of our best statists have too frequently fallen into the error of heading their tables as of supply "from all the world;" whereas, on examination, they are found to embrace only those sources regarding which specific returns can be obtained.

weight of bullion used in the circulation might be assumed,
but it is by no means a settled point, whether this alleged
fall in value has been permanent: certainly up to 1873
whatever fall there was affected both metals in very nearly
equal degree. Beyond this the rapid increase of population and of industry, both in Europe and in the United
States of America, especially of late years, has led to a
great increase in the power to hold metallic money, both
individually and for the purposes of international commerce. But whatever the growing want thus created may
have been, it was more than amply satisfied by the supply
from Russia, California, and Australia.

It should be noticed however that the operations in the
United States and in France were not altogether contemporaneous, and thus when the former resorted to a paper
currency in 1861, the gold set free was certainly available
to supply the continued demand of the latter. But too
much weight must not be given to this consideration, for
its relative value was independently supported by demand
from Asia, and moreover very great progress had been made
in the French operations before that date. The shipments
of gold to the East from Great Britain and the Mediterranean ports which were about £5,500,000 for the five
years ending 1860, amounted to fully £25,500,000 during
the five subsequent years. Though this does not prove
that the supply would have been enough for the wants
both of the United States and France within the period
referred to ending in 1866, it certainly affords reason to
suppose that, at the most, a few years' further production
would have made good the deficiency.

We have before us, however, not merely the extension of
the aggregate currency, but, to a large extent, the substitution of gold for silver, first in the United States of
America, and afterwards in Europe. Every factor in the
equation must tell in the adjustment definitely expressed,
whether familiarly, as the price of silver, or more precisely,
as the ratio which one metal bears to the other. So we
have not only to consider how the gold was obtained, and
what was done with it, but also how silver was extruded,

A A

and extruded so rapidly with so little change in the relative value of the two metals.

5. *Considerations which govern the Transport of Coin or Bullion from one Country to Another.*—Two essentially different considerations have to be held distinctly in mind. 1st, the capacity of a country to receive and retain the precious metals either as bullion or coin ; and 2nd, the means of effecting an exchange of them, at any one time, for value in some other form which can replace the cost of them to the sender, wherever he may require it, in some other country. In every trade it is essential to "find returns," and though these may be made in the form of Bills of Exchange, that only generalises the difficulty, but does nothing to remove it. For these bills must be based on value sent in substantive form directly or indirectly from the country where they are drawn to that in which they are made payable. The subject is often discussed as though bullion would find its own way to the place where it was wanted—a one-sided way of talking, which is very apt to lead to begging the most important part of the question, though there is a very large measure of practical truth in the doctrine that such interchanges are self-adjusting in the sense that they are best and most safely worked out by the unrestricted exertions of those concerned in them.

These two considerations are indeed very closely related. The ability of any country to receive the precious metals without relative depreciation of their value must ultimately govern the transmission to it of bullion ; but the more immediately pressing question will generally be—as in the present case—How to effect its introduction—or in other words, How to get payment for it both promptly and suitably. The chief markets for silver are in Asia, which comprises much the greater part of the population of the world, and, speaking generally, is moreover at a stage of civilisation in which metallic money, coined or uncoined, is far more largely used and hoarded in proportion to the industry supported than in communities where industry is more highly organised. A long course of comparative peace and security has led, especially in India and the regions about

the Malacca Straits, to a great increase in numbers and
in commercial activity.   The suppression of piracy in these
Eastern Seas has been an incalculable gain to humanity.
Imperfect and partial as these advantages are, they are yet
of such a kind that their effects have tended, and will
tend to grow with measured, though accumulating rapidity,
and the power both to pay for and to hold money for
domestic uses is but one sign of a dawning prosperity
which we have good reason to believe is well assured.

6. *Eceptional Causes of Demand for Asiatic Products in
Europe since* 1848.—Over and above these, there have been
a succession of temporary and exceptional causes which
have adventitiously stimulated the demand for Asiatic
produce in Europe since the great discoveries of gold in
1848, and it must be kept in mind that the movement
of an unusually large amount of metallic money does not
so much imply an extended traffic, as a large balance of
value arising over and above the ordinary adjustments
of commerce.

These causes may be summarised in a very few words :
trade with Asia generally had been extended since that
date, with much vigour and success, even before the war
with Russia in 1854 and the interruption of the Black
Sea trade gave a very appreciable stimulus to the effectual
demand for various Eastern products.   In 1855 a far
greater disturbing cause arose from the failure of the
silk crop throughout Europe, throwing a demand upon
China Japan, and India which, for a succession of years
represented an annual value which cannot be taken at less
than £8 to £10 millions.   Then in 1861 came the " cotton
famine " consequent on the war in the United States, the
incidents of which are so recent and so well known that it
is needless to refer to them at length.   One point however
may be noted : the enhanced cost of cotton manufactures
sent to all ports in Asia made a large set-off against cotton
sent from some parts only, while, as the export of silk
manufactures is a mere trifle, the greatly increased quantity
and cost of raw silk was a clear addition to the account
against Europe.   These are only the chief items of a

A A 2

generally expanding trade, which stood out as in excess
of the ordinary value of exports from the East.

7. *The Consequent Movements of Bullion.*—The movements in the precious metals to the East are set forth
in the subjoined note, which it will be seen shows a
considerable positive increase in the export of the precious
metals even after these exceptional causes had ceased to
operate.[1] Looking back for thirty years before 1870, we
have first the outflow of *silver* from the United States of
America, caused by its valuation—as measured in gold
in their coinage—at a lower proportionate rate than that
which ruled in the general market. The difference was
very slight, and not sufficient to put any strain upon the
movements of bullion. It led merely to the retention of
a larger portion of gold in the new world, while silver
passed on in no larger proportion than was required for
current use in the old. The small operation in Holland
in 1847 and 1848, above referred to, had no appreciable
effect on price, but the depreciation of gold, then very generally anticipated, probably influenced the first rise in the
quotations of *silver* in 1849 and 1850 ; but it was not till
1855 that any unusual movement took place in the metal
itself. That year £9 millions were sent out to the East

[1] NOTE III.

*Table showing the Export of Bullion from Great Britain and
Ports in the Mediterranean to the East.*

FROM THE TABLE OF THE ANNUAL SHIFMENTS GIVEN IN THE CIRCULAR OF
MR. G. DE QUETTEVILLE, OF LONDON.

	Gold. £	Ann. Avge. £	Silver. £	Ann Avge. £	Total. £	Ann. Avge. £
1851–1855	4,500,000	900,000	23,000,000	4,600,000	27,500,000	5,500,000
1856–1860	4,706,000	940,000	67,001,000	13,400,000	71,707,000	14,340,000
1861–1865	24,166,000	4,833,000	65,197,000	13,040,000	89,363,000	17,873,000
1866–1870	15,618,000	3,124,000	21,471,000	4,294,000	37,089,000	7,418,000
1871–1875	13,477,000	2,695,000	26,220,000	5,244,000	39,697,000	7,939,000

	Gold.	Silver.	Total.
1876 (1 year)	£3,213,000	£11,096,000	£14,309,000
1877 ,,	3,131,000	16,861,000	19,992,000

The shipments to Egypt are included in these returns, but are not of sufficient amount to affect the general conclusions indicated. There also have
been direct shipments for some years past to China from San Francisco,
which, during 1877, are reported as amounting to about £3,000,000.

from Great Britain and ports in the Mediterranean, followed by an annual export averaging over £13 millions for the ten following years. In 1857 the export was over £20 millions, mostly to China, in payment for silk. In 1858, after the commercial crisis in the preceding year, it fell to within £6 millions, rising again to £16 millions in 1859. In 1861 also the amount fell under £9 millions, but it. rose to £14½, £15, and £17 millions respectively during the three following years of great excitement in the cotton market. In the five years 1862–6, more silver was shipped from Mediterranean ports, chiefly Marseilles, than from London, but it is impossible to say from what quarter the supply was actually drawn. This much is certain, a large balance of gold was retained by France in exchange for silver taken to satisfy a very urgent demand for the East. But it must be remembered that though silver was chiefly taken, gold also, especially since 1861, was accepted in India to a very large extent, though as having no place in the Indian coinage, it was at an unnatural disadvantage. This point will be referred to hereafter.

8. *Exaggerated Enhancement of Prices.*—Looking merely to the quotations of bullion, a superabundant supply apparently made it very easy to make good the deficiency caused by two great failures of natural production; but it may be doubted whether this great facility was any real advantage to those concerned in affording, or in taking, the substituted supply. An urgency of demand totally unchecked by any scarcity of metallic money on the one side, led to an exaggerated inflation of prices on the other. Silk rose to two or three times, and cotton to even four or five times its normal cost, while doubled prices would probably have equally given all the stimulus that could have any effect upon production, without requiring so violent a readjustment of money values in all industries connected with or dependent upon these products. Many drawbacks and comparatively few permanent advantages attend so sudden an influx of " money." Not that this country at all events need grudge the treasure paid to our great dependency, but India during this epoch affords a

strong illustration of the difficulty of usefully employing
wealth in this form so suddenly acquired. Taking the
capital of Western India as an example ; its prosperity
was rapidly advancing before the extreme advance of
prices: its progress since then has successfully continued.
But that period of inflation was marked by a " mania,"
unprecedented in the extent of its waste, folly, and demoralisation, and in the prostration of all healthy energy
which followed the ultimate collapse.

However, as far as the present argument is concerned,
the fact remains that inordinately high prices paid for
silk and cotton, relieved Europe of a superfluity of silver
in a most exceptional manner and to a very large extent.

9. *Cost of Transit as affecting the Relative Values of
Gold and Silver.*—Some points of detail are of so much
importance in reading the indications afforded by movements of the precious metals, that I must again invite
careful attention to them. It has been already shown
(IV. 16) how the charges for transmitting bullion are
counterbalanced by fluctuations above or below the " par "
of exchange, in other words, how they are indirectly
thrown on the general cost, as expressed in Bills of
Exchange, of the commodities for which it is required to
provide payment. If gold and silver are of the same
relative value in two different countries respectively, there
is evidently no inducement to send one more than the
other, but the very slightest difference in these relative
values will influence the preference for one rather than
the other, if there be independently a demand sufficient
to move the metals at all. If we suppose the cost of
transit to be 2 per cent. and the two to be circulating side
by side, say in the proportion of 1 gold to 15½ silver, but
the latter to bear a value of 1 per cent. higher (corresponding to less weight, or 1 to 15·345) at the place of
destination, it would flow out at just half the relative
cost to the exporter. The "gradient of friction" is
already half overcome by the inequality in the relative
values : the favoured metal only would be sent away, when
value was required in this form, but not otherwise. If

the transit charges on gold as the more portable metal
were slightly lower than those on silver it would move
more readily either way. Its "friction" being less, it
could be more cheaply used at any time. It might thus
be in better demand and become relatively dearer. But
this element of value would tell generally in all places,
and it must not be supposed that transit charges or a
difference in transit charges could effect the equivalents
in any one locality only;- international adjustments are
made on the weights of metal actually transmitted. Even
at the cost of transit assumed above, no difference less
than 4 per cent. could cause a movement of the precious
metals without the counter-transmission of a corresponding value in some other form, but when this difference is
attained the two metals will independently be exchanged
the one against the other. Thus, if 17 parts of silver can
be bought here for 1 part of gold and the former sent to
Asia where the equivalents were 16 to 1, it is clear that
the silver could there buy 1·065 part or 6¼ per cent. more
gold. This is more than enough to pay for all the costs
of transit both ways, and an exchange under ordinary
circumstances might be effected at much less than this
difference. It follows, therefore, that the relative values
of gold and silver cannot diverge, except within such
comparatively narrow limits, in any part of the world
open to civilised commerce, without inducing a movement
by which any greater inequality will be reduced by a
process of direct interchange, and consequently any great
change in the relative value of either metal must be
distributed generally without reference to the ordinary
balance of trade in commodities.

The rates quoted in Notes I. and II. do not indicate a
difference between the market and legally fixed relative
values large enough to have moved silver from France to so
distant a destination as India or China, much less to have
moved silver in one direction and gold to pay for it in the
other; but the motive power which caused its transmission
was altogether external to the currency affected. France
had no active part to take. A great stream of bullion was

drawn through the country, and an extremely small difference in value caused gold to be dropped and silver to be taken up. All the costs were borne by the trade, and fell indirectly on the consumers of silk, cotton, and other Asiatic produce.

10. *Commercial Excitement and Consequent Reaction since 1870.*—Let us now again take up the question in 1870. The price of silver was at or slightly under the ratio of $15\frac{1}{2}$ to 1 gold. The outflow of bullion to the East continued on a scale which would have been considered large twenty years previously, gold. however forming a larger proportion of the export than at that time. 'The next great event is the Franco-German war, and the payment of the indemnity of £220 millions to Germany. Glancing merely at economic results, we perceive a great natural rebound of industrial activity after the two great wars in Europe and America, followed by an immense amount of spurious and ill-directed enterprise, which, even more than over-extended efforts, leads to disastrous reaction. England had its share of this perversion of energy, while Germany, flushed with its newly acquired wealth, and aided by nearly a hundred new banks and "Credit" Companies, was pre-eminently distinguished by its attempts to force trade in all directions, without the least recognition of the law that value must depend on a rational adjustment of supply to demand. I need refer specially only to the incidents which more directly influenced Eastern commerce. The great improvements in telegraphy and the opening of the Suez Canal made it easy for any merchant, with the same capital as he had before employed, to carry out a far larger aggregate of transactions in any given time. There was no sound reason whatever for more "distributors" rushing into a business which could have been very greatly extended without the application of any fresh means to it. But this was not the popular notion. If the Suez Canal could have irrigated every parched field in India and restored all the ravages of rebellion in China, it would hardly have sufficed to justify the expectations which induced competitors of all nations to rush into a field

fondly imagined to be new, only because it was opened
to them in a new and more efficient manner. Disappointment was sure to follow, and it fell at last not
only on us, but with even more severity upon our
German and other competitors. The general balances
of trade were still decidedly in favour of the East: the
export of bullion was nearly £10½ millions in 1874, but
casually declined to little over £5½ millions in the following year, with trade generally carried on at unre-
munerative rates, and with the spirit of enterprise
much rebuked by continued want of success.

11. *Introduction of a Gold Currency into Germany, and
Consequent Increased Supply of Silver.*—Germany had for
long desired to establish its currency on a gold basis,
and the large sum received as indemnity money no
doubt induced it to enter immediately on the attempt.
In adopting the ratio of 1 gold to 15½ silver—only
formally retained by the Latin Union—without reference
to the value in the markets opened to all the world,
it started with a "gradient" against the movement it
desired to effect. Had the American equivalents (1 to 16)
been adopted, some portion of the silver discharged might
at first have been taken out by the innumerable channels
of trade, and the task of the Government so far lightened;
as it was every ounce has had to be driven out from the
very first, as it were, with a force-pump.

Holland meantime adopting as equivalent 1 to 15·65,
giving a higher relative value by 1 per cent. for the gold
it wished to secure, reversed, or rather began to attempt to
reverse, its policy of A.D. 1847 to 1849, but seems to have
coined only about £4,000,000 worth on its proposed new
standard. `

The total currency of Germany was comparatively small,
probably not more than a third of that of France, but no
happy course of events aided their task of getting rid of
their superabundant silver, and the inevitable delays in
carrying out a scheme thus worked only brought them on
worse times than ever for such an operation. For in 1876
reports were received of the great success of an extension

of a well-known mine (the Comstock), and of mining enterprises generally in Nevada, to which reference has
already been made (II. 28). It had long been a matter of
general notoriety that these regions in the far West of
America were rich in silver, and the fact was not at first
appreciated that these last new discoveries added also
largely to the yield of gold. There was therefore a large
supply, not merely available if demanded, but which it was
supposed would be pressed upon the market. Prices had
been falling steadily, and by the end of 1875 had reached
about the ratio of $16\frac{3}{4}$ to 1 (4s. 8d. to 4s. $8\frac{1}{2}d.$ per oz.
Br. Std.), and an attempt, or a supposed intention of an
attempt, on the part of Germany to force sales led to a
sharp panic in July, 1876, when silver touched the lowest
price yet known, of 3s. $10\frac{3}{4}d.$ per oz., or a proportion of
20·17 to 1 gold. It rallied, however, shortly afterwards,
and after some fluctuations has settled for a while at about
$17\frac{1}{2}$ silver to 1 gold.

12. *The Practical Lesson enforced by the " Scare " in Silver
in* 1876.—This scare has probably brought home a very useful lesson more effectually than it could have been taught in
any other way. For it has demonstrated to all concerned
the utter futility of the attempt to force transactions in
bullion in excess of the existing balance of value which
could be returned in exchange for it. Practically the run
was on the rate of exchange in India. There was a run
upon bills and any other means of immediately sending
home value, but it was the fall in exchange which forced
down silver, not a natural fall of silver which forced down
exchange. There was much lax discussion on the subject,
and the two very different issues above referred to (§ 5)
were generally confounded together. But in reality nothing
of any permanent consequence, one way or the other, could
be inferred from the results of operations carried out in so
reckless a manner. If Europe could not ·afford to take
cotton at famine prices, neither could India afford any other
means of paying immediately for silver : this was the chief,
though not the sole, cause of the rapid decline, and even
setting aside the ˙extreme rates which were the˙ palpable

result of a panic, there is little doubt that an undue urgency anticipated and exaggerated the relative depreciation which would have been enforced by the normal operation of any natural causes then known to exist.

The balances due in bullion by England to India had indeed been decreased in other ways than by the course of trade. India had borrowed largely in England, getting money there on easier terms; and various charges to be met in England out of Indian revenues had increased from £6 millions to £16 millions annually. Whether the government sells bills on India, or buys bills drawn there on this country is a mere matter of detail as to the best way in which substantive value can be transferred. The only point to be decided is whether, all things considered, the country which pays will be served on better terms by paying in England, where money is superabundant, or in India, where it is comparatively scarce. It is not the place here to discuss whether due economy is exercised in Indian expenditure, but this much may be said: it is assuredly no part of sound policy to adjust the financial arrangements of the country with a view to making a market there for bullion. On the contrary, the better tendency of trade is that it should consist of the mutual interchange of utilities rather than that heavy payments should be habitually made in dead bullion.

13. *No apparent Reason to anticipate Failure in Asiatic Demand.*—These considerations are in a totally different range from those involved in the supposition that Asia was saturated with silver, and had lost the power to absorb it. The sign of such a condition would be a general rise of the money prices of commodities, and a consequent falling off of exports from, and increase of imports into, the country affected. Nothing of the kind has as yet been discerned in India. The falling off in the export is only shown by comparison with periods when the European demand was exceptionally stimulated. The special causes which consecutively led to this enhancement of prices both in India and in China did indeed last for so long a time that general trade had become adjusted to them.

It was natural enough that a change should create some
alarm, but a very little investigation shows the nature of
it. There is no reason to conclude that Asia will take
less bullion than was supposed, only a little more patience
and discretion must be exercised in introducing the
supply; bearing in mind always that, though silver is the
sole legal currency in India, and practically the common
measure of value in Asia generally, gold is largely used in
traffic, and its relative value perfectly well known and
appreciated.

It may be said that the mode in which operations are
carried out does not affect the amounts dealt with, and
that the equation of value must depend upon the relative
quantities of metal and the demand for them as money.
But the truth that there is in this remark is not to the
point. It will not affect the ideal *mean* to which the adjustments of supply and demand must tend, but it does very
greatly affect the steps by which this mean is attained.

Bullion wrongly placed and forced for sale may go for
a time as much below its normal value as any other
commodity, recovering perhaps with a violent fluctuation,
which is an extension of the first evil; and aberrations of
this kind do far more to derange the course of industry
than any change brought about in the natural course of
events.

There has been no difficulty or sign of any difficulty in
making payments in silver, and all accounts from the
interior of India, of which we do know something, agree
in stating that no rise in general prices followed the fall
in silver. Those articles which were suited for export of
course responded at once to the movement in Exchange.
Every dealer in the country knows how the rate for bills
affects prices as well as every changing quotation in the
markets which concern him. All he sees and all he cares
for is that he gets more money for his produce. He will
not trouble himself as to how that desired result has been
brought about, but his keen wits know perfectly well the
immediate conditions which affect his bargain. But except
in so far as prices were governed directly by European

markets there was no reason why there should be any change, and none in fact took place.

14. *Natural Mitigations of a Decline in the Value of Metallic Money.*—The currency certainly could not become redundant from a falling off in the supply of silver, and we may safely infer the same conditions in China and elsewhere. Silver, being cheaper to us, enabled us to offer better terms for all exports, and this has certainly not been counteracted by any general rise in local prices. Speaking roughly, the fall in exchange has been a premium of 10 per cent. in their favour, which no doubt has acted directly to the same extent as a discount against imports, with the apparently satisfactory result, in India, that the inducement on the one side has had a decidedly more marked effect than the discouragement on the other. Shipments have largely increased of products first brought within the range of European demand by this change in the measure of relative value. For this general rise, as it would appear to be from this side, though in fact limited to articles suited for export, had a much more searching and widely-spread effect than that previously induced by demand for some few particular commodities only. Wheat especially promises to become a staple article of trade, nor is it merely drawn out from native stores, but a new branch of industry has been created in many places which it may be hoped will gain strength enough to stand any future adverse changes in the market, and we may be sure that the growers themselves are getting some of the first benefits of the change.

Considered by itself, the normal effects of such a stimulus to the import of bullion would be an increased supply, continued until the aggregate increased quantity led to diminished value, or "purchasing power," shown by generally enhanced prices (I. 22). So that before the advantage gained by such a fall could be wholly lost to the producers the whole quantity of the currency must be increased in the inverse ratio of its total fall in value. Further, over and above all other causes which may enable India to absorb silver, this alone should give place for an effective demand for a weight equal to 10 per cent. of the whole existing currency without any further depreciation of value. All future imports also must be increased by 10 per cent. in weight of metal, and this will affect not merely coined money, but also all bullion used for international exchange. This general "shrinkage" of value will tend to a demand for an increase of quantity proportioned, not to any one year's surplus, but to the whole aggregate held throughout all Asia, and indeed throughout the world.

It is on this principle that we may rely to mitigate the effects of any sudden or extreme decline in the value of silver. But this great world-wide operation cannot be forced. The opportunities for putting it into circulation must be watched and waited for. The progress of accumulation, and consequent decrease in local value must have time to spread by degrees from the centres of trade throughout the countries affected, which will not the less surely absorb *quantity* without violent change in *value*. This implies some check to supply; the experience afforded by the late scare will show that miners cannot capitalise the whole of their property in a few years without making needless and disproportionate sacrifices. Estimates generally were indeed especially exaggerated in respect to *time*, during the recent period of depression. Germany was supposed to want to sell all her silver at once. When the calculation was published that the Great Consolidated Virginia Mine contained 150 to 300 million dollars' worth of ore, it was assumed that the whole of it would be raised and thrown on the market in the shortest possible time. If a mine were like a crop of wheat which must be cleared off the ground that another may grow on the soil, there would be some show of reason for such urgency. In the same spirit a temporary and perfectly explicable dullness of trade and scarcity of local returns at the shipping ports was taken to indicate a panic throughout Asia, and a loss of confidence in the metal, which had been the chief measure of value there from time immemorial.

But it may be said in reply by some of those most

nearly interested : " This is nothing to us. We have got the supply and want to sell it at once." Just so. Every holder of commodities might say the same in turn ; but gold and silver, like all other vendible articles, must abide the natural demand for them, and the necessary cost of production will ultimately govern their exchange value. The longer these principles are neglected the more heavily will the cumulated loss fall in the long run upon those who find they have a supply for which there is no demand, or a demand to satisfy for which they can find no supply.

The vastness of the one great market concerned in the precious metals, and the infinite number of ways in which they can be used, give a larger scope for the adjustments of their values than for those of any other commodities. But this truth tells both ways. Values not only *can*, but *must* eventually be equalised generally throughout the world in spite of any partial attempt to control them.

15. *The Ratio of Value of the Precious Metals may be anticipated and declared, but cannot be controlled by Legal Authority.*—Those who contend that the relative values of the two metals can be fixed by law, do not appear to realise how completely the attempt is beyond the analogies to be found in the practice and customs of all interchange. Higher or lower price means more or less money for a fixed quantity of some other product: or a greater or less quantity of any product may be bought for a fixed sum of money. But to tie down both sides of a bargain is a notion that must be discarded as soon as it is clearly realised. We may talk loosely of a "fixed price" of gold, but that is simply the expression of a definite weight of the metal. The fixed measure of anything by itself may be resolved into a fixed quantity of itself, but in no other sense is the notion of a fixed relative value in any way tenable, except on the assumption that all the terms upon which the several equations of value depend are relatively invariable.

It is indeed sometimes alleged that experience has shown that the relative value of gold and silver can be fixed by law : but the fact is that such authority has been

of avail only as far as it was supported by laws of far
greater and more subtle efficacy.   The crucial question for
a government to decide in order to secure for a time the
concurrent circulation of two metals side by side is,—What
will be the relative price which they will bear hereafter
in the great markets of the world, the one as measured by
the other?—not forgetting to make due allowance for the
effects of its own operations.   If this ratio be determined
with tolerable accuracy there is no reason why they should
not retain for a long time their several places in one
currency.   But the question is, How to adapt these regulations imposed by the State to the course of events upon
which it may indeed exercise some temporary influence,
but which it is powerless in the long run to control.   It is
pre-eminently one for the exercise of a wise forethought;
nor is very minute accuracy always required to secure this
end.   Neither metal will move spontaneously : the nature of
the friction which has to be overcome before any change can
take place has I trust been sufficiently shown.   But when
pressed beyond what these considerations will support, the
argument dreaks down.   Thus it is said : Gold and silver
may be maintained in a currency at a fixed ratio by
adjusting the amount of their issue.   The metal more
valuable in the general market than in the currency may
(it is said) be issued without limit.   No doubt it can be
issued, but it can only be obtained by the State buying it
at the higher valuation, and if the difference be sufficient,
there is no limit to the operation which might be worked
at its cost.   For as much must be bought on the one
hand, as is sold or issued on the other, and relative values
are little affected, though the government loses on every
transaction.   The more dangerous fallacy however lurks
in the contrary notion, that the metal to which too small
a weight is assigned in the local currency can have its
value maintained by limiting its issue.   True again as far as
these terms go, but the conclusions inferred are far broader
than the premises.   If coin is scarce it may be kept at a
local premium on its value as bullion in the general
markets.   So also might a limited issue of paper notes

But in either case, and almost in equal degree, the exchange value will be subject to local influences and delusions from which the general market for bullion is to so great a degree exempt, and in virtue of which exemption the precious metals, each working out independently a world-wide average value, have become pre-eminently money throughout the world. If the United States, for example, were largely to introduce silver into their currency as legal tender money, trusting to keep up the value of it by (ultimately) limiting the coinage, the only probable result would be excessive and futile fluctations. The immediate demand would no doubt cause a great rise in its relative price. But this will be lost as soon as this exceptional (not to say artificial) support is withdrawn, and it does not follow—as it would in a trade under ordinary conditions—that the decline would facilitate export. For the enhanced value arises from local causes, and a fall in price simply brings it to the general level which can be supported in the open market. Governments form no exception to the rule that the dealings of buyers and sellers tend always to raise or depress prices against themselves. There must; be a stronger cause of changing needs behind to justify their operations.

It is hardly needful to insist upon the inevitable futility of any government attempting to retain the dearer of two metals in a currency by the mere dictum of authority; for no legal enactment can be so framed as to do more than ordain that either of two definite coins of two metals respectively shall be deemed a legal tender. The payer, not the receiver, thus has and must have the option as to which he will offer in discharge of his obligations, and his debtor is bound to receive it. To give the choice to the creditor would be, in fact, to lay upon the payer the intolerable obligation of being prepared with both. If the receiver wants the dearer coin he must come to terms with the payer—that is, he must pay a premium for it, and if the difference be considerable nothing could prevent dealers settling their terms and prices beforehand, according to the mode in which payment was to be made, and thus

B B

practically setting aside the legally declared values
altogether.

Before concluding this notice, I desire to refer more
specially to some points directly affecting our Indian
currency, and the trade in Asia generally, in which India
takes a larger and more independent part than is generally
recognised.

These considerations will be found to have important
bearings upon the scheme, which has lately been advocated with much force and ingenuity, to establish, by
general law, a fixed ratio of value between the two precious metals, and suggest some further observations on
the principles involved in the proposal.

16. *Indian Coinage.*—The principles on which equivalent
values must be determined for a voluntary double coinage
may be well exemplified by a reference to our Indian
currency.

The conditions of it as now legally established are
these :—

By the Act XVII. of 1835 of the Indian Government,
gold coins were declared to be no longer a legal tender.
It was thus authoritatively demonetised:

The standard coin is the rupee, weighing, as issued from
the Mint, 1 tola or 180 grains troy of silver, $\frac{11}{12}$ths pure:
this tola being one of the oldest standard weights of the
country, which had in course of time varied, though only
slightly, in the many different states into which India had
been subdivided, but was fixed at this weight on the regulation of the currency. It is thus made exactly equal to
three-eighths ($\frac{3}{8}$ths) of an ounce troy. The Mint, however,
charge a seignorage of 2 per cent. and mintage 1 per mille;
so that 183·861 grains troy have to be taken to the Mint
to procure a rupee, and as long as the coinage is not excessive 102·1 tolas bullion is the equivalent of C.Rs. 100.
If there were a redundancy of coin this element of merely

local value would be lost, and the value of the coinage depreciated accordingly ; as it is, the coin and the weight of silver required to make the coin are normally equivalents, and the weight of the latter must be taken for any comparison between the value of gold and silver bullion.

The price of silver, however, is by no means wholly dependent upon the coinage, for, as the quotations of fine silver show, it is frequently bought as bullion, though the difference is so slight as not to warrant the inference that the coin is unduly scarce, but simply that the metal is otherwise used. Native bankers may prefer to hold their bullion uncoined, at all events at a rate which will admit of their getting it coined with only a very small fractional loss, if ever they should have occasion to send it to the Mint.

The details of these calculations are given below.[1]

During the great pressure for payments for cotton, importers of silver were for a time dependent on the Mint, for the bankers in the country were not disposed to take quite so large a supply; and no doubt, in the districts where coin was superabundant, got quite as much silver as they could immediately manage very much on their own terms. As regards gold, also, the prompt sale of it at its full value was then uncertain, because as it was not

[1] NOTE IV.

The value of the rupee may thus be shown :—

	Grains troy, pure.	Grains troy, standard, ¹¹ths pure.
Quantity of silver required by the Mint	168·539	183·861

	Grains.	Grains.
Seignorage 2 per cent. -	3·371	3·677
Mintage, 1 per cent. ..	·168	·184
	3·539	3·861
Grains troy	165·	180

180 grains troy = 1 tola = 1 Company's rupee weight.
100 tolas pure silver ... . = Rs. 109·09
Seignorage, &c. as above ... 2·29

Gives a price of ... ... Rs. 106·8 or Rs. 106 12as. 9¼pie.

Bar silver, however, is not absolutely pure and 17 B, i.e. 239·240 pure, is taken as fine. This gives an equivalent of Rs. 106 5as. 8³⁶pie (106·355). Practically, a quotation of Rs. 106 4as. for fine silver generally indicates that it is taken to the mint for coinage, and Rs. 106 8as. that it is in demand for other purposes

B B 2

coined or made a legal tender, importers were at the mercy
of dealers, who knew perfectly well that an exceptionally
high price of silver and a low price of gold were in correspondence, and that the one and the other were governed
for the time by the high rate of exchange of bills on England.   As soon as there was a cessation of the extreme
urgency of the demand for cotton, or rather for the means
of paying for it, prices of bullion quickly found their usual
level.   All the extreme quotations of this period are alike
referable to an exceptional *urgency* of demand, and cannot
safely be taken as precedents.

17. *The proposed Introduction of Gold into the Currency.*—
The question of re-introducing gold into the Indian currency has frequently been discussed, but the attempts
made to carry out the design have always failed ; partly
from the mistaken notion that value could be given by
legislative enactment, and partly from a misapprehension
of the principles which govern the relative values of the
two metals.   The result has always been an invitation to
the public to bring gold to the Mint on terms which would
have returned it stamped with a less value than silver
bought at the same cost would have yielded—that is to
say, if 1,000 tolas of standard silver had been taken for
coinage the weight less 2·1 per cent. would have been returned in Rs. 979—as shown in Note IV.   But if this
Rs. 979 had been invested in gold and taken to the Mint
—gold stamped as considerably less—perhaps as Rs. 950
or Rs. 955 only would have been returned for it.   So also
the government has frequently offered to buy sovereigns
at Rs. 10, or at Rs. 10¼ each, when the coin melted down
and sold in the open market would have been worth
considerably more.

The value of the rupee was apparently assumed as $£\frac{1}{10}$,
and the fact that the average rate of exchange for short
bills on England had been 2*s*. per rupee was cited as a
proof of it. Whereas so far as the relative values of the two
metals are concerned, it proves quite the reverse; so long
as the balance of trade is such that bullion is sent from
Europe at all.   The comparison is erroneously made

between a rupee in *India,* and a pound in *England* or
elsewhere. The rate of exchange necessarily includes all
the costs of the whole operation required (IV. 16); and
embraces in addition to the cost in England of the silver
required to make a rupee, transit charges and interest
amounting to 2 or 3 per cent. on that cost. The assumed
$£\frac{1}{10}$ in England, as shown by a bill of exchange drawn upon
England, recouped the sender for the whole. But if the
first cost of the silver had been $£\frac{1}{10}$, or say $£\frac{24}{210}$, a rate of
exchange higher by 2 to 3 per cent. more, or say $\frac{244}{240}$ or $\frac{244}{240}$
= 2s. $0\frac{1}{2}d.$ or 2s. $0\frac{3}{4}d.$ per rupee, would have been required
to yield an adequate return. In fact the silver (183·861
grains) required to make a rupee is not itself worth 2s. in
England unless the price of 5s. $3\frac{1}{4}d.$ per oz. can be obtained,
and the coin itself would not come out at that rate except
at a price of over 5s. $4\frac{1}{2}d.$ per oz. Br. Standard. It will be
seen by Note II. (page 351), that no such price ever was
paid, though notwithstanding this, the rate of *exchange*
was often very much over 2s. per rupee. The charges
of transit should in fact be omitted as altogether irrele-
vant in fixing the relative values of the two metals at
the same place, or at least charged on both equally.

So also as to the notion of getting up gold at a very cheap
rate from Australia. Although the sovereign is legal
tender in England, the colonists must pay for sending it
there. This at once suggests to a banker, who can sell
sovereigns in India, the possibility of one of those fine
adjustments to which I have referred. But the Australian
wants to pay value in England: not in India, with which
he has no dealings. So, however much India may want
sovereigns, it can only get and retain them if the rate of
exchange on England is such that these charges can be
thrown on the exports of Indian produce which convey the
value to England. Whether it can be best afforded by
these, or by the exports of produce direct from Australia,
is a fine question of passing detail for the professional
banker. But to deduct any estimate of such charges from
the relative value of the sovereign, or so to decrease the
value (*i.e.* increase the weight) of the equivalent of any

gold coin which it is desired to introduce, would be to counterbalance the only power which can cause the gold to move at all. Moreover when once sovereigns, or gold, get to England, all these costs for special use are paid for and done with: the sovereign in England is the same as the sovereign in Australia, and the mere difference in the cost of transit from either place to India is extremely small. Silver also may come in like manner to India from ports much nearer than England : from China or Siam, for instance ; but the greater or less charges are all adjusted in the current transaction, which we know has two sides, though one only may come under our notice.

If an opportunity should again arise for coining gold in India, and the State desire that both metals should be brought voluntarily to the Mint, the equivalents must be so adjusted that the same declared values of coin shall be delivered from the Mint for such quantities of either metal as shall be of the same cost to those who bring them to it. If this new element is to be introduced, a weight of gold must be determined which shall correspond with and take up the existing value of the current rupee. It must not be too heavy, or no one will bring gold to be minted, nor must it be too light, for that would be a palpable degradation of the existing standard, entailing an injustice on the holders of all obligations payable in currency, and as has just been stated, might lead to the rejection of the coin, at least at its legal but practically only nominal value. The government must be content to interpret the facts as they come before it, or within the range of reasonable prevision, and not attempt to control them. It is useless to look back to former equivalents. If the common measure of value is changed, the remedy is not to be found by disguising the fact, but by rational action on a clear recognition of it.

The imposition of arbitrary seignorages and restrictions on a coinage cannot have any great effect without entailing the result of localising it, and a currency thus artificially isolated will always be a doubly unstable standard of value. Nor must the practical risk be ignored, that, if it become worth the while of any unscrupulous adventurer to fabricate a perfect facsimile of the rupee, there is a wide choice of places which might now be selected for such a purpose, nor is there any reason to conclude that the difficulties of introducing money, so exactly simulating in all respects that which is a legal tender, would be insuperable.

If the coinage is to maintain that due connection with the world at large which constitutes the highest utility and the best security for any currency, nothing can ensure the concurrent circulation of the two metals, except the permanence of the conditions affecting them severally, both within and outside of the country. But if, as I think there is good reason to believe, certain advantages are to be gained by the introduction of gold into the Indian currency, and further, that its value is more securely based than that of silver (II. 26, 27), there is no reason for an excess of caution in fixing terms which will induce holders to bring it to the Mint. If in process of time circumstances admitted of both receiving full popular recognition and an equal place in the currency, it might then be feasible to make gold the sole standard, provided that a sufficient quantity of it could be procured for this purpose without unduly raising its relative price. It will be long, however, before silver can be superseded as legal tender money in such a country as India, and it will certainly have to be used in any case for a large subsidiary currency. If, on the other hand, silver were to decline further after the equivalent weights had been legally fixed, the gold relatively dearer outside than within the circle of Indian currency would no longer be brought to the Mint, and would flow out of the country as the conditions of trade gave occasion for its export: merely leaving the metallic standard in silver unchanged. Even in this event the attempt, though it might be stigmatised as "a failure" by those who were anxious to get gold into the currency at any cost, would not be likely to have any prejudicial effects, but, on the contrary, would tend rather to mitigate the extreme fluctuations of an exceptionally disturbed epoch.

18. *Expedient of Coining Both Metals Independently.*— It is a question worth considering whether gold might not in some degree be introduced without, at the moment, fixing its equivalent in silver, for there are undoubtedly very strong objections to repeated changes of declared value of legal tender money on the part of government. As there have been lately in the United States "currency prices" and "gold prices," with certain obligations and customs duties payable only in the latter; so there seems no reason why a portion of Indian taxation should not be levied in gold. Part of the large quantity of this metal in the country might thus be brought into ordinary circulation and be at the disposal of the State. Normally, neither metal will go to Europe against the stream of exchange; still, in the possible event of another panic, a reserve in this form might be a useful alternative. In uncertain times it is well to have a choice of resources. A coinage in correspondence with this would have to be of the old well-known weight of tola and half-tola pieces issued at as moderate a seignorage as would cover the cost. As India is not like England, the centre of a vast general trade, there is no sound reason in policy why the coinage should not so far bear its own charges. This would tend to adjust, not indeed permanently, but for the time being more definitely, the relative values of the two metals, and might ultimately afford a good basis for future operations.

There is no reason why two metals should not circulate independently side by side as inconvertible paper and metallic money have frequently done. No doubt a currency appears more symmetrical and complete with both made interchangeable at a fixed ratio. But as they are not and cannot be so fixed, the more simply the true alternative is accepted the better. At present, although gold circulates largely chiefly in the form of small bars or ingots, it has no acknowledged place whatever in the currency of India.

19. *Present Uncertainties.*—In the present state of utter uncertainty as to the future, it is vain to discuss the

question as to what ratio of weight should be determined upon as the most fitting expression of the relative values of gold and silver. It is impossible to predict the next turn of events when both immediate supply and immediate demand are so much under the control of individual interests and discretion.

For India, under any circumstances, to enter into a blind competion with the United States for the purchase of gold would evidently be an error, for an unduly urgent demand might very easily induce a temporary appreciation of it and a relative depreciation of silver to an extent which would greatly aggravate the inconveniences to be apprehended. The results of the recent changes as regards India itself are by no means so disturbing as has been supposed. Local prices are not affected, and the general adjustment of local revenue to expenditure is not disturbed. The most serious item of difficulty is the charge of £16,000,000 now required in gold in England. This is an unquestionable difficulty, and the capital also of some £46 millions of debt incurred in this country is also redeemable only in gold. But we are apt to over-estimate the weight of this loss on an assumed exchange, because it appears so clearly in account, whereas the enhanced cost of other requirements is not seen, though it may in reality entail far more serious expenditure.

Regarded more generally, the effects of the recent changes are magnified, and are indeed. more seriously felt because they partly fall where we have too readily become accustomed to look for certain stability, though in fact that stability has often been more apparent than real. This uniformity in the relative values of the two metals was only obtained because European trade for a considerable period was in such a condition that, speaking generally, mere transfers of bullion, first one way and then the other, were sufficient to adjust the casual balances of trade and rule the course of exchange ; while Asia, where silver was comparatively dear, steadily took off just about the surplus which we could conveniently spare.

These conditions of stability no longer exist. The discoveries of A.D. 1848 and subsequently, upset this balance, though the countervailing causes, which have already been noticed, served to retard the apparent effect of the changed conditions thus introduced. There has been unquestionably, on the other side, a great increase in general industrial wealth, and in the consequent ability to apply larger values of metallic money to beneficial uses. The special inquiry as to the depreciation of silver is involved in the broader question of the future purchasing power of both the precious metals.

The *excess* in value of the rate of production *over* that which was yielded in those days when the ratio ranged between 15 to 16 silver, to 1 gold, has been at least £25 millions for over 25 years, say at least £600 to 700 millions up to 1876. It is well nigh impossible to say how much of the quantity thus indicated has been permanently absorbed without a decrease in value, or what changes in relative value as compared with commodities generally have been caused by this excess; but it has assuredly not passed out of existence. The supply is cumulative from age to age with comparatively slight diminution by loss, waste, and use in the arts. If the production of the next quarter of a century be unchecked it will in all probability yield a quantity which, at the present estimate of value, will be equal to at least £700 millions in excess of that which would have been afforded had the rate of supply remained the same as it was during the first half of the century. This will make together an aggregate of £1,000 to £1,200 millions from the known sources of supply in Europe and America. The proportion of gold to silver in these aggregates has varied, and may yet vary greatly, and this vast quantity, which will have to be placed throughout the world, will also inevitably tend to modify the relative demand; for it is impossible to foresee or to control the choice which will be exercised when both metals are offered in unprecedented abundance.

20. *Proposal of a general Fixed Ratio.*—To meet the apprehended danger of a decline in silver, it has been urged

by a very ardent school of financiers that all nations should
agree to take gold and silver only at a certain fixed ratio
of value, viz., 1 to 15½. I shall not here enter at length
into the arguments set forth to support this proposed
revolt against laws of value conceived according to the
motives and traditions which have influenced mankind
from time immemorial, but we may well ask why we are
called upon to attempt so strange an innovation. If the
supply of silver present and potential be in excess of the
wants of the world, we shall only disguise the fact for a
comparatively very short time by stimulating an artificial
demand for it. Ultimately the cost of production must
govern its exchange value—meaning of course the highest
cost which will have to be paid in order to obtain the
whole quantity required. If this necessary cost really be
below the proposed, or the present, ratio, an artificial
stimulus will merely be a bonus to miners, at the future
expense of the buyers and subsequent holders. Further, as
regards present holders whether states or individuals:—if
there really be an excess, the value is already depreciated,
disguise the fact as we may; and there is no reason why
others should be called upon to undertake this loss, especially in a way which will tend eventually to aggravate
the evil. There are, as I have shown, great natural mitigations to over-rapid depreciation, but these are thrown
away if a demand is created which simulates value but
does not dispose of quantity, and thus neither adjusts the
weight of the supply to the demand, nor tends to put any
timely check upon excessive production.

21. *Independence of Asiatic Traffic in the Precious Metals.*
—It is urged, however, that if silver be not supported, it
may be utterly rejected in a blind panic by all the nations
of Asia: that gold would then be insufficient to supply
the great void thus created, and that the consequent appreciation of the sole standard of value would lead to consequences of the most alarming character. But those who
know anything of the immobility of the East will have no
fear whatever on this score. There is not more, but far
less, likelihood of a panic from any such cause there than

in Europe.   Indian bankers have plied their trade long
before the north of Europe had learnt the arts of commerce
save in their rudest forms.   There is no considerable village
where a *hundi* (draft) cannot be obtained on any other
district throughout the country.   The instinct of money-
dealing which especially distinguished the Jew and the
Lombard in the Middle Ages carries the Hindoo, in spite
of his own religious prejudices and dread of the " black
water " of the ocean, to every part of Arabia and even to
Eastern Africa, where Mahommedan civilisation has taken
the place of the lower forms of native barbarism.   We may
be quite sure that the bankers of Hindostan know all that
we know about the production of the precious metals in
the mines of Europe and America, and probably a good
deal more which we do not know about Asiatic sources of
supply.   They may not know in terms the economic law
of " rent " or of " supply and demand," but they do know
quite well that when production pays largely it is likely
to increase, and to fall off when it no longer gives a profit.
Long experience makes them distrust the permanence of
sudden and violent changes.   They will continue to buy
gold or silver bullion according to their own judgment,
without the slightest reference to our currency laws,
further than they may effect the actual supply or demand
at the moment.   Of any such changes they will certainly
take the utmost advantage which the market affords: they
are shrewd and for the most part very cool bargain drivers.
China also has the tradition of ages for the free alternative
use of the precious metals, and the very fact that the
country has not any formal currency system makes it more
utterly out of the question to influence the relative value
of gold and silver in any other way than by actual purchase or sale.   Even if all Europe were to adopt the fixed
ratio of 1 to 15½, the only consequence would probably be
that Asia would take the gold and leave the silver to the
" new " world.

But that they should reject silver altogether is equally
beyond the limits of probability.   They will buy it on
their own estimate of its value, though not on any ratio

fixed for them, and quote wise aphorisms on the folly of haste while they take the utmost advantage of any undue urgency of sellers. And as regards the currency, strictly speaking, no fluctuation in metallic money can cause a change in prices in any way equal to those with which all classes are familiar so far as regards their own personal experiences. Whether there be a general rise in prices is indeed a very great question and always one which it will require very wide and careful investigation to answer, the more so because it is a remote cause usually overlooked amidst the more special and urgent causes which lead to a change in the price of any one commodity. Further, as regards the relative depreciation of silver, gold then seems to be rising even more clearly than anything else; and, though holders of silver may wish that they had had gold, its apparent dearness at the time will check their demand for it. To the general apprehension it will not be silver that has fallen, but gold, and prices generally that have risen ; and at the worst such a change is not of a kind likely to excite general alarm in the way suggested. An ignorant panic would be far more likely to excite popular indignation against the dealers in food and other commodities.

22. *Movements of Bullion in India.*—The statistical abstracts relating to British India, annually submitted to Parliament, give some very suggestive indications of the movements of bullion. Thus it appears that from A.D. 1867 to 1875, £113 millions of treasure were imported against an export of £17 millions only, leaving a balance of £96 millions retained in British India. These returns may not be altogether complete, but there seems no reason to doubt that they are good proof so far as they go, and rather under than over-state the extent of the traffic. Now the total export from European sources (as given in Note II.) was only £77 millions, and a large portion of this certainly went to China and the Malacca Straits. The Indian detailed returns are not quite contemporaneous with those made here, but are sufficiently so for all practical purposes in this context. They show that out of a total

of £76 millions worth of silver, received during A.D. 1866 to 1875, £29 millions were from England and £5 millions from other parts of Europe, in all £34 millions. At least £25 millions from China and over £4 millions from Ceylon (probably for the most part transhipments), leaving £12 to £13 millions from miscellaneous sources. While of £39 millions of gold, £16 millions were from China, £11¾ millions from Australia, £8½ millions only from Europe, and about £3 millions from other sources. It is in this last item of miscellaneous trade, carried on by numerous small craft from Africa, the Persian Gulf, the Red Sea, &c., that omissions are very probably made, which in the aggregate would come to a considerable amount.

The coinage of silver for these years is £51 millions, being about two-thirds of the whole supply, but 50 per cent. more than the whole receipts from Europe. It may be added that there is a note-circulation of about £10 and 12 millions. This coinage, however, is probably melted down in an unusually large degree. The seignorage does not protect it in this respect, for though 2 per cent. is a heavy charge on a large bullion operation, it is a very small one for a trustworthy assay of 2 or 3 ounces of silver ; and that is what it practically comes to with the many millions of the poorer classes, who in good times like to have their savings in the form of ornaments, and have them made directly from the standard coin. These returns afford also a very definite proof of the extent of the large and independent traffic in gold entirely unsupported by any demand for the legal currency of the country. If the question of its coinage should be again taken up in India, there is no doubt that large supplies will be forthcoming providing a due value is assigned to it. But it is needless now to enter further into the details of this difficult and very technical question.

23. *The Ratios of Value will best be worked out by Free Competition.*—The more fully the subject is investigated the stronger appear to be the reasons for trusting to the operation of natural laws rather than to expedients however ingeniously contrived, or however well and boldly worked

out. I need not repeat the arguments set forth in the foregoing treatise, by which I have endeavoured to show that
a currency is soundly based only when it rests ultimately
upon the widest average which the world can afford, worked
out by the untrammelled interaction of supply and demand.
I have not denied that less perfect currencies can be got
to work, and believe that doctrines exaggerated in this
respect have given colour to many of the fallacies which
still prevail on the subject. Still, I may repeat, the
question in the present day is not what forms of currency
can be got to work in some sort of way, but what will afford
the best attainable basis for the great system of industrial
and commercial organisation which is being developed
around us. This is of far more consequence than any
casual loss which may arise from the depreciation of one
of the precious metals. No one will deny that a demand
artificially stimulated will support the relative value of the
weaker of these metals for a considerable period. But
just in the degree that production was so stimulated would
be the ultimate fall when supply at the increased rate had
to be disposed of finally. The mere prospective falling off
of demand will not stop supply, on the contrary will tend
rather to increase it; that will be brought about only by
such a general rise in prices as shall render mining less
profitable, and bring the test of the cost of production to
bear on every mine with increasing severity. Even if the
demand for coinage could be regulated at a fixed ratio of
relative value, that would only afford an undue—because
necessarily only a temporary—stimulus to the production of
that metal which was the cheaper with reference to that
fixed ratio. Even if every coin issued contained a fixed
proportion of gold and of silver there would yet be a limit
to the demand for each severally. If gold and silver are
independently variable it is clear they will be variable also
with reference to any combination of gold and silver, and
the fixed price of this " electrum " would be just as certainly resolved into a mere expression of relative weights.
The metal which could be produced most largely at a profit
upon its proportional fixed value would be in excess, the

other relatively scarce. If one, say gold, were to become
relatively scarce in this manner, no power on earth could
prevent its acquiring a premium; demand creates demand
and induces a confidence in stability, so that this premium
would tend to augment. The less costly metal, say 15½
parts silver, would seek for its counterpart in vain, but
who could prevent its production, if 16 or 17 or more
parts could be produced at a profit as compared with the
1 part of gold. It would willingly be sold at a discount.
The artificial nature of the arbitrated ratio would thus
become glaringly apparent, and, as regards any question
of relative value, utterly worthless and ineffective in the
long run. Reverse the supposition if you will, and write
silver for gold, and gold for silver, the argument holds
equally good. The expedient ignores the true conditions
of the problem and must end in confusion, unless indeed
the course of events be such as to render it unnecessary
and useless.

The two metals circulating side by side independently,
as they have done from time immemorial, will each find its
own true level far better and more evenly without any such
interference. Nations or governments who have to deal
practically with the question must exercise their own timely
discretion as to any acts which may affect the supply or
demand of either, bearing in mind that though they may
very easily do much to perturb the present, they can do
little or nothing to control the future course of monetary
adjustments.

24. *Relative Cost of Production must ultimately govern
the Relative Value of Gold and Silver.*—The fundamental
fallacy which lies at the bottom of all arbitrary proposals
to regulate the value of the precious metals is, that
because their uses as money are special and peculiar, therefore they are not subject to the same laws of value as those
which govern all other things. Captivating as the error
has been to many very acute minds, it is hardly more than
a mere verbal mystification. Of course money measured
in money cannot give any intelligible evidence of its own
worth, or afford any indication of a change in its own

value. But as all things are measured by money, so money in its turn is measured by that which it will buy; and ultimately, the necessary relative cost of production governs all supply according to conditions which Nature imposes upon all mankind : and further, all traffic in its widest sense comes at last to an interchange of supply, and thus laws of physical necessity underlie the laws. which control all relative values.

This is why all who study the higher problems of value feel that well-devised and trustworthy statistics of general prices, which have hitherto been rather a matter of intelligent curiosity, may become a matter of serious importance : for by their aid only can we test the stability of money itself, which is not inherently more than a common measure of all other relative values.

Because the value of the precious metals is highly generalised and independent of the transient accidents which affect most other commodities, it seems to be inferred that value is in some way independently inherent in them. But this is in nowise the case. It is surely governed by the aggregate influence of countless agencies, ever acting both in the present and upon the accumulated stores of ages. Hence it is that the effect of these agencies, though gradually produced and often at the moment obscure, is ~~evidently~~ worked out with such irresistible power. The total quantity yielded must be adapted to the total effectual wants of the world ; and an addition to any previously existing quantity can only be taken into the common fund, either by an extension of the uses found for it ; or by such a reduction in the units of value into which the whole may be divided, as shall leave the value of the aggregate unchanged ; that is, by a decrease of the purchasing power of every such unit and a corresponding rise in all prices. But when all other things become dearer in relation to gold and silver, it becomes less and less worth while to produce any given quantity of them. And thus it is that the production of every mine severally, and therefore of each metal separately, must be ultimately

governed by what the world will give in commodities
which gold or silver can buy.

Thus, though gold measured in silver, or silver measured
in gold, give but a barren indication of value; the inducement to produce either is effectually regulated by the
relative returns—as measured in those things which
directly minister to the wants and pleasures of mankind—
that can ultimately be obtained for the labour devoted to
this rather than to any other kind of employment.

Assuming as a probable fact that the production of gold
and silver will be in excess of the wants—fully admitting
them to be increasing wants—of the world at large, it
follows that the more directly a decline in value arising
from such excess is brought to bear upon production, the
better for all the vast interests concerned in the stability
of money values. For, I repeat, this excess will be cumulative. The question must not be argued as though the
large supply of recent years had been so disposed of and
consumed as to be out of the account altogether. Delay
in the application of the only efficient remedy will lead
only to more violent fluctuations hereafter, and render the
ultimate adjustments of values and prices more difficult.
In other words; leave the price of gold measured in silver,
or silver measured in gold to adjust itself relatively, as all
prices will and must adjust themselves to the future
relative value of metallic money [II. s. 11 and 23] : and
though the apprehended increase in quantity can only be
met by a decrease in value, still this decrease, affecting as
it does so vast an aggregate, will itself create the best
outlet for this increase in quantity.

Until we can see that the production of both metals is
brought immediately under the influence of the law of
supply and demand : in other words until it is held clearly
in check by the difficulty of getting adequate returns for
the poorer class of mines indifferently, we cannot but feel
uncertainty as to their fitness as standards of value for
any lengthened periods; though there seems no reason
whatever to doubt that both of them, as effectually as

heretofore, will serve as common measures of value for the current interchanges of commerce and industry.

The present generation may have more than its share of doubt and difficulty to undergo, but there is no legacy which it can leave to posterity better than a currency soundly based on that stability of value which a world-wide average, freely worked out, will give to the precious metals.

*** The foregoing remarks were written in the summer of last year, and now, in the beginning of 1878, I have little to add to them. The extent to which the fall in the price of *silver* has led to its transmission to the East has far exceeded general expectations. Last year's returns have been added to Note III. The change in international values, or more strictly speaking, in international valuations, by checking exports from Europe to Asia, and stimulating imports to Europe from Asia, has largely increased the differences in value which are normally payable in the precious metals. The tendency of general and more remotely operating causes will be gradually to work down these differences ; and this should be the more carefully noticed, as it is likely to be forgotten amidst the more conspicuous and pressing influences of the moment.

Meantime the utmost uncertainty continues to exist on all sides as regards the future available supply and demand. The now well known "Bland Bill" for remonetising silver in the United States currency seems likely to become law. The ratio of value of gold to silver, to be fixed under it, has been the subject of some discussion. A dollar of 425 grs. troy, which was proposed, gives a ratio of nearly 16½ (16·473) to 1. The trade dollar of 420 grs. (which has been coined in San Francisco specially to compete with the Mexican dollar in China and the Eastern Seas), gives rather more than 16¼ (16·279) to 1. But the original silver dollar, or more strictly speaking the dollar of A.D. 1837, seems likely to be adopted, which is less than 16 (15·988) to 1. (§ 3, page 348.) This would be about on a par with the prices which were paid in the first half of A.D. 1874, and about 8 per cent. higher than the average quotations during the past year.

It is surely a backward step in monetary policy for the United States, after having attained the advantages of a standard based on gold, to commit themselves to all the uncertainties of a double standard, with the probability that they will drift into a depreciated and depreciating standard of silver. The step, however, does not seem to have been taken so much with the view of relieving debtors at the expense of creditors (though that feeling, no doubt, has had something to do with the adoption of the lighter rather than the heavier dollar) as from the notion that the country could be very greatly enriched by using the vast stores of silver which the Pacific States afford to increase the "money" in circulation. It is not to be wondered at that the farmers in the West should fail to perceive that such money must decrease in value as it increases in quantity. There are too many examples of belief in the seductive delusion that such money is real wealth. Moreover, rising prices are always popular with certain classes who are well able to make themselves heard. The Western farmer suffers, in fact, from the protective system. The protected interests drive hard bargains with him, and leave him very bare of money. It is a great stroke of craft to leave him in the belief that more "money" will put more dollars into his pocket, which is indeed true—to the very letter.

It must be clearly recognised that there are two distinct questions before us, viz., the effects of the aggregate increase of *both* gold and silver, and the probable ratio of value which one metal will bear to the other. The partial adoption of silver in the United States will both tend to stimulate production and to increase the native demand for it; but so much the more gold will be available for export, which will tend to the depreciation of that metal also in Europe. When the quotations of silver vary, it will be difficult to determine whether it is owing to a rise

in the one metal or a fall in the other, or to a fall in both
in unequal proportions. The tendency, however, of the
double change will be to cause their values to converge;
that is, to raise at all events the nominal value of silver;
and this is no doubt for the advantage of the mining
interest for the time being. On the other hand, Germany
has still to dispose of a considerable balance of the silver
rejected from its currency; and it appears further that the
Bank of France, out of a total of £81,000,000 of bullion,
holds 34½ millions, or over 42 per cent. in silver.

On the assumption, however, that as long as the United
States Government is a large buyer, the price will be
somewhat enhanced, the effect will be to reverse *pro
tanto* the recent conditions of our trade with Asia. The
stimulus to production and the discouragement to importers
there will both be diminished; so far the tendency will be
to reduce the balance which it can give in return for
bullion. A pressure, though probably not of any very
great severity, will thus fall upon those industries which
have lately been favoured. The hardships entailed by
such changes are real and much to be regretted; but the
only true remedy is to submit ourselves to conditions
which we cannot possibly control. The energy which
shows itself in the work of production is of no avail
unless it is guided by the intelligence which can adapt
its methods and its results to the changing circumstances
with which we have actually to deal. It is this practical
intelligence which must have free scope, especially in such
times of difficulty and uncertainty as the present.

It is strange how again and again the fallacies of the
old mercantile system crop up. Very lately, in addressing
one of our learned societies, the speaker went out of his
way to remark, " Will America, in selling its cotton, sugar,
and tobacco, to the extent of £20,000,000 or £30,000,000,
take an equal or greater amount of our manufactured
goods in return ? " The Board of Trade returns show even
larger figures, giving an export of £71,000,000 against
imports from this country of £16,000,000 only. Are we
to assume that this balance of £55,000,000 is not paid for

by the products of British industry. It is true we hold
a large amount of the United States debt, and to some
extent their export goes to pay the interest due on our
capital advanced. But for the rest, are we generally
bankrupt, and do not pay our commercial debts? Or has
the heathen Chinee so far imbued our giant offspring with
sentiments of filial piety that he makes a gratuitous offer
of the amount to the old country? The absurdity which
is drawn out in the replies was latent in the question
itself. The fact is, that we do and must pay in the products of British industry sent to all quarters of the globe
in exchange, not the less real because it is indirect, for
other products which are consumed in the United States.
If our direct imports were reduced, all those interested in
the exports which served to pay for these products would
suffer, or at least be likely to suffer just as much as if the
export were made direct to the States. Even if our direct
export to the States were increased, one effect would be
that the means immediately available for the support of
these various trades would be curtailed. For instance,
coffee sent from the Brazils to New York is paid for by
bills drawn on London. These are bought in the Brazils
by those who have sold British manufactures there; but
New York has to send value to London to pay these bills
drawn for its account, and can now do so out of its large
supplies sent to England. If these last were to cease, the
means of paying for manufactures sent to the Brazils
would cease also; nor can we assume that they could pay
us at once in coffee, for the presumption is that we have
a sufficient supply of that article already. The compensations for all such changes as come about in the natural
course of events are constantly found by the activity of
commerce, if only artificial barriers are not set in the way
of the new adaptations required; but we must not hark
back on the old fallacy that a trade with any country is
insecure merely because from our ignorance we cannot
trace exactly how it is balanced.

How widely extended and efficacious these indirect
channels may be is indeed singularly well illustrated by

our trade with the United States. Locally, indeed, they have adopted a policy of protection far more to their own national loss than to ours, but the great external traffic in which they are concerned cannot be restricted ; and over and above the great excess of value sent to us in products, a large amount of their treasure is further sent to us for such indirect transactions as have just been described.

I refer to this subject more especially at this juncture because the large supply of treasure which is being produced, and must be distributed throughout the world, will tend very greatly to stimulate indirect traffic of this nature. The owners will ever be seeking an outlet in any and every market which can afford them returns for it in any way. Money in this substantive form is thrown upon the world, and is in the main only adapted for those primary uses which were set forth in Chapter I. of this book. It will be a very searching pioneer to open up new trades under new conditions. It both stimulates, and is capable of affording support to new enterprises in many and various directions ; and though the real value of mere metallic wealth is altogether misconceived and exaggerated in popular estimation, it would not the less be an error to neglect this advantage which may afford much compensation for many of the losses and inconveniences which the disturbance of the common measure of value will entail. Whether we will or not, the old courses of traffic will be peculiarly liable to be deranged and in some cases superseded altogether. The gaps thus made are too apt to engross all our attention, to the exclusion of new and growing interests which have an equal claim upon our regard.

Those who intelligently advocate the full freedom of trade do so not from any love of change for the sake of change, but from the well-assured conviction that our prosperity depends upon the continuous adaptation of our labour to the ever-varying conditions of society (III. 6). Protection, however disguised, claims a vested interest in a perpetuity existing only in a moribund imagination which can dream only of the past, but is unable to realise either the living present or the promise of the future. The accession of "metallic wealth," if appropriately used as a medium and agent of exchange in opening up new channels for industry, may do something to promote the sum of general prosperity ; though if regarded as in itself constituting wealth, its increase will be found only a bitter mockery and a delusion.

THE END.